E. W. Edersheim

The Laws and Polity of the Jews

E. W. Edersheim

The Laws and Polity of the Jews

ISBN/EAN: 9783337134747

Printed in Europe, USA, Canada, Australia, Japan

Cover: Foto ©ninafisch / pixelio.de

More available books at **www.hansebooks.com**

THE LAWS AND POLITY OF THE JEWS.

The Laws and Polity of the Jews.

BY

E. W. EDERSHEIM.

London:
THE RELIGIOUS TRACT SOCIETY,
56, Paternoster Row; 65, St. Paul's Churchyard; and 164, Piccadilly.

UNWIN BROTHERS, THE GRESHAM PRESS, CHILWORTH AND LONDON.

TABLE OF CONTENTS.

PART I.
POLITY OF THE JEWS.

CHAP.	PAGE
I.—THE KING	1
II.—PRIESTS AND LEVITES	13
III.—PROPHETS	27
IV.—JUDGES AND COURTS OF LAW	37
V.—MILITARY LAWS	52
VI.—TAXES AND TRIBUTES	66

PART II.
DOMESTIC LAWS.

VII.—PROPERTY AND INHERITANCE	73
VIII.—SLAVES AND SERVANTS	86
IX.—WIVES AND CHILDREN	99
X.—POOR LAWS: DEBTOR AND CREDITOR	110
XI.—TRADE	122
XII.—SICKNESS AND DEATH	130

PART III.
THE TEN WORDS: MORAL LAWS IN DAILY LIFE.

XIII.—THE "TEN WORDS": IDOLATRY	143
XIV.—THE "TEN WORDS" (*continued*)	153
XV.—THE CLEAN AND THE UNCLEAN	162
XVI.—HOSPITALITY: THE STRANGER	171
XVII.—MUTUAL RIGHTS AND OBLIGATIONS	178

INTRODUCTORY.

"Sic in Sina lex divina
Reis est imposita,
Lex timoris non amoris
Puniens illicita.

* * * *

Nos distractos sub peccatis
Liberet lex caritatis,
Et perfectæ libertatis
Dignos reddat munere."

Apud Daniel, Thes. Hymnol. v. 422.

ONE of the first needs of a nation, after emerging out of barbarism, or settling in some land, would be the enactment of a code of laws suitable to the character of the people and of the locality. These laws would be rarely unalterably fixed, but capable of being either modified or enlarged, according to what might be felt requisite, at that or at any later period, in the consolidation or extension of the state. And the memory of the Lawgiver would be cherished to all generations as the true founder of the nation, by reason of his having given it stability, and furnished that order without which its establishment would have been impossible.

In accordance with this is the early history of the Jews as a nation. For, when brought out from the bondage in which they had been held in Egypt, and when about to take rank as a nation in the land where they had formerly been but a family, they were furnished with a code of laws exactly suited to their own character, and to that of their country. Only, unlike the laws of other nations, the Pentateuch legislation was perfect and complete, neither to be added to, nor to be diminished.[1] Nor could it have been otherwise, since the laws had been given by that God Who changeth not.[2] Further, whereas in ancient heathen states the fundamental ideas of law and polity underwent not only modifications but entire changes, according to the various kinds of government introduced, the fundamental principles of the Jewish nation remained unchanged under judgeship, royalty, or republic, until the final dispersion of the nation. The reason for this immutability of the Jewish code of laws is most important, as it not only throws light on the events of Old Testament history, but also explains to us the real necessity and object of the nation itself, and gives dignity and value to laws in themselves often seemingly—but only seemingly—unmeaning. And this grand principle, for which Israel became a nation, and for violating which they suffered punishments which, viewed by themselves, might appear almost disproportionate to the offences committed, was the *Theocracy*, or royal rule by God Himself over the nation. This Theocracy was the rule of God to Israel in an especial sense, not only as typical of the time when the final establishment of God's Kingdom on earth would be an outward as well as an inward reality, but to teach men in those ages, as well as in our days, that there is a Power higher than themselves, that each wrong done will surely bring down its own punishment, that verily there is "a reward for the righteous; verily He is a God that judgeth in the earth."[3]

In a general sense, the whole world is a Theocracy, since God is truly its King, and nothing can take place on it without His direction and permission. But as applied to the history of Israel, the word must be taken in a particular sense. Not as though it were hereby implied that, while the Jewish nation existed, God left the rest of the world purposely in ignorance of Himself, or preserved His creation simply for the benefit of the Jews, as in later times the Rabbis held; but that He chose the people to keep alive the knowledge of Himself in the midst of universal idolatry. For this purpose it was that He made a

[1] Deut. xii. 32.   [2] Mal. iii. 6.   [3] Psa. lviii. 11.

INTRODUCTORY.

special revelation of Himself by giving them a code of laws, the very essence of which was His Kingship, and the only security from whose penalties, implicit obedience on their part to His rule.

Bearing this important principle in mind, we can understand how disobedience to God would bring down upon Israel such severe punishments as captivity in the case of the nation, or instant death in that of individuals. For, as has been well noted, disobedience was really high treason, since it was an offence against the covenanted King; while its most outrageous form, Idolatry, was a denial of His being the One True God, of His rights and rule, as well as, on the people's part, of their solemn engagements and responsibilities. More than this, God was not only their King in the generally accepted sense, but their Deliverer from Egypt, their Founder as a nation, and the real Possessor of their land. From Him each man held his property; and it was therefore inalienable, and must always revert to its original owner. This accounts for such provisions as tithes, offerings, and the Sabbatical and Jubilee years. Again, we find in this the reason for the absence of any kind of substantial reward for patriotic or virtuous deeds. Contrary to the custom of all heathen nations, who celebrated the return of their heroes with triumphs, games, crowns, or lands, the Jew was taught to expect no reward other than the good esteem of his fellow-countrymen. As a matter of fact, the only expressions of popular estimation for the great recorded in the Old Testament are lamentations for a leader or king, and in some cases a triumphal reception on the part of a band of women with songs and dancing. These expressions are, however, in no wise commanded or contemplated in the Pentateuch code—rather is the contrary commended. The object of this exclusion of individual exaltation undoubtedly was, not only to render more marked the contrast between the Jewish idea of a nation as a whole, and the heathen views current at that time, which regarded a people as an aggregation of units, but to vindicate the higher moral principle, that virtue and heroism are intended to be the ordinary, not the extraordinary, life of a nation, while cowardice and evil-doing, as deformities, are to be shunned and detested.

The Theocracy by no means excluded the rule by judges, kings, or priests. On the contrary, the code made ample provision for all these; stipulating, however, that such offices must be held as under the Supreme Ruler, and filled by persons obedient to the laws, and ministers of God. As this special feature has been fully treated of by other writers, it need here only be remarked that the Mosaic legislation by no means—as it has been falsely asserted—contemplated a hierarchy. In fact, not only was the tribe of Levi so circumscribed in position that it was utterly impossible for it to arrogate to itself power over the other tribes, but from the time of Moses to that of the Maccabees only one priest, Samuel, is found ruling the Israelites.

In conclusion, attention should be directed to a few distinctive features of the Theocracy, and to its special agencies, as illustrated by the history of Israel.

The Mosaic code did not utterly ignore all former institutions and customs, but adapted and modified several ancient practices, probably handed down from the time of the Great Dispersion after the Flood. Among these should be noted sacrifices, the avenging of blood, and vows; though of course the moral element in all these was something quite new to the generation of the Exodus. For, gradually, as the nations had sunk deeper into idolatry, the meaning these institutions had originally conveyed to their ancestors had become lost, or so intermixed with fable that it was almost impossible to separate the false from the true. This required a Divine Revelation, such as was granted Israel at Mount Sinai. At the same time, the separation between Israel and the rest of the world became more strongly marked by the way in which crime was viewed by the Mosaic code, and by the character of punishments introduced. These punishments were of two kinds: some were administered directly by God Himself, as childlessness, and the so-called waters of jealousy; others by the appointed judges, and, unlike

INTRODUCTORY. xi

heathen codes, for such offences as swearing falsely, idolatry, etc. A most marked feature in the criminal laws, distinguishing them very clearly from heathen or even mediæval legislation, was the absence of torture, and of any shameful death. This alone would go far to establish the Divine origin of the Pentateuch code.

Of all the special agencies by which God asserted His rule over Israel, and His disposal of events, the most important was the Prophetic Order. Besides this special agency, there were the answers by Urim and Thummim—by means of mysterious light on the stones of the High Priest's breastplate—and the Lot. But the last two agencies were seldom employed, except in the earliest times, for public undertakings, or in worship on some solemn occasion.

What immense moral influence the knowledge of the personal rule of God over the nation must have exercised, cannot now with truth be estimated. For, as we may estimate the strength of forces most clearly in their decay, even so it is chiefly from the darker pages of Jewish history that we learn what the people must have been, so long as they acknowledged God as their King. When they had turned aside to idolatry, they lost their meaning as a nation, and their laws, instead of being a protection to them, became not only burdensome, but witnesses against them. With this part of their history we have happily not to deal, but with the Divine code as elaborated in the Pentateuch for the rule of the nation by a perfect law. We can now, therefore, proceed to a more close examination of the Laws and Polity of the Jews, as originally designed by their Great King, they "having a shadow of good things to come,"[1] and, until Christ came, their "righteousness," if they observed to do all these commandments before the Lord their God, as He had commanded them.[2]

From the limited size of this book, it has been impossible to do more than sketch in outline the leading features of the Jewish code of laws. Here at the outset the reader must be

[1] Heb. x. 1. [2] Deut. vi. 25.

reminded that the laws of a nation cannot furnish him with that nation's actual history, but will only serve to point to what it was intended to be, what is historical about such a code merely referring to that period when the legislator first framed the laws. To the student of Biblical antiquities, then, the Pentateuch legislation can but serve as a starting-point, from whence he may survey Israel ideally, and mark how quickly the ideal was neglected, and the Invisible despised, and finally rejected.

In studying the history of a nation, the first object perceived by an outsider would be the structure and the directors of the state. Accordingly, the First Part of this book has been devoted to the Polity of the Jews, dealing in the first instance with its ruler, the King (Chapter i.), then sketching its Priesthood (Chapter ii.), and thirdly, its Prophets (Chapter iii.). These three chapters, therefore, deal with the great state directors. To the Polity also belong the Judges and Courts of Law, in which last must be included the Criminal Law of the Pentateuch (Chapter iv.). Next, the nation must be considered in relation to other nations, in peace and in war (Chapter v.); while finally, the individual Israelite is viewed in his relationship to the state—his dues, taxes, and tributes (Chapter vi.).

The Second Part deals with the Domestic Life of the Israelite. To an outsider the first thing here perceived would be his outward possessions—his land and his property inherited from his fathers (Chapter vii.). Secondly, as the stranger becomes more intimate, he is introduced to the Israelite's household—his slaves and servants (Chapter viii.); and finally to his wife and children (Chapter ix.). As the Jew must be holy in all his domestic relations, so must he likewise show himself holy and merciful to the poor, and to his debtor (Chapter x.); as also just and true in his commercial dealings (Chapter xi.). Even beyond these particulars, in those circumstances of life most trying: in sickness, in death, and in mourning, he must remember his holy calling, and not sorrow as the heathen did, even as though he had no hope, but as befitted one whose God was the Ever-Living, and to Whom all lived (Chapter xii.).[1]

[1] Luke xx. 38.

The Third Part concerns the Moral and Social Life of Israel. Here the all-pervading motive is shown to be Love, manifested to God in reverent obedience, to man in self-abnegation and unselfishness. As the great foundation on which the whole structure is built stand the Moral Laws, revealed in the Ten Words. These, considered in regard to man, show him his two-fold duty—to his superiors (Chapter xiii.); and to his equals (Chapter xiv.). Nor do his obligations end here. The "Words" lead to results—to a holy life, to the abstaining from all that is unclean in food (Chapter xv.); to the duty of hospitality and friendship to the brother afar off, the stranger to man, though no stranger to the God of all the world (Chapter xvi.). And finally, as summing up in some measure all that had gone before, the Pentateuch furnishes rules for the most humble avocations, to show that over small things as well as over great there watches the all-seeing eye of God, to the exclusion of all mean and petty revenge, to the maintaining of the dignity of both man and beast, to the avoiding of respect of persons, to the searching out and discovering of secretly cherished malice (Chapter xvii.).

And over all these laws—over the Political, the Domestic, and the Social Life of Israel—was to be written as a golden motto, *Holiness unto the Lord.* For all could and should be equally holy; nothing short of this could serve the redeemed of the Lord. And so even in the darkest hour of trial the prophet Zechariah could see, afar off, the day approaching when everything in Israel should be equally holy—from the bells on the horses to the bowls before the Altar in the Sanctuary, and when all who served God would be His people in name and in deed: "in that day there shall be no more the Canaanite"—the idolater, the denier of God—"in the house of the Lord of hosts."[1]

[1] Zech. xiv. 20, 21.

PART I.

Polity of the Jews.

THE KING.

THROUGHOUT the Old Testament runs, as its connecting line, this grand thought: the Kingdom of God ruleth over all—that Kingdom of God which now "is not meat and drink," but for whose coming Christ has taught us to pray; and which, though it is "not with observation," is nevertheless a fact, a motive-power, and that for which the creature waits, till Christ shall be revealed from heaven. This world-wide principle of the Theocracy was taught to men of old by the history of Israel, not fully, but in measure as they were able to bear such knowledge. But, while the Kingdom on earth was, ideally and really, to be like the Kingdom of heaven, the precise form of government was to be defined as should in after ages be judged most expedient. Accordingly, the Pentateuch furnishes neither express permission nor prohibition of rule by judges, by priests, by prophets, or by kings; but it gives ample provisions for regulating the conduct of those set in authority, no matter what office or title such might claim.

The Book of Deuteronomy, as is implied in its name ("second law"), expands and explains many laws briefly alluded to in the Books of Exodus, Leviticus, and Numbers. Of the antiquity and authority of this book, there is most indubitable evidence; and one of the strongest arguments against the many hypotheses hazarded by writers as to its more recent age, is to be found in the laws laid down for regulating monarchical government in Israel. An uninspired writer, living during the time of the later kings, could scarcely have ventured thus to express himself. Besides, these provisions are in themselves eminently archaic, and mark such an ideal state of affairs as we know from the history never did exist. For, when royalty was established in Israel, and the King chosen in the manner prescribed, so far had the people fallen from their obedience to God and trust in Him, that their King, instead of being a good gift from God, and fulfilling what had been appointed for the Jewish monarch, was sent to them in anger, as a scourge and punishment.[1] Yet they learned not the lesson taught them even now, so that royalty, instead of bringing them back to God, finally led them farther away from Him. And throughout the whole later history of Israel, we may trace the gradual decay of the state from that time when, choosing to be like the other nations, governed by a visible king, God gave them their heart's desire, but sent leanness into their soul.[2]

While Israel was in the desert, the supreme power was vested in Moses. He by no means used it despotically, but associated with himself first his brother Aaron, and afterwards Joshua, who had been selected by Divine command for this; and who personally, by his uprightness and courage, had proved himself well suited for the position of leader and arbitrator. After the death of Moses, Joshua was appointed to the chief command. During his rule, the Holy Land was conquered and divided by lot among the tribes; a civil war averted; and the worship of God in the Tabernacle, and throughout the whole country, established by a solemn oath and covenant. After his death, the Israelites began to feel the need of some central authority, to be acknowledged and obeyed by all. Surrounded and harassed by enemies on every side, both within and without the land, torn by tribal jealousies and dissensions, it seemed as if the brief periods of peace under the Judges only heralded the advent of more disastrous times. The selfishness and half-heartedness of tribes whose possessions were not those devastated or threatened, brought down sharp rebuke (as of Reuben and Gad in the Song of Deborah),[3] and even severe chastisement (as of the men of Penuel and Succoth

---

[1] Hosea xiii. 11.   [2] Psa. cvi. 15.   [3] Judg. v. 15-17.

by Gideon).[1] When at last the rule of Samuel had restored peace to Israel, so thoroughly disorganized and faithless had the people become, that, dreading the prophet's death, or his authority delegated to his sons, the elders requested the aged seer, in the name of Israel, to make them a king. The manner of their demand was not only peculiarly offensive to Samuel, but dishonouring to God: "Behold, thou art old, and thy sons walk not in thy ways: now make us a king to judge us like all the nations."[2] We know the consequences of their request, and of their practical renunciation of the rule of God. A King after the manner of the nations was given them: fine in appearance, courageous even to rashness in war, but arrogant and despotic. Yet the people, in their blind desire to rival the nations around, heeded not the yoke they had laid on their own shoulders; and when at last their eyes were opened, and they began to realise what their king truly was, the knowledge came too late. For his army and foreign alliances made the monarch all-powerful, and the history of the nation soon became that of its ruler.

In order to understand clearly what royalty implied in Israel, we must first consider the Ideal King—if the term may be used—as described in the Book of Deuteronomy;[3] and then gather together the notices of royal power and display, as preserved in the historical books of the Old Testament.

1. The Mosaic law guarded most carefully against the exclusive usurpation of power by either king or people.[4] This is expressly insisted upon in the words defining how the King was to be chosen. He was to be Divinely appointed, yet this appointment was to be ratified by the people also; and until the King was recognised as such by his subjects, he could neither claim nor exercise authority. This is illustrated by the case of Saul, the first King, who, though anointed by Samuel, and acknowledged by part of the nation, had no power to enrol an army to deliver Jabesh,[5] and was only universally

[1] Judg. viii. 4-17. [2] 1 Sam. viii. 5, etc. [3] Deut. xvii. 14-20.
[4] Ibid. xvii. 15. [5] 1 Sam. xi.

received and obeyed after he had defeated the Ammonites, and rescued that city. The ideal King, then, must be God-chosen and man-acknowledged; and it was in the union of these two rights that an even balance of power was to be preserved. This mode of proceeding excluded all undue influence by votes, and was equally opposed to purely aristocratic and democratic government.

2. The King must be an Israelite: "One from among thy brethren shalt thou set king over thee; thou mayest not set a stranger over thee which is not thy brother."[1] This provision, of course, referred to Israelitish descent on the father's side only. Many instances are forthcoming of kings whose descent on the maternal side was non-Israelitish. Thus, the great-grandmother of David, Ruth, was a Moabitess; the wife of King Ahab and mother of Jehoram and Ahaziah, Jezebel, a Tyrian. But in no instance did a foreigner rule the land till the time of the Herods, when, the country having become a Roman province, that Idumæan family obtained the sovereignty over it from the Emperor.

The tribe from which most of the monarchs sprang, and which was set apart as royal, according to the blessing of the patriarch Jacob, was that of Judah.[2] The first Levite King, in the sense of supreme ruler, was Judas Maccabæus; but the domination of his family, the Asmonæans, was not of long duration. In fact, priestly interference in the choice of a monarch was unthought of, and the only High priest who took at all an active part in the elevation and coronation[3] of a king was Jehoiada. This action, however, was simply due to the peculiar position of the "seed-royal" at that time.

3. "He shall not multiply horses to himself, nor cause the people to return to Egypt, to the end that he should multiply horses: forasmuch as the Lord hath said unto you, Ye shall henceforth return no more that way."[4] The reasons for this stipulation are obvious. In the first place, the Israelites were to be pre-eminently an agricultural people, who for ploughing, etc.,

---

[1] Deut. xvii. 15. [2] Gen. xlix. 10. [3] 2 Kings xi. [4] Deut. xvii. 16.

would use only oxen, and, perhaps, sometimes asses.[1] In wars of a defensive character, which were to be the only ones undertaken by Israel, horses would be, for most intents and purposes, practically useless. Situated as Palestine is—bounded on the west by the sea, north by a chain of mountains, east and south by deserts unsuited for the forage of horses—the main use to which they could have been put would have been in state chariots, or magnificent processions, such as were common in later times.[2] But Eastern state, or ostentation, was directly opposed to the Divine purpose in royalty. Beyond this, an alliance with Egypt, such as must necessarily follow from friendly intercourse and trade with that country, of world-wide celebrity as a horse-market, was always most disastrous to Israel. The Egyptians would (and, as appears from the subsequent history, actually did) lead the Israelites into wars of which they alone reaped the benefits, while their Jewish allies were weakened and injured, and finally fell a prey to Egypt itself. For all reasons, then, practical and political, this command guarded against a very possible danger, and, if obeyed, would have insured the permanent good, if not continuance of, the Jewish Kingdom.

4. "Neither shall he multiply wives to himself, that his heart turn not away."[3] Herein lay an important distinction between the Theocratic King and the Oriental despot, part of whose pride and greatness consisted in the size and splendour of his harem. The wisdom of this proviso will appear most clearly, when it is considered that not only was it contrary to the generally received practice of monogamy among the Israelitish people, but also that it must of necessity create a distinction between prince and people, which could only prove injurious to public morals and manners. Besides, the wives of the King would naturally be princesses, and therefore heathens. What harm such foreign wives as those of Solomon,[4] or the Queen Jezebel, did in bringing in idolatry, and turning aside

---

[1] 1 Kings xix. 19; 1 Sam. ix. 3.
[3] Deut. xvii. 17.
[2] 2 Sam. xv. 1.
[4] 1 Kings xi. 1-8.

the hearts of King and people, is only too well known. Further, a large seraglio would, without doubt, require an immense income to sustain, as well as make a court luxurious and effeminate—in short, exactly contradict the meaning of Israel's existence, and lead the monarch and his subjects to folly and eventual ruin.

5. Consistent with the injunctions already noted is the one against accumulating riches: "neither shall he greatly multiply to himself silver and gold."[1] The full force of this command lay in the words "to himself." A king's revenue would of necessity be large, for he would have officers to pay or to reward, a certain state to keep up, and many demands on his treasury for public undertakings. Accordingly, these are not the special dangers which this clause was intended to avert, but such as: 1. Useless trade, as bringing in foreign luxury, and creating a desire for splendour and show. 2. Inequality of position, such as must necessarily arise from inequality of possession. 3. Avarice, and hoarding for his own family, instead of laying up for the benefit of the public in the Sanctuary, as seems to have been the custom.[2]

6. The last restriction laid upon the king reads as follows: "And it shall be, when he sitteth upon the throne of his kingdom, that he shall write him a copy of this law in a book, out of that which is before the priests the Levites: and it shall be with him, and he shall read therein all the days of his life; that he may learn to fear the Lord his God, to keep all the words of this law and these statutes, to do them: that his heart be not lifted up above his brethren, and that he turn not aside from the commandment, to the right hand, or to the left: to the end that he may prolong his days in his kingdom, he and his children, in the midst of Israel."[3] The king, according to this, must rule after the appointed laws; and, in order to secure his obedience, he must have an exact copy of them, and study them diligently all the days of his life. He was therefore in no sense a lawgiver, since he could neither make nor alter the laws.

[1] Deut. xvii. 17. [2] 1 Kings xiv. 26. [3] Deut. xvii. 18-20.

THE KING.

Nor, indeed, was this ever attempted all through Old Testament history. Even when bringing in the idolatrous worship of the golden calves, King Jeroboam did not put the worship of the calves as such forward, but professed to sacrifice to God Himself through them.[1] He would not bring in what was entirely novel, but rather strove to infuse the ancient spirit into the new form. The worship of God not being a thing under his supreme authority, his attempt to make it such naturally ended in failure.

Gathering these notices together, and supplementing them from the historical books, an adequate conception can be formed both of what royalty in Israel really became, and what it was originally intended to be.

First, then, it should be noted that the King united in his own person all the powers of the state. He alone could declare war, or make peace. Being permanent and hereditary ruler, he could be of far more service to the state than the Judge, who, being only raised up for extraordinary needs, could but *appeal* for help to his fellow-countrymen, not *demand* it. Next, the King had full command over the country by means of his standing army. Beyond this, he was the supreme judge, the arbitrator of difficult questions, and the appointer of punishment.[2] This privilege would, of course, be open to gross abuse, as when King Saul ordered the destruction of the whole city of Nob;[3] while the opportunities for fomenting discontent afforded by the inconveniences of this primitive mode of administering justice were so taken advantage of by Absalom, that by means of them he succeeded in raising a formidable insurrection against his father.[4] This King David seems to have perceived and felt, for he afterwards appointed regular judges, though still reserving to himself the final power of condemning and acquitting.[5]

Monarchy was to be hereditary, on the condition of obedience to the Divine ordinances. This is implied in the

---

[1] 1 Kings xii. 28. [2] Ibid. iii. 16-28. [3] 1 Sam. xxii. 11-19.
[4] 2 Sam. xv. 2-6. [5] 1 Chron. xxvi. 29.

words: "that he may prolong his days, he and his children, in the midst of Israel."¹ By this law the rights of both king and subject were equally guarded, and the succession secured to those only who proved themselves worthy of ruling. That this actually was the case appears from the history of both Judah and Israel. Saul having proved unfit to reign, the kingdom was after his death, by Divine appointment, and with the glad assent of the tribes, taken from his family, and given to David and his descendants.² Rehoboam, David's grandson, having refused to agree to proposals from ten of the tribes, made that their hardships might be alleviated, lost two-thirds of his kingdom, which was transferred by the revolted tribes to Jeroboam. But the family of the usurper did not long reign; for, having led Israel into idolatry, they had forfeited a main condition of their sovereignty, and were speedily removed from the throne, through Divine overruling of events. The later history of both kingdoms amply bears out what had been foretold—that the Divine law would be vindicated, and that the King whose heart turned away from following God should be destroyed, both he and his sons.

The heir to the throne was not necessarily the first-born, though such an one would generally be selected. Polygamy would, of course, here create much difficulty. So it did in the case of David's sons, Absalom and Adonijah, both of whom found it hard that a younger brother, son of a mother of inferior rank, should have been made heir instead of them. In after times the eldest son was generally elected,³ or, if he had predeceased childless, his next brother. During a minority, or sickness, a regent was appointed.⁴ When the country became tributary to Egyptian or to Assyrian power, the Kings of Israel and Judah were deposed or elevated according to the pleasure of their suzerains, though these puppet-kings were generally taken from the royal family.⁵ In the Kingdom of

---

[1] Deut. xvii. 20.   [2] 1 Sam. xvi. 1-12; 2 Sam. v. 1-3.
[3] 2 Kings i. 17; iii. 1.   [4] 2 Kings xii. 2.
[5] 2 Kings xxiv. 17; 2 Chron. xxxvi. 3, 4, 10.

Israel, succession was often interrupted by revolts of chief captains, or by popular insurrections, when the whole of the deposed monarch's family might be put to the sword.[1] In Judah the succession remained uninterrupted in the family of David.

A limit to despotism also lay in the knowledge of the laws possessed by each Israelite; in the inalienable rights of property; and in the prophetic office. Even Queen Jezebel could only procure the confiscation of Naboth's vineyard by false accusation and murder. The prophets further, with their permitted freedom of speech and access to court, must, by their solemn warnings and denunciations, have proved no inconsiderable bar to the exercise of absolute power. Again, the practice seems to have existed that, on the accession of each new monarch, a covenant was entered into both by him and by his subjects.[2] It was for refusing to ratify one proposed to him after his coronation that King Rehoboam lost the Ten Tribes; whom, by Divine command given through a prophet, he was not allowed to make war against, nor punish in any way for their revolt.

Nowhere is the Israelitish King termed, or in any way regarded as "the father of his people." Rather was he their "brother;" and in accordance with this view of the relationship of sovereign to subject, King David, when receiving the assembly, rose to his feet in token of respect, and addressed them as "my brethren."[3] This was in accordance with the Theocratic principle, that One was their Father, even He in heaven, and that all they on earth were brethren.[4]

The royal revenues were considerable, and derived from various sources, chiefly no doubt from royal domains (mostly, probably, confiscated property).[5] Another great source of income would be the herds, the camels, the asses, and the flocks, for which they had a right to a portion of the pasture in the wildernesses.[6] Beyond this, there were the King's tithes;[7] free

---

[1] 2 Kings x. 1-7. [2] 2 Sam. v. 3. [3] 1 Chron. xxviii. 2.
[4] Matt. xxiii. 9. [5] Ezek. xlvi. 18; 1 Chron. xxvi. 26, 28.
[6] 1 Chron. xxvii. 29, 31. [7] 1 Sam. viii. 15.

gifts;[1] a certain fixed proportion of booty taken in war;[2] dues and tribute from dependent states,[3] and trade in special articles of foreign luxury.[4] Part of these revenues, of course, went to pay the royal officers, who were very numerous, and often persons of wealth and position.

The principal court officials seem to have been:—1. The prime minister or chancellor, also called the "recorder,"[5] and "he that was next to the king;"[6] the "scribe," or secretary;[7] the captain of the host;"[8] the captain of the Cherethi and Pelethi, or royal bodyguard;"[9] the "counsellors;"[10] "he over the tribute;"[11] the chamberlain;[12] the cupbearer;[13] the friend of the King,[14] probably courtier; the head of the royal household, or steward, etc.[15]

The manner of enthroning the Israelitish king was not clearly defined, nor could there have been any fixed ceremony, the circumstances of each new accession being generally so totally different. In the early days of the monarchy, Kings were solemnly anointed with the holy oil, and being so consecrated were holy, and might not be touched with impunity.[16] After the accession of Solomon, however, the only monarchs thus installed were Jehu,[17] the Israelitish King who dispossessed the family of Ahab, and in Judah Joash,[18] son of Ahaziah, and Jehoahaz,[19] son of Josiah. In each case the anointing had a special significance attaching to it, mainly by reason of the peculiar circumstances attending the accession. Hence many writers have inferred that the "anointing"—oftentimes the act of the people—was an extraordinary ceremony, only performed when the King required special sanction, as may be inferred from the case of Jehoahaz, who was elected in preference to his elder brother Eliakim; or when a new dynasty was being

[1] 1 Sam. x. 27.
[4] 1 Kings ix. 26, 28.
[7] 2 Sam. viii. 17.
[10] 2 Sam. v. 15.
[13] Neh. i. 11.
[16] 2 Sam. i. 14.

[2] 2 Sam. viii. 7.
[5] 2 Sam. viii. 16.
[8] Ibid. viii. 16, 18.
[11] 2 Sam. xx. 24.
[14] 2 Sam. xv. 37.
[17] 2 Kings ix. 1.
[19] Ibid. xxiii. 30.

[3] 2 Kings iii. 4.
[6] 2 Chron. xxviii. 7.
[9] Ibid. viii. 18.
[12] 2 Kings xxii. 14.
[15] 1 Kings iv. 6.
[18] Ibid. xi. 12.

founded. On ordinary accessions,[1] the King was proclaimed sovereign with popular acclamations, with blasts of trumpet, and by being mounted on the royal steed, and led in a state procession, after which the notables gave him the kiss of homage, to which reference is made in the second Psalm.[2]

To the Jewish King due respect and obedience were paid. Before him the Israelite dismounted, or fell on his face in token of homage.[3] As he passed through the streets, or along the city walls, he was entreated for audience, or to rectify some injustice.[4] He dwelt in a splendid palace, and was waited upon by young men of good position, who received their education together with the princes.[5] To sit at the King's right hand was an honour only conferred on his especial favourites, a mark of the greatest esteem and regard.[6] The pleasure-gardens and summer-palaces of royalty are often referred to,[7] as well as the court musicians, whose duty it was to be in attendance while the King was at table, or at night to sooth his restless hours.[8] Sumptuous was the provision made for the royal household,[9] and splendid the King's table, at which it was an honour to be a regular guest.[10] Even in death the monarch was exalted above his subjects, for in Judah the royal family only might be buried within the city of David; and frequent mention is made of the Kings' sepulchres, as well as of their splendid funerals, which were made occasions of public mourning, lasting for several days.[11]

The insignia of royalty, though not particularly described in the Pentateuch, are frequently referred to in the historical books. Among them were the royal crown or diadem;[12] the sceptre;[13] the throne;[14] the bracelets;[15] and the purple mantle.[16] Probably part of the investiture was the girding on of a sword, and to this ceremony may refer the expressions, "strengthening the

[1] 1 Kings i. 32–40.   [2] Psa. ii. 12.   [3] 2 Sam. ix. 6.
[4] 2 Kings vi. 26, etc.   [5] 1 Kings xii. 8.   [6] Ibid. ii. 19.
[7] Jer. xxxix. 4 ; Cant. viii. 11.   [8] Eccl. ii. 8 ; Dan. vi. 18.
[9] 1 Kings iv. 22, etc.   [10] 2 Sam. ix. 7, 8.   [11] 2 Chron. xvi. 14.
[12] 2 Sam. xii. 30.   [13] Esther v. 2.   [14] 1 Kings x. 18.
[15] 2 Sam. i. 10.   [16] 1 Macc. vi. 15.

right hand," [1] and "girding the sword on the thigh," [2] used with reference to God's anointed ones.

Such, in some measure, was royalty in Israel in the days before the Exile. After the return from Babylon, when the country had become, first a Syrian, and finally a Roman province, a Jewish King from among his brethren ceased to be a possibility. Yet the nation still cherished the hope of an Israelitish Messiah-King, a mighty Deliverer from, and Leader against, all Israel's foes. And even the Apostles, after three years' teaching from our Lord, could not divest themselves of the idea that He would eventually, if not then speedily, restore the Kingdom—the world-kingdom—to Israel.[3] So they and the Jews of old, as well as we in these days, had to learn through bitter disappointment that Christ's Kingdom was not of this world, neither came with observation,[4] but was "righteousness, and peace, and joy in the Holy Ghost." [5]

[1] Isa. xlv. 1. [2] Psa. xlv. 3. [3] Acts i. 6. [4] Luke xvii. 20. [5] Rom. xiv. 17.

CHAPTER II.

PRIESTS AND LEVITES.

THE priesthood in Israel, as designed by God, and portrayed in the Pentateuch, was one of the most important institutions of the Mosaic Code. Its distinction from the monarchy consisted chiefly in its being, necessarily, a permanent, immutable office, and as such quite above popular choice or interference. The relationship between priest and people, then, was very unlike that which existed between King and subject. For, whereas the monarch was simply the elder brother, the priest stood between the congregation and God in a twofold relationship. As regarded the people, he was God's minister and messenger; in reference to God, he was the nation's representative and mouthpiece. Standing as he thus did between God and Israel, the priestly office would be strictly a *religious* one, and this in the sense of binding again to their Great King those who, without this mediator, might and would have lapsed into idolatry.

The need of a priesthood, in the sense of a link between the Visible and the Invisible, had been felt from the earliest ages; and, as in so many other cases, this human need was recognised and met by the Divine appointment. In patriarchal times each head of a family acted as priest to his own household, building altars and offering sacrifices. But when these families had expanded into tribes, and finally into a nation, the need of a uniform and fixed mode of worship, and of persons whose life-business it would be to superintend the devotions of Israel, was fully recognised, and the want supplied. In other countries, such as Egypt,[1]

---

[1] Gen. xli. 45.

Midian,[1] even in the land of Canaan,[2] priests had long since been the spiritual, often also the temporal, rulers, over their fellow-countrymen. But when on Mount Sinai Moses was directed to set apart his brother Aaron and his sons for the priestly office, there was a peculiar significance in the institution at that time, and to that people. For God had just vouchsafed a revelation of Himself to Israel, which would distinguish that nation to all ages from every other one, and which had brought the Jews into a relationship with God such as had never been enjoyed since the Fall. Israel was now to become to God "a kingdom of priests, and an holy nation,"[3] "a peculiar treasure above all people." According to this view, if Israel but obeyed God's voice, and kept His covenant, there would have been no need of a priesthood. Yet, though this obedience was set before Israel as a possible frame of mind, it never became a real one. Even with the firmest intention of serving God, the whole of the nation could scarcely have been expected to succeed in being always so perfectly holy as to be worthy of approaching God. The priests, however, who were not to entangle themselves with the affairs of this life, not to contract any defilement, nor to do anything unworthy of their high position, might fitly act as representatives of the holy community—be to Israel, so to speak, what the Most Holy Place was to the Tabernacle, that building whereof each part was holy, the sanctity of the Most Holy being distinct from that of the other courts not so much in kind, as in degree. This explains the great difference between the Israelitish priesthood and that of heathendom. The Jewish priests were not separated from the rest of the nation, in that they were regarded as the sole depositaries of Divine truths, initiated in sacred mysteries their fellow countrymen could never hope to learn. They were simply typical, representative men, whose whole lives were devoted to the one object of serving God, and who in virtue of this life-consecration stood between God and sinning man, acting on behalf of the one and of the other—teaching in their lives the great lesson

[1] Exod. ii. 16.   [2] Gen. xiv. 18.   [3] Exod. xix. 4-6.

of *Holiness to the Lord.* In short, as the prophet Malachi preached to the apostate priesthood in after ages, this was their true office and work: "For the priest's lips should keep knowledge, and they should seek the law at his mouth: for he is the messenger of the Lord of hosts,"[1]—his lips must teach what he himself has known, for the words he has to speak are not his own, but his Lord's, Who gave him the commission.

The Pentateuch legislation did not introduce the priesthood, then, as something quite novel, but rather expanded those views of worship which had come down from the patriarchal ages, further adding what was necessary to ensure its permanent usefulness and beauty. And as the royalty in Israel was symbolic and typical, so also was the priesthood, for it pointed forward to Him who was the Mediator of a better covenant,[2] even Christ, made a priest for ever after the order of Melchisedec.[3]

THE LEVITES.

The tribe selected for the service of God in holy things was that of Levi, the descendants of the third son of Jacob. Their separation dates from the Exodus, when they were chosen by God in the place of the firstborn sons of all Israel. It has been supposed by some, though without sufficient reason, that their selection was on account of the assistance they rendered Moses after the sin of the golden calf in executing vengeance on the idolaters.[4] The earliest notice of their being devoted to the service of God does not, however, occur till after the first census taken in the wilderness—that of men able for war. Injunction was then given not to number the tribe of Levi, but to give them the supervision of the Tabernacle and its vessels, and to appoint their camping-place immediately round it.[5] In Num. iii. 12, 13 it is distinctly stated that the Levites were taken instead of the firstborn, and this "because all the firstborn are Mine; for on the day that I smote all the firstborn in the land of Egypt, I hallowed unto Me all the firstborn in Israel,

---

[1] Mal. ii. 7.   [2] Heb. viii. 6.   [3] Heb. v. 10.
[4] Exod. xxxii. 26-29.   [5] Num. i. 47-53.

both man and beast, Mine shall they be." From this verse it has been conjectured that till the rearing of the Tabernacle sacrifices might be offered by any Israelite, and that the choosing of the tribe of Levi was only rendered necessary by the establishment of the central sanctuary, of which they were the custodians. This hypothesis is, of course, unsupported by the history. The more likely explanation seems to be that in them Israel would have a perpetual memorial of their deliverance from Egypt, and of their consecration as a nation; while this tribe in particular was selected, partly on account of the fact that Moses and Aaron belonged to it, and partly on account of its compactness and smallness.

The *duties* of the tribe of Levi—which as a tribe is distinguished from the family of Aaron—were clearly defined in the Pentateuch. In the wilderness they were to have the charge of the fabric of the Tabernacle, and of its vessels, and the honour and responsibility of removing them, carefully covered by the priests, from one camping-place to another.[1] When the Tabernacle was set up in any place, the Levites were to act as porters or doorkeepers, as well as to assist the priests in certain offices. After the entrance into Canaan, and especially after the appointment of the Temple ritual, the services performed by the Levites became more important. Besides being porters in the Temple buildings,[2] they were formed into a choir, and became the leaders in sacred music, both vocal and instrumental. To them we owe many of the most beautiful Psalms (those for the sons of Asaph, and of Korah). Their general position in regard to the service of the sanctuary is thus characterised in the Book of Chronicles, as keeping "the charge of the tabernacle of the congregation, and the charge of the holy place, and the charge of the sons of Aaron their brethren, in the service of the house of the Lord;"[3] in the Book of Numbers[4] as "the service of the ministry, and the service of the burden in the tabernacle of the congregation." This "service" began from their twenty-fifth or thirtieth year, and lasted till their fiftieth year.

[1] Num. iii. iv.   [2] 1 Chron. xxiii.   [3] Ibid. xxiii. 32.   [4] Num. iv. 47.

The tribe of Levi consisted of three great families: those of Gershon, of Kohath, and of Merari. From the second of these families—that of Kohath—Aaron and his sons were chosen for the priesthood. The other Levites were consecrated by the laying on of hands, and by the offering of special sacrifices.[1] As regarded their social position, they were not given any tribal territory in the land of Canaan, and this because "the Lord is his inheritance, according as the Lord thy God promised him."[2] The Levites were thus placed on quite a different footing from the rest of the nation, each member of which, being an independent landed proprietor, derived his influence solely from his inalienable possession. In a state purely agricultural, where all property was in kind, the most influential persons would naturally be those who were the largest landowners. But this influence the Levites could not hope to obtain. All the land allotted to them consisted of forty-eight cities, the dimensions of which were limited to a very small area. As these were scattered throughout the length and breadth of the land, it would have been impossible for the tribe to muster in any great force, and so obtain the mastery over their fellow-countrymen. The only real influence they could hope, then, to obtain, would be a personal, not substantial one, gained by reason of a holy life, or by superior knowledge. But even thus they were limited by being forbidden to keep others in ignorance of holy things. They had specially to teach what they themselves had learned concerning the law of God. In other branches of knowledge, any Israelite might compete with the Levite. For example, not Levites, but members of the tribes of Judah and Dan were chosen to superintend the making of the Tabernacle and of its furniture.[3] The office of judge did not of necessity belong to them, while they were—at least in the time of Moses—excluded from military appointments.[4] Outwardly, then, their position differed vastly from that of re-

---

[1] Num. viii. 5–12.   [2] Deut. x. 8, 9.
[3] Exod. xxxv. 30, 34. Comp. 2 Chron. ii. 13, 14.
[4] Deut. xxvii. 14–26; xxxiii. 10.

ligious orders in other countries; in fact, we find them classed with the poor, and the command is given not to forsake them.[1]

The forty-eight Levitical cities were allotted to the tribe after the land of Canaan had been divided by Joshua. They comprised the six cities of refuge, and forty-two other towns.[2] Of these forty-eight thirteen were appropriated by the priests, ten by the rest of the family of Kohath, thirteen by the Gershonites, and twelve by the Merarites. These cities, situated throughout the length and breadth of the land, were merely intended to supply the immediate wants of the Levites. In order, however, to secure them more effectually to the tribe, a Levite who had sold his house or land was allowed to redeem it at any time when he had wherewithal to do so, and was not obliged to wait till the Jubilee year before his property returned to him, as an ordinary Israelite must do.[3] The only other source of revenue to the Levites was that of tithes.[4] These, which seem to have been given even in patriarchal times,[5] though periodically due, and binding on the nation, were very irregularly paid in later times, and seem almost to have been regarded as a sort of alms.[6]

Very few instances, and these mainly of individuals, occur in which the tribe of Levi is noticed from the time of the allotment of their cities to that of King David. After that monarch had been established firmly on the throne, the Levites were appointed to offices and service in the Temple. In the time of Rehoboam, when, through the influence of Jeroboam, the worship of the golden calves had been introduced into Israel, the Levites dwelling in the revolted provinces forsook their cities and possessions, and came to Judah and Jerusalem, having been deprived of their offices by the usurper-king.[7] The influence exercised by the Levites over the people at this period must have been very considerable, for it is recorded that "after them out of all the tribes of Israel such as set their

---

[1] Deut. xii. 19. etc. [2] Josh. xxi. [3] Lev. xxv. 32.
[4] Num. xviii. 21-24. [5] Gen. xiv. 20. [6] Mal. iii. 8.
[7] 2 Chron. xi. 13, 14.

hearts to seek the Lord God of Israel came to Jerusalem, to sacrifice unto the Lord God of their fathers."[1] After this period the Levites do not again play a prominent part in Old Testament history, until the time of the zealous Ezra, and of Zerubbabel and Jeshua.[2]

From these historical notices it will appear that, in later times, the Levites made no attempt to arrogate to themselves power. But such was not the case at the time of the separation of the tribe. Great jealousy was then excited by the choice of Aaron and his sons for the priesthood, and the secretly cherished enmity at length broke out into open rebellion against Moses and his brother.[3] The ringleader in the conspiracy was Korah, a member of the family of the Kohathites, and the movement evidently occasioned great alarm.[4] The awful judgment that overtook the conspirators effectually awed the whole assembly; and the memory of it was for ever preserved in the "covering for the altar,"[5] made from the censers of those who had been burned, significantly termed "sinners against their own souls." The miracle of Aaron's rod blossoming silenced for ever all opposition to the choice of his family for the priesthood, and henceforward no attempt was made to dispute his right, either on the part of the Levites, or on that of any other tribe.

An account of the "separation" of the Levites is given in detail in the Book of Numbers.[6] From this it would appear that the ceremony there described was a final one, *i.e.* not repeated in after ages. The Levites were first sprinkled with "water of purifying," their flesh carefully shaved, and their garments washed. Two young bullocks were then taken, for a sin and a burnt offering, and the Levites brought before the Tabernacle, where the "whole assembly of the children of Israel" was gathered together. They were next set apart by the laying on of the hands of the elders of Israel, and "offered to the Lord" by Aaron; after which they laid their hands on the bullocks, which were then sacrificed as an atonement for them.

---

[1] 2 Chron. xi. 16.   [2] Ezra iii. 2; vii. 11.   [3] Num. xvi.
[4] Ibid. vers. 4-11.   [5] Ibid. vers. 36-40.   [6] Ibid. viii. 5-26.

THE PRIESTS.

The selection of the family of Aaron for the priesthood dates from the forty days spent by Moses on Mount Sinai.[1] They were chosen "from among the children of Israel," and particularly for the ministry of the sanctuary. This service was to be hereditary, and to be performed precisely in the manner appointed by God. In no sense were the priests to be free agents—in fact, most severe punishment would visit such as dared transgress even the letter of the law. Thus were they to act as representatives alike of God and of Israel, and in falling short of this terribly high standard would they bring with their sin its own condemnation and punishment.

The Book of Leviticus furnishes most minute details of the duties, responsibilities, penalties, revenues, and dress of the priests. From it, and other notices in the Books of Exodus and Numbers, a correct estimate can be formed of the general position and aim of the priesthood in Israel. But as this subject belongs more properly to the Ritual Law,[2] only such part of it as concerns the relation of priest to people, and the barest outline of the social position of the former, can here be given.

The Hebrew word for priest, *cohen*, probably signifies "a minister," "one who stands to minister," and as such is used in the Old Testament to designate the family of Aaron. The principal duties of the *cohen* were, of course, connected with the service of the Sanctuary. Of this the most honourable part, that which was, in fact, the very essence of his ministry, was the offering of sacrifices, which were to be brought by Israel as atonement for their sins, or as thank-offerings, etc. Beyond the actual slaying and burning of animals in sacrifice, it was the duty of the priests in the Sanctuary to burn incense on the golden altar in the Holy Place,[3] to clean and fill the lamps on the golden candlestick,[4] to pronounce the blessing,[5] and to

---

[1] See *Rites and Worship of the Jews*.
[2] Exod. xxviii. 1. [3] Ibid. xxx 7. [4] Lev. xxiv. 1–4. [5] Num. vi. 23–26.

THE PRIESTS. 21

change the shewbread every Sabbath day.[1] These duties constituted part of the regular services, and were to be entered upon with reverence—manifested by bared feet—and with renewed self-consecration—symbolised by lustrations, abstinence from wine or strong drink, etc. Besides these offices, the priests had various other functions, which they alone could perform. The silver trumpets which announced the Sabbatical and Jubilee Years were kept and blown by them,[2] and a town wherein murder had been committed by some unknown hand must be "reconciled" through a ceremony which could but be performed by the priests.[3] Further, they were to pronounce judgment on the leper,[4] as well as to declare sentence in the case of a woman required to drink the so-called "waters of jealousy." In other matters their responsibilities as teachers and arbitrators were very great. The priests were those charged to keep the book of the covenant, and to teach the people out of it. To them Kings were to apply for instruction in their duties. As regarded matters of public safety and health, according to the prescription of the Pentateuch, the priests were to act as sanitary officers, pronouncing sentence on infected houses, garments, etc.[5] They must, therefore, have been required to possess a certain knowledge of medicine, as well as of natural history.

At the head of the priesthood, and, indeed, of the whole tribe of Levi, stood the High priest, or Chief priest (*ha-cohen haggadol*), who must be a lineal descendant of Aaron. The office was intended to be for life, and involved unusual responsibilities and privileges. As the head of his brethren, the High priest had a general superintendence of the service of the sanctuary, and of the tithes, a tenth part of which was to be given by the Levites to the priests.[6] The most solemn part of the service on the Day of Atonement, that of sprinkling the blood before the Mercy-Seat, might only be performed by the High priest, and he alone of all Israel might enter the Most Holy Place on that day once every year.[7]

[1] Lev. xxiv. 5–9.   [2] Num. x. 8.   [3] Deut. xxi. 1–9.   [4] Lev. xiv.
[5] Lev. xiv.   [6] Num. xviii. 25–28.   [7] Lev. xvi.

The revenues of the priests were not at first considerable, but were well secured to them. Besides the tenth part of the tithes given by the Levites as an "heave-offering," the priests were to receive certain dues from the congregation. Of these dues may be mentioned the "ransom-money" to be paid for every firstborn Israelitish son,[1] though it seems doubtful whether in the earlier ages this money—five shekels of the sanctuary—was regularly demanded, or whether it was not rather a reserve fund that might be levied for some religious undertaking, such as for repairing or building the sanctuary. However this may be, the priests possessed, as sources of regular income, the "first-fruits" of food, both in its natural and in its prepared state, certain parts of the animals and other offering brought for sacrifice, as well as the shewbread which had been removed from the golden table.[2] Certain portions of the sacrificial food might be eaten by the priest's family also, by a widowed daughter who had returned to her father's house, by slaves, either purchased or else born in the house; but not by strangers, nor by hired servants.[3] But no priest's daughter married to a layman might eat this food. In the matter of sacrificial portions, a distinction was made between holy and most holy food, of which the former might be freely eaten by the priest's family, provided it were not kept too long, while of the latter only the priests themselves might eat, generally only within the sanctuary.[4] Of ordinary, *i.e.* not sacred, food the priest might freely eat of clean animals, but on no account of that which "dieth of itself, or is torn with beasts."[5]

In order to secure the holiness of those who ministered to the Lord in their persons and in their family life, it was enjoined that no member of a priestly family having certain bodily deformities might minister in holy things.[6] Nor might any one venture to perform priestly duties who was sick, or defiled in any way.[7] The penalty for disobeying this command was being "cut off"—a terrible punishment, implying banish-

---

[1] Num. xviii. 16; comp. ch. iii. 46-48.   [2] Ibid. vers. 8-14.   [3] Lev. xxii. 10-13.
[4] Num. xviii. 10.   [5] Lev. xxii. 8.   [6] Ibid. xxi. 17-23.   [7] Ibid. xxi. 1-8.

ment from God, as well as loss of the privileges enjoyed by an Israelite. The reason for such awful judgment is furnished us: God was to be sanctified in those that approached Him, therefore all they that did so must be perfectly holy—outwardly as well as inwardly.

In his domestic relations also must the priest be holy.[1] No tonsure must he make upon his head, nor incision in his flesh as token of mourning; nor might he cut and round the corners of his beard. The High priest might not, on the death of any relation, however near, rend his garments, nor dishevel his hair,[2] though an ordinary priest might do so in token of mourning for father, mother, brother, maiden sister, son, or daughter[3]—according to the Talmud, also wife. The wife of a priest must be a woman of good character,[4] that of the high priest a virgin, and an Israelite.[5] The daughter of any priest convicted of adultery must be burned to death.[6]

While engaged in the services of the sanctuary, the priests were to be barefooted, and to put on special symbolic garments,[7] described in Exodus xxxix. 27-29. From this passage it appears that there were four distinctive priestly garments: the under-garment of byssus, or "fine linen of woven work;" the cap or "mitre" of fine linen; "breeches," reaching to the knees, "of fine twined linen;" and a girdle of many colours, made of the same materials as the veil before the Most Holy Place, viz., fine twined linen, and blue and purple and scarlet needlework. When not ministering, the priest wore the garments of the ordinary Israelite.

The dress of the High priest was both magnificent and costly.[8] Besides the common priestly garments, he wore four others, distinguishing him from the ordinary *cohen*. Of these

[1] Lev. xxi. 1-5.   [2] Ibid. vers. 10, 11.   [3] Ibid. vers. 1-4.
[4] Ibid. ver. 7.   [5] Ibid. ver. 13.   [6] Ibid. ver. 9.
[7] Everything connected with the priestly garments was symbolic. Thus, their number, four, was symbolic of that Name Jehovah, (written in Hebrew in four letters), by which God had revealed Himself to Israel. The colour of the "byssus" was symbolic of holiness, and of glory, etc. Comp. Bähr, *Symbolik des Mos. Cultus*, vol. ii. p. 71, etc.   [8] Exod. xxxix. 22, etc.

the first was an upper, sleeveless garment, reaching below to his knees, and with an opening above to admit his head, the colour being hyacinth. This "robe of the ephod," as it was termed, had an embroidered hem, of "pomegranates of blue, and purple, and scarlet, and twined linen," separated by "bells of pure gold," which were to make a tinkling when Aaron went into the sanctuary.[1] Over this "robe of the ephod" the High priest wore the "ephod" itself, a short garment in two pieces, the one covering the back, the other the breast, down to the waist. The ephod was fastened above by shoulder-pieces of gold, in which were set onyx stones, "graven with the names of the children of Israel," and below with an embroidered girdle. The ephod and the girdle were of "gold, and blue, and purple, and scarlet, and fined twined linen," and fitted close to the upper part of the body.[2] On the ephod again the High priest wore the "breastplate," a square, "doubled" piece of "cunning work," made of the same materials as the ephod, and fastened to the shoulder-pieces above by golden chains, and to the "girdle of the ephod" by a lace of blue, and golden rings. In this breastplate were set twelve precious stones, on each of which was engraved the name of a tribe, and in the midst of the breastplate the Urim and Thummim, to be upon Aaron's heart, when he went in before the Lord.[3] Further, the High priest wore on his head, besides a kind of turban called "the mitre," a diadem or "plate of the holy crown," of pure gold, on which were engraven the words, *Holiness to the Lord*. This "plate" was fastened to the "mitre" by a lace of blue.[4]

The special service by the High priest alone once every year on the Day of Atonement, that of offering the sin-offering for himself and for the people, and of sprinkling the blood before the mercy-seat, was to be performed in the plain garments of an ordinary priest,[5] to indicate that on that day he approached God as a sinner, and not in his priestly capacity.

---

[1] Exod. xxviii. 35.   [2] Ibid. xxxix. 1–7.   [3] Ibid. xxviii. 30.
[4] Ibid. xxxix. 30, 31.   [5] Lev. xvi. 4.

THE PRIESTS.

The ceremony of consecrating Aaron and his sons to the priesthood took place after the rearing and sanctifying of the Tabernacle, and was performed by Moses according to Divine command. The priests first underwent the legal lustrations, were robed in their sacred garments, and Aaron anointed with the holy oil. A bullock was then offered as a sin-offering, and two rams, one as a burnt-offering, the other "of consecration." Aaron and his sons were next touched with the blood of the ram of the consecration, and the altar likewise sprinkled. The wave-offering was then brought, and waved on the hands of Aaron and his sons, after which they were sprinkled with the anointing oil, and with part of the blood from off the altar. The ceremony was brought to a close, after a watch of seven days on the part of the priests at the door of the Tabernacle, by the offering of various sacrifices for Aaron and for the people, when, as Moses and Aaron blessed the congregation, "the glory of the Lord appeared unto all the people; and there came a fire out from before the Lord, and consumed upon the altar the burnt-offering and the fat: which, when all the people saw, they shouted, and fell on their faces." [1]

As regards the after history of the priesthood, it need here only be mentioned, that the distinctive priestly service, that of offering sacrifices, was performed on some extraordinary occasions—though not, of course, in the Sanctuary—by prophets; as, for example, by Elijah on Mount Carmel.[2] On this occasion the prophet's act was owned by God; hence it was not one of which He disapproved. On the contrary, the prophet then stood before the sinful people as a representation, a picture, of what they themselves might have been: the holy nation of priests, united (as symbolised by the twelve stones), offering to God acceptable sacrifice—purified by water, and meetly prepared for the heavenly fire. In the same sense is each Christian, as St. Peter has taught, one of a royal priesthood,[3] whose sacrifices are not of bulls and goats, but of their

[1] Lev. ix. 23, 24.   [2] 1 Kings xviii. 30–39.   [3] 1 Peter ii. 9.

own bodies, presented as a living sacrifice, holy, acceptable unto God, which last is reasonable, or, spiritual service.[1]

And still further, beyond all the gorgeous ritual, and deeper than the outward observances, there was a typical meaning. For they—the priesthood, the sacrifices, the Tabernacle and Temple—all pointed forward to Him Who, "because He continueth ever, hath an unchangeable priesthood,"[2] even to One Who, "being come an high priest of good things to come, by a greater and more perfect Tabernacle, not made with hands, that is to say, not of this building; neither by the blood of goats and calves, but by His own blood, He entered in once into the holy place, having obtained eternal redemption for us."[3]

[1] Rom. xii. 1.   [2] Heb. vii. 24.   [3] Ibid. ix. 11, 12.

CHAPTER III.

PROPHETS.

THROUGHOUT the history of the Kingdom of God in the Old Testament, the agency most powerful for good was that of the prophetic order. It was, so to speak, the centre power of the whole; and this power is acknowledged even by those who would fain deny its usefulness. No one, then, can form a true or adequate conception of the life, political or domestic, of Israel, without there standing out in the foreground the "Man of God," that mysteriously God-inspired servant, who could peer into the future, and read its pages, even as others might those of the past; and whose most awful warnings not even an idolatrous king, nor a rebellious nation, dared silence, or treat with contempt.

The English word "prophet" has three Hebrew equivalents, each differing in signification. The most usual designation, *navi*, or "weller forth," seems to point to the prophet as a man speaking in the Spirit of God, pouring forth the Word of the Lord as revealed to him. The other two names, *choseh* and *roeh*, the "seer," are somewhat kindred in meaning, and mark the prophet as the "seer" of, and "gazer upon," the Divine vision—*navi* thus referring to his outward mission, *roeh* and *choseh* to his inward calling and preparedness. The three designations are frequently used interchangeably; while from 1 Samuel ix. 9, it would appear that "seer" (*roeh*) was the ancient name for him "that is now called a prophet" (*navi*)—or, as one has explained it, that designation which anciently but expressed the *form* in which the revelation was made was now changed for one that penetrated beyond the form to its *source*, even to God Himself.[1]

The prophets mentioned in the Old Testament were not, however, always the servants of the true God. Sometimes Holy Scripture speaks of the "prophets of Baal," and of those who are false, deceiving prophets. All the Old Testament prophets, however, true or false, have this in common: they profess to be the mediums of Divine communication, those to whom the Deity—whomever such may acknowledge—has revealed what ordinary mortals cannot see. Of course, in the case of God's prophets, this claim was a just one, in that of false prophets an unfounded one. But more than this, the prophets of Jehovah claimed to be, and were, something greater than merely foretellers or magicians. They were spiritual men—"men of the Spirit,"[2] who "spake as they were moved by the Holy Ghost."[3]

The prophets of the Lord, then, must not be looked upon merely as foretellers—as those who by Divine revelation could read the future, and announce certain events as assuredly coming to pass. This was undoubtedly part, but perhaps not the chief part, of their mission. They were specifically "watchmen,"[4] those who made a hedge round Israel, whose office it was to hear the word from the mouth of God, and give warning to, and save from ruin, the rebellious nation.[5] But their work did not end here; for this part of their mission could have been performed by one not Divinely inspired. The prophets pointed forward to the advent of the Messiah, and kept alive in Israel the hope of His appearing, and of the glorious time when the rule of God would not have to be vindicated by wars and judgments, but when all should know Him, from the least unto the greatest. Thus, as men Divinely inspired, having perfect freedom of speech, and liberty of access even to the court of the most idolatrous kings; delivering their message without the slightest fear, painting in burning colours the sins

---

[1] Compare Lange, *Bibel Commentar* on 1 Sam. ix. 9.
[2] Hosea ix. 7. [3] 2 Peter i. 21. [4] Ezek. iii. 17. [5] Ibid. xiii. 5.

alike of King and people, and drawing aside the veil from a future most awful, as recompense most just for guilt unrepented of, not to be bribed nor influenced by the great—they were the ceaseless witnesses of God against idolatry, and the preservers of the true faith, alike in prosperity and in adversity.

The Mosaic legislation, foreseeing the need that would arise for the prophetic order, provided for the security of the prophet on the one hand, and for that of the people on the other. From Deut. xviii. 15, it appears that the office of the prophet was to be like that of Moses on Mount Sinai—the medium of Divine communication, into whose mouth the words of God were to be put, and who was to speak all that he was commanded. Such a person was what the Israelites themselves had specially desired, and to him they must hearken; for if they refused to do so: "I will require it."[1] On the other hand, "the prophet which shall presume to speak a word in My Name, which I have not commanded him to speak, or that shall speak in the name of other gods, even that prophet shall die."[2] Yet this death was not to be by the hand of man; it would be from the Lord, who would vindicate His word and His truth, alike in the case of the false prophet and of the true. Thus viewed, the punishment, which must come from God, would be also apparent to man: it would be of such a kind, and in such a manner, as would be recognised by all. The truth of a prophecy was thus to be ascertained: "When a prophet speaketh in the Name of the Lord, if the thing follow not, nor come to pass, that is the thing which the Lord hath not spoken, but the prophet hath spoken it presumptuously."[3] Nowhere, therefore, is it laid down that the prophet was responsible to man. He was simply God's mouthpiece—as the New Testament explains it: "No prophecy ever came by the will of man: but men spake from God, being moved by the Holy Ghost."[4] In accordance with this principle, even when the false prophet Hananiah was deceiving and leading astray the Israelites, during the reign of Zedekiah,

---

[1] Deut. xviii. 19.   [2] Ibid. ver. 20.   [3] Ibid. ver. 22.   [4] 2 Peter i. 21.

the prophet of God, Jeremiah, did not flatly contradict his words, but submitted them to the test ordained by Moses: "the prophet which prophesieth of peace, when the word of the prophet shall come to pass, then shall the prophet be known, that the Lord hath truly sent him."[1] In the same manner did Jeremiah, not only negatively, but positively, vindicate the reality of the Divine commission entrusted to him: "Hear now, Hananiah; the Lord hath not sent thee; but thou makest this people to trust in a lie. Therefore thus saith the Lord: Behold, I will cast thee from off the face of the earth; this year thou shalt die, because thou hast taught rebellion against the Lord. So," adds the history, as though this were the logical sequence of the other, "Hananiah the prophet died the same year in the seventh month."[2]

Historically speaking, the activity of the prophets of Jehovah may be said to have extended over the period from Samuel to the return from Babylon. The use of the word "prophet" is not, however, confined to that period, but in the Old Testament is employed as a designation for Abraham,[3] for Moses,[4] for Aaron,[5] for Miriam,[6] and for Deborah,[7] etc. But in these instances the term "prophet" or "prophetess," seems rather to designate one to whom the will of God is revealed—in the case of Aaron, for the office of spokesman; in that of Miriam, for that of an inspired singer—not, as in later times, a man whose life was entirely and consciously dedicated to distinct and prophetic work. The prophets, as an order, may be said to have been established in Israel in the time of Samuel. To his lifetime also may be traced the establishment of the so-called "schools of the prophets,"[8] colleges or settlements where men of any age, though generally young, married or unmarried, were taught the Divine will, and trained to be the teachers and spiritual guides of the people. These "schools of the sons of the prophets" were probably so termed from their president, or "father," being a prophet. The history does not seem to imply

---

[1] Jer. xxviii. 9.   [2] Ibid. vers. 15-17.   [3] Gen. xx. 7.   [4] Deut. xxxiv. 10.
[5] Exod. vii. 1.   [6] Ibid. xv. 20.   [7] Judg. iv. 4.   [8] 2 Kings iv. 1.

that these "sons of the prophets" were possessed of predictive gifts, although they were sometimes despatched on prophetic errands, which they executed with faithfulness.[1] The false zeal and religious curiosity of the "sons of the prophets" at the time of the assumption of Elijah,[2] prove how far they often were from being "men of the Spirit," as well as does their utter dependence on their head for direction and help in difficulties or dangers.[3] The chief stations for the "schools of the prophets" were Ramah,[4] Jericho,[5] Beth-el,[6] and Gilgal.[7] In these settlements they seem to have lived in common, and to have worked for their needs, their more pressing wants being supplied by the generosity of the devout in Israel.[8]

As regarded *the character* of the prophet of Jehovah, it was most necessary, to begin with, that he should be a man of a pure and a holy life. He whose spiritual eyes were opened to behold Divine realities must have his outward and carnal eyes closed;[9] the lips which had been given God's message to utter must have been purified, even with hot coals from off the sacred altar.[10] In short, the prophet must become another man, with a new heart.[11] He must have no will of his own in matters which concerned his message and calling, but must obey to the letter whatever he might have been commanded by God. Thus, he must not shrink from loathsome or unlawful food,[12] from walking barefoot long years,[13] nor from doing anything, however repulsive to his natural inclinations. The message he was charged to give, or the prediction he uttered, was not of his own framing and devising: it was the Word of the Lord, which, coming from Him, could not return "void," but must be delivered to those to whom it had been sent.[14] It would have been useless for the prophet to attempt to disobey, or to ignore the "Hand,"[15] the "Strong Hand"[16] of

---

[1] 2 Kings ix. 1-10. [2] Ibid. ii. [3] Ibid. iv. 38-41; vi. 1-7.
[4] 1 Sam. xix. 19. [5] 2 Kings ii. 5. [6] Ibid. ii. 3.
[7] 2 Kings iv. 38. [8] Ibid. iv. 42. [9] Num. xxiv. 3, 4.
[10] Isa. vi. 6. [11] 1 Sam. x. 6, 9. [12] Ezek. iv. 14, 15.
[13] Isa. xx. 2, 3. [14] Isa. lv. 11. [15] Jer. xv. 17.
[16] Isa. viii. 11; Ezek. viii. 3.

God, for nothing could withstand it. The prophet Jonah might try to flee to Tarshish from the presence of the Lord,[1] but his attempt would be vain, for, in the words of the prophet Jeremiah, God was stronger than he, and would prevail. The prophet could not keep back his message, whatever might come upon him in consequence from man, or however it might seem to be spoken into the air. Vain, then, were the efforts of man to silence the prophet, for he was mastered by an overwhelming power. So, in the anguish of his soul, after a night spent in the stocks, when brought forth out of them by his persecutors, Jeremiah could not keep back his message, but could only thus make his complaint to God: "Since I spake, I cried out, I cried violence and spoil; because the word of the Lord was made a reproach unto me, and a derision, daily. Then I said, I will not make mention of Him, nor speak any more in His Name. But His Word was in mine heart as a burning fire shut up in my bones, and I was weary with forbearing, and I could not stay."[2]

Yet, though the prophet was constrained to deliver his message faithfully, the form of it was intensely sympathetic, full of human tenderness, often most loving and entreating. For, before the prophet's far-seeing eyes were immense dangers—calamities coming thick and fast upon his own people, who all blindly courted their ruin, misled by idolatrous rulers, by false prophets, by false signs and wonders. Earnestly, as seeing these things, did the prophet warn, exhort, and entreat; now speaking on behalf of God to his fellow-countrymen; again, as mouthpiece of the nation, beseeching God to avert His judgments, and to pardon their iniquities. Little mattered it to him what calamities overtook[3] him personally, since the Lord was with him to deliver him, whose most glorious title was that of servant to Jehovah. Life-work thus God-dedicated and God-protected was more than recompense for all dangers, even for death.

The gift of prophecy was neither hereditary, nor yet confined to any especial tribe. It was strictly an extraordinary agency;

---

[1] Jonah i.   [2] Jer. xx. 8, 9.   [3] Ibid. i. 19.

and though not necessarily connected with the power of working miracles, was usually attended by some "sign," as token of its Divine origin (as in the case of the remarkable recovery of King Hezekiah),[1] or by some symbolic action (as the rending of the altar at Beth-el).[2] The manner in which the prophet was called to his office would be by a vision,[3] or by some other inward communication. But no single message might be delivered without special revelation, which often required a mind and body prepared for it in solitude and prayer. The manner of announcing the Divine message was, of necessity, clear and concise. For instance, Elijah suddenly appeared, and as suddenly disappeared, having his message prepared before he came upon the scene.[4] At another time, Elisha's message was not furnished beforehand, but a musician was employed to bring upon him "the Hand of the Lord."[5] Again, the message might be delivered in the form of a dialogue (as in the case of Hananiah), or even of a writing left after the prophet's death.[6]

In other directions the activity of the prophetic order made itself felt. As sacred writers, chroniclers, and poets, they recorded events from their own standpoint, seeing below the surface the fundamental principles of justice vindicated, God's rule more firmly established, and the best and highest ends of the Theocracy served. Often they were only bidden write what was afterwards to be known by Israel, this task being sometimes dictated by them to an amanuensis or scribe (as Baruch acted to Jeremiah).[7] The prophets' service for God was likewise acknowledged by Him in various ways, such as by a supply of food for daily needs,[8] or by the power, so often granted them, of working miracles,[9] or by deliverance from threatened danger.[10]

Further, the prophet must be a man whose understanding was ripened, and whose mind was readily receptive of the message

---

[1] Isa. xxxviii. 8.   [2] 1 Kings xiii. 1-5.   [3] Isa. vi. 1, etc.
[4] 1 Kings xvii. 1, etc.   [5] 2 Kings iii. 15.   [6] 2 Chron. xxi. 12.
[7] Jer. xxxvi.   [8] 1 Kings xvii. 6.   [9] Ibid. xvii. 14.   [10] 2 Kings vi. 13-23.

entrusted to him. In every instance, save that of the child Samuel, who is described as wise above his years, the prophet was of mature age, and usually, though not necessarily, a learned man.[1] In every instance, also, except in that of Jonah, the message of the prophets was delivered to Israel, though often the predictions uttered by them concerned Israel's allies or enemies. Repentance for the sin denounced by the prophet might stay,[2] or even avert the coming judgment;[3] but from Old Testament history it seems too true that such repentance from fear was by no means that "godly sorrow which worketh repentance to salvation not to be repented of;"[4] but rather that the prophet was only resorted to in cases of direst necessity,[5] while, when possible, he was ill-treated, imprisoned, and even slain.[6]

With regard to their mission to the two kingdoms after the separation under Rehoboam, it is remarkable that the prophets in Israel, who were far more numerous than those in Judah, arose at all times when the northern kingdom had sunk deepest in idolatry, and had renounced most entirely the worship of the One True God. On the other hand, at least during part of Judah's history, the prophets in the southern kingdom were the preachers of, and aiders in, the great spiritual revivals, under such kings as Jehoshaphat, Hezekiah, etc. But, when Judah's cup of iniquity was filling up, and when, harassed on all sides by enemies, there was most need of a faithful prophet, then it was that such were most cruelly persecuted, even unto death, by the degenerate kings.[7]

In dress the prophet was distinguished chiefly by his simplicity, his raiment being poor, even to coarseness. The distinctive garment seems to have been the prophet's "mantle,"[8] and a "garment of hair,"[9] fastened with a leather girdle.[10] His dress was sometimes symbolic,[11] while even domestic

[1] Comp. Amos vii. 14.
[2] 1 Kings xxi. 29.
[3] Jonah iii. 10.
[4] 2 Cor. vii. 10.
[5] 1 Kings xxii. 7.
[6] Ibid. vers. 26, 27.
[7] 2 Chron. xvi. 10; xxiv. 20, 21.
[8] 1 Kings xix. 13.
[9] Zech. xiii. 4.
[10] 2 Kings i. 8.
[11] Isa. xx. 2.

PROPHETS.   35

events were not without their meaning to the nation at large.[1] The outward call to the office might be in various ways: as in the case of Elisha, by the casting of Elijah's mantle upon his shoulders.[2] Disobedience to the letter of the commission necessitated instant death, since the prophet could in no sense be termed a free agent—that is, while he was engaged on his errand.[3]

From 2 Kings iv. 23, it would appear that the prophets were accustomed to teach the people—probably explained the Law, and warned their hearers against idolatry and disobedience to God—on new moons, and on Sabbaths. This teaching and warning was delivered in open places: "in the gate" of the city,[4] at the Temple gates,[5] in the Temple courts;[6] while their special messages, to individuals, were delivered in the king's palace,[7] in the open street,[8] or conveyed by a chosen messenger.[9] In all ages, even the most idolatrous, the prophets were regarded with awe and fear, and after their decease splendid sepulchres were reared to such of them as had fallen victims to the fury of offended monarchs.[10] Of these the New Testament speaks, and this tardy acknowledgment serves in the mouth of our Lord as another witness against that generation which betrayed and murdered Him to Whom all the prophets had given witness.[11]

In the Kingdom of Israel, the prophets' bitterest foes were the sovereigns of the land. Queen Jezebel sought to exterminate them altogether,[12] and even when the presence of Elijah or Elisha was absolutely necessary for the safety of city or state, their lives were often in imminent danger.[13] Truly, it required great and strong faith, as seeing Him who is invisible,[14] to uphold that sure word of prophecy, that light shining in a dark place.[15] For it must indeed have seemed hard that they, who by their righteousness alone saved the

[1] Ezek. xxiv. 18.   [2] 1 Kings xix. 19.   [3] See 1 Kings xiii.
[4] Amos v. 10.   [5] Jer. vii. 2.   [6] Ibid. xix. 14.
[7] 2 Sam. xii. 1.   [8] Jonah iii. 4.   [9] 2 Kings ix. 1.
[10] 2 Chron. xxiv. 20, 21.   [11] Matt. xxiii. 29-31.   [12] 1 Kings xviii. 13.
[13] 2 Kings vi. 31.   [14] Heb. xi. 27.   [15] 2 Peter i. 19.

nation, should be always blamed as the cause of trouble, and of national disaster.¹

The prophetic order, as a continuous body, may be said to have ceased after the return from the Exile, being no longer needed as an extraordinary agency. The names of prophets or seers recorded in the Old Testament from Samuel to the return from the Exile are thirty-six in number, which are thus chronologically arranged:—

A.—*Prophets whose Writings are not recorded in the Old Testament Canon.*

UNDER WHICH KINGS.	NAMES.
David and Solomon	Samuel. Gad. Nathan.
Rehoboam and Jeroboam	Ahijah, Shemaiah, Iddo.
Asa, Baasha, and Jehosaphat	Azariah, Hanani, Jehu, Micah, Jehaziel, Eliezer, Oded.
Ahab to Jehoash	Elijah, Elisha, Micah.
Jehoash	Zachariah.
Jeroboam II.	Jonah.
Ahaz	Oded.
Hezekiah	Huldah.
Jehoiakim	Urijah.

B.—*Prophets whose Writings are in the Old Testament Canon.*

NAMES.	DATES.	NAMES.	DATES.
Obadiah	about 885 B.C.	Zephaniah	about 627 B.C.
Joel	,, 809 B.C.	Habakkuk	
Amos	,, 790 B.C.	Ezekiel	,, 595 B.C
Hosea		Daniel	,, 695 B.C.
Isaiah	,, 758 B.C.	Haggai	,, 520 B.C.
Micah	,, 725 B.C.	Zechariah	,, 520 B.C
Nahum	,, 712 B.C.	Malachi	,, 414 B.C.
Jeremiah	,, 627 B.C.		

¹ 1 Kings xviii. 17.

CHAPTER IV.

JUDGES AND COURTS OF LAW.

BY the Judges of Israel we generally understand those specially raised up warriors and leaders, who defended the people from their foreign foes on the one hand, and on the other administered sharp punishment to evil-doers within the land; and whose period of activity extended over the troublous times between the death of Joshua and the accession of King Saul. It is not, however, these heroes that are now to be described, but other personages, corresponding to our modern judges and magistrates, whose office it was to administer justice, to settle disputes, and to see that their sentences were carried into execution. Such men are termed in the Old Testament "elders." As the criminal laws occupy a considerable portion of the code of Moses, it is most important to have a clear understanding of the position and functions of these magistrates.

The institution of judges dates from the visit paid to Moses by his father-in-law,[1] the Midianite priest-ruler Jethro; and was rendered necessary by the over-great burden of responsibility borne by Moses alone, which must, his visitor well knew, cause him "to wear away."[2] The system then indicated by Jethro was made a national institution at Taberah, when, by Divine command, Moses was to gather seventy men of the elders of Israel, whom he knew to be elders of the people, and officers over them.[3] These men were brought to the Tabernacle of the congregation, where "the Lord came down in a cloud," and "took of the spirit that was upon him"

[1] Exod. xviii.   [2] Ibid. ver. 18.   [3] Num. xi. 16.

(Moses),[1] and gave it unto the elders, in order that they might "bear the burden of the people with thee, that thou bear it not thyself alone."[2]

The judges thus appointed, whose office was sanctioned by God's visible Presence and blessing, were "elders"—that is, heads of their families, and chief men of their respective tribes, honourable on account of their age and position, and to be revered for their wisdom and understanding.[3] From Exodus iv. 29-31, it would appear that the "elders" were from earliest times regarded as the representatives of the people, to whom application must be made before undertaking any enterprise of importance. As such responsible personages, they would have to be "known among your tribes."[4] Further, the seventy elders selected at Taberah were charged by Moses, and the charge was recorded for the benefit of all future judges : "Hear the causes between your brethren, and judge righteously between every man and his brother, and the stranger that is with him. Ye shall not respect persons in judgment; but ye shall hear the small as well as the great; ye shall not be afraid of the face of man; for the judgment is God's : and the cause that is too hard for you, bring it unto me, and I will hear it."[5]

That this primitive method of administering justice, first ordained in Israel during the wandering in the wilderness, was resorted to after the settlement in Canaan, is very evident. Nor was the system found a defective one, either in a Theocratic, or in a social, point of view. For the various incidents of legal proceedings preserved to us in the Old Testament but serve to point out most clearly, that the ruling principle of Jewish justice was that of considering the offender, not as an outlaw, but as a disobedient child; and the object of punishment, not wreaking vengeance on the sinner, but putting away the sin. And, beyond this, the lesson to be taught was, that sin had a bearing wider, an end more destructive, than the ruin of one individual, that in the sin of the one man the whole land

---

[1] Num. xi. 25.   [2] Ibid. ver. 17.   [3] Deut. i. 13.
[4] Ibid.   [5] Verses 16, 17.

suffered, for it was rendered by this offence defiled, unworthy to be the habitation of the pure and holy God, and that, therefore, sin put away cleansed the land. Such was the meaning of the words by which the laws for murder were summed up: "Defile not therefore the land which ye shall inhabit, wherein I dwell: for I the Lord dwell among the children of Israel."[1]

The "elders" or judges were to be appointed "in all thy gates;" that is, every city, as well as every tribe, was to have magistrates, to "judge the people with just judgment."[2] These officials possessed full power to condemn to death, to administer corporal punishment, and to fine individuals for certain stated offences. Should a case prove too hard for the magistrates "in judgment, between blood and blood, between plea and plea, and between stroke and stroke, being matters of controversy within thy gates,"[3] the judge—not the criminal—was permitted to appeal for a decision to a higher court, to be "in the place which the Lord thy God shall choose." This court of appeal—if it may be so called—would give the final judgment, and the sentence thus obtained was not to be declined from, " to the right hand nor to the left,' on pain of death. The judges composing the supreme court were to be either "the priests the Levites," or any other chief magistrate there might be "in those days:" King or High priest indifferently. The number of these arbitrators is not furnished us, but it seems clear from this and from other passages that more than one judge was required to constitute the tribunal.

The mode of administering justice in each of the cities of Israel, as described in the Book of Ruth,[4] is truly primitive, even patriarchal. From this we learn that the judges sat daily (except, according to the Talmud, on Sabbaths) in an open place near the gate, probably close to the market,[5] where most of the inhabitants would usually congregate, and where,

[1] Num. xxxv. 34.   [2] Deut. xvi. 18.   [3] Ibid. xvii. 8.
[4] Ruth iv.   [5] 2 Kings vii. 1.

probably, the majority of disputes would arise. When any disagreement occurred, or any act of violence was done, both plaintiff and defendant were at once, without ceremony, obliged to appear before the elders. These dignitaries carefully but quickly investigated the matter, heard the witnesses, and pronounced sentence orally, which judgment was then and there carried into execution. The elders who acted as magistrates do not seem to have received a salary—perhaps to have done so would have been considered beneath their dignity. Special injunctions were given them not to wrest judgment, nor to respect persons, nor to take gifts: "for a gift doth blind the eyes of the wise, and pervert the words of the righteous."[1] Of course, in a court consisting of several judges, differences of opinion were sure, occasionally, to arise between the brother-magistrates. But an elder who differed in judgment from his associates was bidden beware lest he "speak in a cause to decline after many (*i.e.* the majority) to wrest judgment;"[2] while at the same time he was neither to countenance, nor yet to pervert the judgment of the poor in his cause.[3] He must be treated with respect by all his fellow-citizens: he must not be cursed,[4] but before him, as his neighbours did to Job in his prosperity, the young men were to hide themselves, the aged arise and stand up, the princes and rulers hold their peace.[5]

The local courts do not appear to have been thoroughly organized and superintended by the rulers of the state till the time of David, who appointed six thousand officers and judges, from the tribe of Levi, throughout the length and breadth of the land.[6] Previous to this, judgment in difficult cases had been delivered at some stated place (as Deborah was wont to do for Israel, "under the palm tree of Deborah, between Ramah and Beth-el in Mount Ephraim"),[7] or "in circuit," the supreme judge visiting the various great centres

---

[1] Deut. xvi. 19.   [2] Exod. xxiii. 2.   [3] Ibid. vers. 3 and 6.
[4] Ibid. xxii. 28.   [5] Job xxix. 8-10.   [6] 1 Chron. xxiii. 4.
[7] Judg. iv. 5.

of justice once a year.¹ From the time of Solomon onwards justice was regularly, and without the delays attendant on the former systems, administered by appointed officers, although the King possessed at the same time the right of exercising a supreme authority, and could, without the consent of the real judges, imprison those with whom he was displeased,² and even order their execution (as King Manasseh did).³ But such "shedding of innocent blood" was by no means permitted or countenanced in the earlier times. In the Mosaic days the judge was God's vicegerent, and the very criminal respected, "not to be put to shame." Imprisonment under the Mosaic law, as a punishment, was unheard of, was in wilderness-days an impossibility: the offender might only be kept "in ward" till the trial came on. Every opportunity was afforded him for making amends to the party he had injured, or for escaping; and a sentence of death might only be pronounced after the most irrefragable evidence, not only of the murderer's guilt, but of his criminal intentions, had been produced. Yet, in spite of these humane provisions in the law under which all still professed to live, grievous were the complaints of wrong or partial judgment on the part of sufferers under the degenerate Kings, when the judges are described as loving gifts, as neglecting the cause of the fatherless and widow,⁴ as taking bribes,⁵ as turning aside the poor in the gate, and as judging for reward.⁶

Besides the judges, there were certain "officers," *shoterim*, selected for aiding in the preservation of order. The duties performed by these men seem to have varied at different periods, and they appear alike as superintending the labours of the children of Israel while in Egypt,⁷ as officers of justice,⁸ as representatives of the tribes,⁹ and as making regular proclamation to the Jewish army before an engagement.¹⁰ The LXX. render the word *shoterim*, "scribes," and doubtless

---
[1] 1 Sam. vii. 16. [2] 1 Kings xxii. 27. [3] 2 Kings xxi. 16.
[4] Isa. i. 23. [5] Amos v. 12. [6] Micah iii. 11.
[7] Exod. v. 6. [8] Deut. xvi. 18. [9] Ibid. xxix. 10.
[10] Ibid. xx. 5–9.

they were, at any rate, in later times, chiefly employed as secretaries, although this implied other duties besides merely transcribing.

An undoubtedly just sentence could not well, in the Israelitish courts, have been obtained without witnesses. These must be, at least, two or three in number, if their testimony was to have any weight: "One witness shall not rise up against a man for any iniquity."[1] More than this, witness-bearing was a necessity, and the neglect of it a sin for which an offering must be brought.[2] But although, when evidence was being given, no oath was required to be taken, to bear testimony was a most solemn and awful responsibility. Terrible was the punishment that overtook the false witness. To him would be done "as he had thought to do to his brother," and "thine eye shall not pity; but life shall go for life, eye for eye, tooth for tooth, hand for hand, foot for foot," that so the evil might be "put away from among you."[3] According to the teaching of the Rabbis, to whom capital punishment was a judgment too awful to visit anything but the most heinous crime, a false witness was only to be put to death if the sentence he had brought upon his neighbour had not yet been executed; if the unjustly accused were already dead, the witness escaped his punishment from the hand of man —since, as they argued, one had already suffered, why should a second? In Mosaic times this logic would scarcely have been deemed sufficient. According to the Pentateuch code, on the witnesses depended in great measure the responsibility of the judgment given. It was "from their mouth," that "he that was worthy of death was to be put to death." The solemnity of their share in the trial was still further increased by their being obliged to take the first steps in executing the sentence: "the hands of the witnesses shall be first upon him to put him to death, and afterward the hands of all the people."[4] It has been conjectured that the meaning of this

[1] Deut. xix. 15.
[2] Lev. v. 1, etc.
[3] Deut. xix. 19-21.
[4] Deut. xvii. 6, 7.

provision was to give witnesses an opportunity for retracting their testimony as untrue, and for owning that their opinion had been too hastily formed.

In cases of controversy, wherein witness-bearing was impossible—*i.e.* where there was no circumstantial evidence—an oath, called "the oath of the Lord,"[1] was resorted to. The words rendered in the Authorised Version indifferently "oath" are in Hebrew two distinct designations: *shevuah*,[2] a simple, ordinary oath; and *alah*,[3] an oath containing an imprecation, (as in after times: "God do so to me," etc.). According to Exodus xxii. 7–11 the oath (*shevuah*), which contained the Divine Name, was to be employed in defending one's self against charges of stealing or losing the property of a neighbour, which had been entrusted to the accused. Swearing the oath—whether *shevuah* or *alah*—was accompanied by certain formalities, such as lifting up the hand to heaven,[4] and was considered to be binding for ever.[5] The oath alluded to by our Lord in His Sermon on the Mount, by the Temple, by Jerusalem, or by one's head,[6] was unknown in the time of Moses, and would not have been considered binding in a court of law.

An extraordinary measure for obtaining a decision in a disputed case was that of "casting the lot;" but this practice was seldom resorted to. The trial of Achan,[7] in which the lot separated the guilty man from the rest of his brethren, belongs more correctly to the category of military offences than to that of criminal proceedings. Perhaps by his theft he had deliberately placed himself under the ban in which Jericho lay. As proof that Achan's sin was no ordinary offence, it may be noted that not only he, but all his family and his possessions, suffered death for it.[8] In ordinary trials, the testimony of witnesses, unbiassed, not bribed, above all things, not tortured, showing in this also how Divine

---

[1] Exod. xxii. 11. [2] Josh. ii. 12. [3] Deut. xxix. 12.
[4] Gen. xiv. 22; Exod. vi. 8; Deut. xxxii. 40. [5] Ps. cx. 4.
[6] Matt. v. 34–36. [7] Josh. vii. [8] Verses 24, 25.

was the spirit of the Jewish laws in opposition to those of the heathen nations around—was first heard; or, if this failed, a solemn oath was sworn, he that had sworn falsely bearing his own iniquity, and receiving his punishment hereafter from the hand of God.

The punishments prescribed by the Mosaic law may seem, and have often been represented as being, of a severity disproportionate to the offences committed. But this objection to the criminal code will vanish if the fact be considered (as has been well observed by many writers on the subject), that the punishment for a crime must be viewed, not only in connection with the offence itself, but also with the state of popular feeling concerning that offence at the time the laws were laid down. Thus if, at the time of framing the code, a moral crime be regarded with abhorrence by the nation, death will not be considered too severe a punishment for it. At the same time, the more uncommon such an offence may be, the stronger will be the measures taken by the lawgiver to prevent its becoming common. Besides these considerations, it must be remembered that certain of the punishments prescribed in the Pentateuch legislation are to be viewed more as *principles*, or *limits* of action, than as actually intended to be carried into execution. As one of these principles, attention must be specially called to the law of *retaliation*, as expounded in such passages as Leviticus xxiv. 17–22, etc.[1] That this principle and fact is true in the physical, as well as in the moral, life of man, there is daily the most indubitable evidence. But as forming part of a criminal code, to be continually put into practice by man, it is, as has been well noted, next to an impossibility.[2] Of course, what one man does to another he has a right to expect to receive himself—as he sows, so he must reap. But to repay an injury done by a similar act of violence can neither compensate for that injury, nor yet be of

---

[1] Exod. xxi. 23-25; Deut. xix. 21.
[2] Salvador, *Gesch. der Mos. Instit. u. des Jüd. Volks*, Vol. ii., Book iv. chap. i. p. 30.

any real service to the state. To God belongs such judgment, not to man. Viewed, then, in connection with our Lord's explanation of this law of retaliation—called by divines, *jus talionis*—in His Sermon on the Mount,[1] wherein He expressly preceded those words by the statement that He had come, not to destroy, but to fulfil the Law,[2] we are warranted in explaining that the carrying out of this law (which, as being Divinely given, was to be used), implied, rather than wrong for wrong, the recompense of the injury done *up to that point*. According to this view it can be understood that what Moses intended by "an eye for an eye," etc., was, that the loss of this organ must be repaid by money, or by anything else, of or up to the same value, and that by this means both parties should be reconciled. For by such a punishment the offender could not feel himself likewise an aggrieved person, but be dissuaded from a repetition of his crime, not so much from fear of punishment, as from a sense of what was due to his neighbour from himself.

Punishments by man for the various crimes enumerated in the Pentateuch might only come upon the offender himself: "the fathers shall not be put to death for the children, neither shall the children be put to death for the fathers: every man shall be put to death for his own sin."[3] It was for neglecting this admonition (afterwards obeyed by a more reflecting monarch, King Amaziah of Judah[4]), as well as compassing the infamous murder of Naboth himself,[5] that vengeance came upon the house of Ahab.[6] That the moral responsibility of parents was by no means lessened, but rather increased, by this proviso, may be seen by comparing the admonition attached to the second commandment[7] with the fuller exposition given in Ezekiel xviii.

The Book of Deuteronomy[8] lays it down, that by punishment for sins committed the community were to be benefited in

---

[1] Matt. v. 38, 39.   [2] Ibid. ver. 17.   [3] Deut. xxiv. 16.
[4] 2 Kings xiv. 5, 6.   [5] 1 Kings xxi.   [6] 2 Kings ix. 26.
[7] Exod. xx. 5.   [8] Deut. xix. 19, 20.

two respects. First, by this means "the evil was to be put away"—a principle to be viewed as similar to the secondary meaning of sacrifices for sin to the offerer: *i.e.* the sanctifying of what had been defiled, not the prevention of the recurrence of the crime. Secondly, the admonition of those who were not concerned in the offence: "those which remain shall hear, and fear, and shall henceforth commit no more any such evil among you." The moral element in the Mosaic punishments, then, was not vengeance—that belonged to God [1]—but a restoration of the equipoise which had been disturbed. Hence absence of all torture, since the offender's dignity was by no means to be impaired, and, in receiving his sentence, it was his sin which was primarily condemned, though this of necessity included the sinner also. Lingering or infamous death was unheard of: the criminal was "a brother," and, while rank was not to be considered, the punishment must not be too grievous, "lest then thy brother should seem vile unto thee." [2]

The utmost penalty of the law was *death*, which was to be suffered for such crimes as deliberate murder,[3] improper or disrespectful conduct to parents,[4] manstealing,[5] adultery, immoral conduct,[6] lying assumption of the prophetic office,[7] profaning the Sabbath,[8] blasphemy,[9] idolatry,[10] witchcraft,[11] soothsaying,[12] disregard of the sentence of the supreme judge.[13] All these offences were classed in one category, as being dishonouring to Israel as the people of God, and therefore as violating the fundamental principles of the Theocracy. The mode of executing the sentence differed according to the heinousness of the crime. Some idolaters were to be slain with the sword; but the most usual death for this sin, as well as for other offences, seems to have been that by stoning, in which punishment all the spectators were required to assist, the putting

---

[1] Deut. xxxii. 35.   [2] Ibid. xxv. 3.   [3] Exod. xxi. 12.
[4] Ibid. xxi. 15, 17.   [5] Ibid. xxi. 16.   [6] Lev. xx. 10.
[7] Deut. xiii. 5, etc.   [8] Exod. xxxi. 14.   [9] Lev. xiv. 16.
[10] Deut. xvii. 2.   [11] Exod. xxii. 18.   [12] Lev. xx. 27.
[13] Deut. xvii. 12, 13.

away of the sin being thus made a national act. Stoning was an instantaneous death, and might be accomplished in one of two ways: either by the casting of enormous stones (*sakal*), or by piling a heap of stones on the criminal (*ragam*). In this punishment the first and chiefest part was taken by the witnesses.[1] Another, and more summary, mode of administering justice was lawful in the case of a murderer who had fled from the consequences of his crime. Here the punishment of death was allowed to be inflicted on the criminal by the next of kin to the murdered man, styled the *Goel*, or "avenger," "whenever he shall meet him"—*i.e.* outside his city of refuge.[2]

Burning was the punishment for him who had married both mother and daughter,[3] as well as for adultery on the part of a priest's daughter.[4] But it seems most probable that this punishment, as well as that of hanging, was only executed on the corpse of the sinner, after he or she had been slain with the sword. After a criminal had been hanged, care must be taken to remove the body from the gibbet before nightfall: "for he that is hanged is the curse of God," therefore "thou shalt in any wise bury him that day that thy land be not defiled, which the Lord thy God giveth thee for an inheritance."[5] Crucifixion was not sanctioned by the Mosaic law, although it was countenanced by the Eastern monarchs at the time of Mordecai.[6] The "hanging" by which the Gibeonites avenged themselves on the seven sons of Saul was probably crucifixion.[7]

Next to death, the most severe chastisement that could come upon an Israelite was to be "beaten with stripes." This punishment was to be administered in the presence of the judge, the "wicked man," "worthy to be beaten" lying down, and receiving on his back [8] a "certain number" of strokes.

[1] Deut. xiii. 9, 10; Lev. xxiv. 14-16, etc. [2] Num. xxxv. 9, etc.
[3] Lev. xx. 14. [4] Ibid. xxi. 9. [5] Deut. xxi. 22, 23.
[6] The LXX. render the words "Hang him thereon," Σταυρωθήτω ἐπ' αὐτοῦ, "Let him be crucified on it." (Esther vii. 9, 10.)
[7] 2 Sam. xxi. 9. [8] Prov. x. 13

The limit set to these stripes was forty: "lest, if he should exceed, and beat him above these with many stripes, then thy brother should seem vile unto thee."[1] The "stripes" were administered with whips made of thongs of ox hide, afterwards perhaps with " scorpions "[2]—whips provided with sharp hooks at the ends, whose touch resembled a sting by a scorpion.

A milder punishment was by fining,[3] which was done by confiscating the property of the offender up to a certain proportion of what he had lost or stolen, or by his paying for the time he had caused another to lose, or for the injury he had inflicted. These fines were limited in amount, from one hundred shekels for the graver offences, to thirty shekels for injury done to a slave by an ox, and even to smaller sums, according to the value of what had been destroyed. A thief who had stolen an ox, killed and sold it, must restore the owner five oxen, and "four sheep for a sheep;"[4] but should the "theft be certainly found in his hand, he shall restore double" only.[5] The reason for the last provision was, as has been conjectured, that, as the thief had not yet parted with what he had stolen, he might have been repenting of his evil deed, and planning to restore the stolen animal to his master. The owner whose ox had gored a person to death not only lost his animal, which must be immediately destroyed, and whose flesh might not be eaten, but was also fined a sum of money as "ransom of his life," if he had known that the ox "was wont to push with his horn in times past," and yet had not "kept him in."[6]

Punishment by the hand of God is described as "cutting off,"[7] "rooting out,"[8] "plucking off,"[9] and was for such sins as serving Moloch,[10] turning after "familiar spirits" or wizards,[11] not being circumcised,[12] neglecting the Day of Atonement,[13] or the Passover,[14] or eating leaven during this Feast,[15] and

---

[1] Deut. xxv. 1-3.
[2] 1 Kings xii. 11, 14.
[3] Exod. xxi. 18, etc.
[4] Ibid. xxii. 1.
[5] Ibid. ver. 4.
[6] Ibid. xxi. 28-30.
[7] Exod. xxx. 33.
[8] Deut. xxix. 28.
[9] Deut. xxviii. 63.
[10] Lev. xviii. 21.
[11] Ibid. xx. 6.
[12] Gen. xvii. 14.
[13] Lev. xxiii. 30.
[14] Num. ix. 13.
[15] Exod. xii. 15, 19.

using the blood and certain portions of fat of animals slain.[1] This "cutting off" was probably neither banishment, nor yet excommunication, but some punishment which it is impossible now to specify—perhaps an early death, or childlessness—at any rate, one which the sinner was worthy to receive, since he had voluntarily separated himself from the congregation of the Lord.

Besides these punishments, mention is made in the time of Ezra of separating persons "from the congregation of those which had been carried away," together with forfeiting "of all their substance."[2] This would imply exile from the land of Palestine. The "ban," or "devoting" of certain districts, nations, or individuals, seems to have been a religious ceremony, requiring as its issue the extermination and destruction of what was included in it.[3] It was a Divine judgment on idolatry.

In later times the kings or rulers of Israel were accustomed to imprison all those persons who were in any way troublesome to them.[4] The dungeons were sometimes, in fact, generally, underground, or even a dry cistern might serve the same purpose.[5] In this horrible place the prisoner would be usually fastened—to the wall perhaps—with chains,[6] his diet being bread and water.[7] He was not, however, forbidden to receive visits from his friends and relatives—a custom which seems to have been also permitted in New Testament times,[8] and by the Romans, since one reason for the reward rendered to those good and faithful servants who, inasmuch as they did it unto one of the least of Christ's brethren, did it unto Him,[9] was their visiting Him when "sick and in prison."

To sum up the criminal laws of the Jews, it may be noted that the offences punished under the Mosaic law were not only civil but moral ones. They were chiefly :—

[1] Lev. vii. 25, 27.
[2] Ezra x. 8.
[3] Josh. vi. 17, 18, etc. Comp. chap. vii.
[4] Jer. xxxviii. 6.
[5] Jer. xxxvii. 16 ; Gen. xxxvii. 20.
[6] Jer. xl. 1.
[7] 1 Kings xxii. 27.
[8] Acts xxiii. 16 ; xxiv. 23.
[9] Matt. xxv. 35.

As against God: Blasphemy, idolatry (with all the unnatural crimes it implied), witchcraft and soothsaying, prophesying falsely.

As against Man: Murder, permanent injury to another by reason of carelessness, or through deliberate malice, man-stealing, theft and robbery, false witnessing, calumny, profane or frivolous language, adultery and all immoral conduct, offences against parents, disobedience to judges, etc.

Suicide was a very uncommon crime, and rarely contemplated by the Israelites till later times,[1] when the practice seems to have obtained of leaving the corpse unburied till evening, to mark abhorrence of the sin.[2]

For manslaughter, flight to one of the six cities of refuge was permitted.[3] Within "the borders" of that city the manslayer was obliged to remain till "the death of the high priest, which was anointed with the holy oil." After this had taken place he might "return into the land of his possession," without any fear of falling a victim to the next of kin of him whom he had slain. But if, at any previous time to this, the manslayer ventured "without the border of the city of his refuge," he might at once be slain by the *Goel*, who in that case would "not be guilty of blood." For murder by an unknown hand a religious ceremony, performed by the priests and the elders, was enjoined, that "so the guilt of innocent blood" might be put away "from among you."[4]

Different, indeed, in all respects to this "holy and just and good"[5] law of God, was the mockery of a trial allowed to the Lord Jesus Christ on that awful night before His crucifixion. Hurriedly summoned in the palace of the High priest, members of the Sanhedrim of Jerusalem, that central council which in the law of Moses was to decide what no other assembly could do, disregarded the fact that even the two witnesses brought against Jesus could not agree between themselves, and declared the Lord to be worthy of death for making Himself the Son of

---

[1] 2 Sam. xvii. 23. [2] Josephus, *Jewish Wars*, iii. 8, 5.
[3] Num. xxxv. 10-32. [4] Deut. xxi. 1-9. [5] Rom. vii. 12.

God.¹ The guilt of innocent blood,² so lightly taken by them upon their own selves and upon their children, branded them as the betrayers and murderers—not the judges and condemners—of the Just One.³ Yet, as our Lord taught His disciples both before and afterwards, in these very things the Scriptures must needs be fulfilled.⁴

Nor is the penal code of the ancient Jews without its lesson to the present time. For to us all comes the solemn warning and meaning of these penalties suffered for wrong done, but raised from the moral into the spiritual atmosphere of the Christian Dispensation: "He that despised Moses' law died without mercy under two or three witnesses: of how much sorer punishment, suppose ye, shall he be thought worthy, who hath trodden under foot the Son of God, and hath counted the blood of the covenant, wherewith he was sanctified, an unholy thing, and hath done despite unto the Spirit of grace?"⁵

[1] Matt. xxvi. 57-67; Mark xiv. 53-65; Luke xxii. 54-71; John xviii. 19-24.
[2] Matt. xxvii. 25. [3] Acts vii. 52. [4] Luke xxiv. 25-27.
[5] Heb. x. 28, 29.

CHAPTER V.

MILITARY LAWS.

THE laws of the Jews which relate to military expeditions, as having been those most impugned, and regarded as unnecessary in their severity by modern critics, are, perhaps, those to which most attention should be paid. At the outset, it must be admitted that these laws deal with a part of Jewish state-existence very different from that which has just been under consideration. This must necessarily be the case where matters of war, not of peace, enemies, not brethren, are being contemplated. But it is not this point that has proved a stumbling-block to many. It has been argued, that while some nations were doomed to wholesale destruction, others whose sins and wickedness came little short of that of their neighbours, not only escaped this judgment, but were actually protected by express command of God. Here, according to these critics, is an unaccountable partiality, which does not at all match with a perfectly just and equal law. Such an argument, and many more for which there is neither time nor space in this book, rest, without doubt, upon an entire misunderstanding of certain obvious facts, which may be gathered partly from the sacred text itself, and partly from those records of history contemporary with the giving of the Mosaic law, which have been preserved to our days.

That war is a necessity, when a nation is in its infancy, and has not only to make for itself a position, but actually acquire its territory, is a fact that none can dispute. Further, such a war must be by its nature, to a great extent, an aggressive one, though it can scarcely be characterised as just unless some weighty reason can be assigned for its being entered into. Now the entrance of Israel into Canaan, and their taking possession of the Promised Land, implied, of course, such an aggressive war. But for this war there was a necessity, and it is this necessity—a religious one—which is the feature of the Jewish military laws put in the foreground. For this war of conquest, then, reasons were assigned, which place it on quite a different footing from other enterprises apparently similar, and which, connecting it with the fundamental principle and reason of the Mosaic code—the Theocracy—make it a religious war, necessary both as vindicating the sovereignty of God over the land of Canaan, and as the fulfilment of long-threatened, most righteous judgment on its inhabitants. Yet though the cause for the war might have been just, it was possible that the mode of carrying it on might prove very much the opposite. To provide against this danger, regulations were made, to ensure on the one hand the *subdual* of the land, by reason of Him Who was the Captain of the Lord's host,[1] and on the other, for the same reason, to prevent Israel from imitating the horrible cruelties practised on their conquered foes by the nations around.

When Abraham first, by Divine command, quitted his home and entered the land of Canaan, it was already, but thinly, peopled by the Canaanites and the Perizzites.[2] These aborigines permitted the patriarch and his descendants to dwell in their country without molestation, to dig wells therein, and to pasture their flocks in the meadows or the wildernesses. No land, however, could be claimed by any of the family of Abraham until it had been purchased,[3] or obtained by the slaughter of its owners for some offence given (as at the town of Shechem).[4] However obtained, such possessions of land evidently continued to belong to the children of Israel even after their descent into Egypt, since there exists no record of resistance on the part of the Canaanites to the burial

---

[1] Josh. v. 13–15.   [2] Gen. xiii. 7.   [3] Ibid. xxiii. ; xxxiii. 19.
[4] Ibid. xxxiv.

of Jacob, or of his sons, in the cave of Machpelah.¹ After the death of Joseph, however, the Israelites apparently abandoned almost entirely their intercourse with the Promised Land. There are, it is true, notices in the Book of Chronicles of various expeditions undertaken during the sojourn of Israel in Egypt, such as that which resulted in the building and fortifying of Beth-horon the Upper and the Nether, and of Uzzensherah, by a granddaughter of Ephraim.² This successful expedition had, however, been preceded by a disastrous raid on the part of four sons of Ephraim into the land of the Philistines, in which all the four perished.³ Again, in 1 Chron. iv. 22, certain descendants of Judah are spoken of "who had the dominion in Moab." Jewish tradition⁴ also has it that, after the burial of the eleven patriarchs in the cave of Machpelah, a few Israelites, in particular Amram, afterwards father of Moses, remained for some time in the Holy Land before returning to Egypt. But beyond these isolated notices there is no record of any attempt to maintain intercourse, friendly or otherwise, with the Canaanites.

But during the four hundred years of Israel's sojourn in Egypt the "iniquity of the Amorites,"⁵ and of the nations inhabiting the land of Canaan, was being slowly filled up. As has been well pointed out,⁶ of all the nations of antiquity none was so degraded, none so cruel and abominable in their rites as the Canaanitish aborigines. From their land, far and wide, spread the most abject and sunken idolatry, and any intercourse with them must have been fatal to the life, both moral and religious, of the Jewish people. The Canaanites were, so to speak, in great measure responsible for the sins of the nations around : and therefore in exterminating them the death-blow would be struck at the great head of the kingdom of darkness. Far from considering that justice was imperfect in those days, that it was "an unchecked passion," . . . "moral in its hatred of evil, but

---

[1] Gen. l.; Acts vii. 15, 16.   [2] 1 Chron. vii. 24.   [3] Ibid. ver. 21.
[4] *Book of Jubilees*, chap. 46.   [5] Gen. xv. 16.
[6] By Dr. Edersheim, in vol. iii. of the *Bible History*, p. 109.

without clearness, and blind and dim in its notion of persons,"[1] it may safely be asserted that at no time has justice shown herself more discriminating than in thus selecting the leaders of, and instigators to, idolatry as those on whom alone judgment was to be executed. And in what peril Israel would be placed by disregarding the Divine commission entrusted to them, may be gathered from the solemn warning given in the Book of Deuteronomy: "Take heed to thyself that thou be not snared by following them, after that they be destroyed from before thee; and that thou enquire not after their gods, saying, How did these nations serve their gods? even so will I do likewise. Thou shalt not do so unto the Lord thy God: for every abomination to the Lord, which He hateth, have they done unto their gods: for even their sons and their daughters they have burnt in the fire to their gods."[2]

The wars commanded by God, therefore, were not merely aggressive. They had for their aim and object the destruction of the most degraded and degrading form of heathenism then existing. In these wars God Himself would be the Great Leader of the Israelites; He it was Who should "cast out many nations before thee, the Hittites, and the Girgashites, and the Amorites, and the Canaanites, and the Perizzites, and the Hivites, and the Jebusites, seven nations greater and mightier than thou."[3] The children of Israel, for their part, acting under Divine command, must "smite them and utterly destroy them," "make no covenant with them, nor show mercy unto them," might not make marriages with them—the reason being thus emphatically given: "For they will turn away thy sons from following Me, that they may serve other gods: so will the anger of the Lord be kindled against you, and destroy thee suddenly."

Besides the seven Canaanitish nations, the Amalekites were to be utterly destroyed.[4] Nor from contemporary notices does their fate seem to be unmerited; for from these it appears that the Amalekites were desert wanderers, highway robbers, and

---

[1] Mozley's *Lectures on the Old Testament:* "Exterminating Wars," p. 99.
[2] Deut. xii. 30-32. [3] Ibid. vii. 1-4. [4] Exod. xvii. 14.

murderers. They are represented as smiting the hindmost of the children of Israel when they came forth from the land of Egypt, when they were faint and weary.[1] They were utterly reckless: "he feared not God." These features were not united to any of the nobler qualities of the Arab tribes in our days. On the contrary, the account of their raid against Ziklag in the time of David,[2] their drunken orgies after their expedition on account of the spoil taken, and their cruel desertion of a sick slave, sufficiently show how fully deserving they were of the awful judgment pronounced on them—the blotting out of their name from under heaven.

While these nations were to be utterly destroyed, war was forbidden with certain others, and their territory secured to them by Divine command. Of these, three kingdoms are expressly mentioned. The Edomites, as being the descendants of Esau, to whom God had given Mount Seir for a possession, were not to be meddled with;[3] and even when their king had uncourteously refused to allow Israel to pass through his land, Israel, instead of resenting the insult, must "turn away from him."[4] Again, war was not permitted with the Moabites,[5] the descendants of a daughter of Lot, and the land occupied by this nation at the time of the Exodus was secured to them "for a possession," in exactly the same manner as that in which Israel acquired the right to possess the land of Canaan. The third people protected from war were the Ammonites, descended from another daughter of Lot.[6] It seems probable, that the reasons for protecting these nations were not merely that their ancestors had been connected with the patriarch Abraham, but that at the time of the Exodus they were fairly in possession of territory not originally destined for the Jewish people. The prohibition would not, of course, be binding on the Israelites should a contest arise in which either of the three nations was the aggressor. Nor could they claim land which had formerly been their own, but which had been wrested from them by

---

[1] Deut. xxv. 1-19.   [2] 1 Sam. xxx.   [3] Deu'. ii. 4-7.
[4] Num. xx. 14-21.   [5] Deut. ii. 9-12.   [6] Ibi', vers. 19-23.

some nation not the Israelitish, at a period prior to the Exodus. That disputes of such kind did afterwards arise, appears from the historical books, the time seized by their hostile neighbours being, of course, that of Israel's disunion, when there was no strong hand to rule, and each man did that which was right in his own eyes. The most noticeable instance of war with one of the three nations is that in which Jephthah headed the children of Israel against the king of Ammon.[1] The contest, which was courted by the king of Ammon, had assigned as its cause the fact that, when Israel had come out of Egypt—three hundred years before—they had taken possession of the kingdom of Heshbon, formerly belonging to Ammon, but at the time of the Exodus ruled by Sihon the Amorite.[2] This being produced as a legitimate reason for war, in answer to the ambassadors sent by Jephthah, that Jewish captain at once replied in terms straightforward and explicit, showing the king that it was not Ammon's, but Sihon's, land which had been subdued, and summing up his explanation with the words: "Whomsoever the Lord our God shall drive out before us, them will we possess. And now art thou anything better than Balak the son of Zippor, king of Moab? did he ever strive against Israel, or did he ever fight against them, while Israel dwelt in Heshbon and her towns, and in Aroer and her towns, and in all the cities that be along by the coasts of Arnon, three hundred years?"—that is, if the king of Moab has not demanded land which, before we came out of Egypt, had belonged to him, what right had Ammon to do so? "Why, therefore, did ye not recover them within that time? Wherefore I have not sinned against thee, but thou doest me wrong to war against me: the Lord the Judge be judge this day between the children of Israel and the children of Ammon." In spite of this remonstrance, the king of Ammon insisted on fighting; but the war ended most disastrously for him, for the Lord delivered the Ammonites into the hands of Jephthah, so that they were smitten from Aroer to Minnith "with a very great slaughter."[3]

[1] Judg. xi.   [2] Ibid. ver. 13.   [3] Ibid. vers. 14–33.

But even after this war Ammon and its neighbours did not suffer Israel to dwell peaceably. For in the time of David there are records of wars with all the three nations: with Moab, with Ammon, and with Edom, in all of which doubtless these kingdoms, not Israel, were the aggressors.[1] In the case of Ammon, at any rate, the war was provoked by the gross insults heaped on King David's ambassadors.[2] But although in these instances, and no doubt in many others, war was a necessity, forced upon the Israelites—as were those with the Philistines, Midianites, etc.—yet that it was far from being pleasing to God, may be inferred from the fact that David, the man after God's own heart, was not allowed to build the Temple because he had been "a man of war," and had "shed blood."[3]

It should further be noted that, except in the cases of Jericho and Ai, Israel was not the aggressor throughout all the war attending the entrance into Canaan. The war with Sihon furnishes a notable example of this.[4] For, Israel only acted on the defensive; and had not the king of Heshbon first come out against them, he would have been left in the peaceable possession of his land.

Turning our attention now more particularly to the regulations laid down for the conducting of warfare, it appears that the Pentateuch code evidently contemplated fighting as a strictly religious duty, to be undertaken against such as were God's enemies. The laws detailed in Deut. xx. fully bear out this statement. The Israelites, when they went out to battle, were bidden not to fear the number, the horses, and the chariots, of their enemies [5]—the last two being defences which, as has already been shown, were forbidden them, as unnecessary in the wars alone to be undertaken—"for the Lord thy God is with thee." When the battle was about to begin, a priest was to deliver a short exhortation,[6] after which the *shoterim* were to proclaim liberty to retire from the fight to all those who had built a new house, but not dedicated it; planted a vineyard, and

---

[1] 2 Sam. viii.; x. [2] Ibid. x. 1–5. [3] 1 Chron. xxviii. 3.
[4] Num. xxi. 21. [5] Deut. xx. 1. [6] Ibid. ver. 2–4.

MILITARY LAWS. 59

not eaten of it; married a wife, but not taken her.[1] These persons being dismissed, the battle might begin.

According to the Pentateuch, every male above the age of twenty was bound to fight for his country.[2] Josephus, indeed, limits the period of military service to the age of fifty;[3] but this does not seem to have been rigidly adhered to, since it is recorded of the veteran Caleb that he was still vigorous for war at the age of eighty-five.[4] Leaving this question, it seems probable that there were "lists" or "genealogies,"[5] kept by the *shoterim*, of those who were fit for battle, and that from these lists, at any rate in the earlier times, a certain number would be selected for whatever expedition was to be undertaken.[6] These forces would be summoned by messengers, and, when the war was ended, be at once disbanded. That this system was the cause of serious evils to the nation there is evidence in the tribal jealousies, and at the same time the selfishness, so characteristic of the time of the Judges. But this grievance was, to a great extent, done away with after royalty had been introduced into Israel. From the time of Saul onwards, a standing army was gradually formed, commanded by competent leaders.[7] Besides these forces, there was the royal bodyguard—the Cherethi and Pelethi—while foreign mercenaries were frequently employed, or foreign soldiers, such as the faithful Gittites in King David's time, enlisted.[8] The leaders of the army were styled the "captains of the host," and might be one or more in number.[9] Under the "captains of the host,"[10] were other military officers, the "captains of thousands,"[11] "of hundreds,"[12] "of fifties." To the commander-in-chief a secretary—*sopher*, scribe—seems to have been attached, whose business it was to "muster the people of the land."[13] The numbering of the people by Joab,[14] in obedience to David's

---

[1] Deut. xx. 5–9.   [2] Num. i. 3.   [3] *Ant.* iii. 12, 4.
[4] Josh. xiv. 10, 11.   [5] Num. xxvi. 2.   [6] Judg. xx. 10.
[7] 1 Chron. xxvii.   [8] 2 Sam. xv. 18.   [9] Ibid. xx. 23.
[10] 2 Kings ix. 5.   [11] 2 Sam. xviii. 1.   [12] 2 Kings i. 9.
[13] Ibid. xxv. 19.   [14] 2 Sam. xxiv.

command, which brought upon the nation such terrible judgment, was probably a military census.[1]

If in later times the Israelitish army received any pay (of which there is no distinct evidence), it most probably would be in kind. The history would rather seem to imply that the Jewish soldiers had to support themselves,[2] and were only furnished with the necessary weapons of war, since on one occasion only is mention made of certain officers being appointed "to fetch victual for the people."[3] Mercenaries were occasionally hired, and paid with money,[4] but doubtless with respect to the national troops the plunder they might obtain would be deemed amply sufficient pay. In certain cases, when the city or district was under the "ban," no booty might be taken: the gold and silver were dedicated to God, and everything else, including even men and animals, must be utterly destroyed (as in the case of Jericho).[5] But after any ordinary town had surrendered, what each man acquired he was allowed, to a certain extent, to keep—that is, of spoils of metals, raiment, etc. A fixed proportion of the booty was the king's share,[6] while the men, women, and cattle captured were divided into two parts, of which one half was given to the victorious soldiers, the other "to the congregation."[7] Of the share allotted to the men of war one five-hundredth part must be given to the priests, who also received the one fiftieth part of that given to the congregation, as "a tribute" and "heave-offering" unto the Lord.[8]

Terribly cruel, indeed, was the vengeance taken in those days on a conquered foe, even by the more merciful Israelites —not, however, that for these deeds of violence the Mosaic law was in the least responsible. Generally all the men were slain,[9] while the women and children were carried into captivity, or even slaughtered. In some instances the prisoners taken were fearfully mutilated,[10] but this mode of proceeding was not Israelitish, but genuinely heathenish. In many instances also the

[1] 1 Chron. xxi.   [2] 1 Sam. xvii. 17, 18.   [3] Judg. xx. 10.
[4] 2 Chron. xxv. 6.   [5] Josh. vi. 21.   [6] 2 Sam. viii. 7.
[7] Num. xxxvi. 25, etc.   [8] Ibid. ver. 29, 37.   [9] Deut. xx. 13.
[10] Judg. l. 6.

towns were utterly destroyed,[1] and even the chariot horses horribly maimed.[2] But in comparison with the cruelties practised by the neighbouring nations,[3] the Israelites might well appear merciful.[4] Further, it must be remembered that extreme measures were, to a great extent, necessary, both to maintain the dignity and position of the nation, and also on account of the kind of enemies with which Israel had to contend. Killing prisoners was, so to speak, almost forced on them. To keep captives *en parole* was an impossibility, since they would escape on the first opportunity.[5] Again, it must not be forgotten that war in those days meant extermination, and that it was sent only in judgment for the sins of Israel and of the other nations.

When a town was to be besieged, the Israelites were bidden first to offer peace, doubtless by means of ambassadors.[6] These were then, as now, held sacred, and to insult them was equivalent to a declaration of war.[7] If the offer of peace were rejected, the siege was at once proceeded with in due form.[8] But even in war the Israelites might not act without considering the needs of their foes. All fruit-bearing trees growing around the city, or any which could be used for food, might not be cut down and used by the besiegers against the town, but only such as were known not to be "trees for meat."[9] This provision is in most marked contrast to the actions even of such a nation as the Romans at the much later period of the great Jewish war, whose ruthless wasting of their enemies' land Palestine attests to the present day. Finally, after the city had surrendered, all the women, children, cattle, and "all that is in the city,"[10] might be saved, except the possessions of the Hittites, Amorites, Canaanites, Perizzites, Hivites, and Jebusites, who being, with the Girgashites, under the ban, "thou shalt utterly destroy."[11]

The *camp* of the Israelites was probably circular, and would

---

[1] Judg. ix. 45. [2] 2 Sam. viii. 4. [3] 2 Kings viii. 12.
[4] 1 Kings xx. 31. [5] Comp. 1 Kings xx. 39. 40.
[6] Deut. xx. 10. [7] 2 Sam. x. 4. [8] Deut. xx. 12.
[9] Ibid. ver. 20. [10] Ibid. vers. 13-15. [11] Ibid. vers. 16-18.

be surrounded by the baggage waggons.[1] During the leadership of Moses and of Joshua, each tribe encamped by itself, and went out to battle headed by its own captain,[2] a custom which was probably continued up to the time of the monarchy. While a battle was being fought, some of the soldiers were left in the camp to tarry "by the stuff." According to a statute made by David, these persons were entitled to an equal share of the spoil with those that went down to the battle.[3] At night, guards were set to sentinel the camp, who were relieved at the different "watches."[4] The holiness of the soldiers in camp was to be most rigorously maintained,[5] and the custom seems also to have obtained that after a war was over the army must undergo legal purification.[6]

Before undertaking a military expedition, Israel generally asked counsel of God,[7] either by Urim and Thummim, or by a prophet.[8] In later times this ceremony—then become only a form—was dispensed with. It seems to have been customary that the army should be accompanied by a priest, whose duty it was to give the exhortation before the battle, and in whose charge were the silver trumpets which gave the signal for the combat to begin.[9] This done, the charge was made in a manner truly Oriental, the Israelites shouting their war-cry, and impetuously rushing on their enemies.[10] Stratagems[11] and ambushes[12] were occasionally resorted to, but as a general rule the attack was made in a line, which, however, might be, and sometimes was, surrounded by a more crafty foe. The fight was usually hand to hand, and a life and death struggle, no quarter being either asked or given. The *rappel*, or the retreat, would be sounded by trumpets;[13] while after the war the return of the victorious army was celebrated with shouts of joy, in songs and sacred dances, oftentimes a trophy being erected in memory of the victory.[14] Burying the slain was

---

[1] 1 Sam. xvii. 20. [2] Num. ii. [3] 1 Sam. xxx. 24, 25.
[4] Judg. vii. 19. [5] Deut. xxiii. 10-14. [6] Num. xxxi. 13-20.
[7] 1 Sam. xiv. 37. [8] 1 Kings xxii. 6. [9] Num. x. 2; 2 Chron. xiii. 10, 14.
[10] 1 Sam. xvii. 52. [11] Judg. vii. 16. [12] 2 Sam. v. 23.
[13] Ibid. xx. 22. [14] 1 Sam. xv. 12.

considered a sacred duty [1]—in especial, a general was buried with splendid funeral honours, the king sometimes following the bier as chief mourner.[2]

The Israelitish army was originally composed solely of infantry. These soldiers wore no distinctive uniform, but were summoned from their ordinary occupations, often hastily, by the king's messengers,[3] by the blast of a trumpet,[4] or by the setting up of a standard.[5] Cavalry were first brought into the army by King Solomon, who built several magazine cities, in which were kept military stores, and which are described as "cities of store," "cities for his chariots, and cities for his horsemen."[6] The chariots here referred to are supposed to have been those taken by his father David from the Syrians.[7]

The armour worn by the Israelitish soldiers must have been very simple, so as to leave the person considerably exposed. The different portions of it more particularly mentioned are: the helmet;[8] the shield,[9] which was sometimes carried on the back; the breastplate or coat of mail,[10] a short military garment made of iron scales, covering both the back and the breast, and to which was attached an additional jointed piece of armour,[11] to protect the lower part of the body. It was through the joints of this last piece of armour, or between it and the breastplate, that the arrows which mortally wounded King Ahab at the battle of Ramoth-gilead penetrated. In the time of the Maccabees the coat of mail, instead of being made of iron scales, was of chain armour. The soldiers' legs were covered with greaves, made of brass, or of some other metal.[12] Josephus also speaks of the soldiers' shoes, "full of thick and sharp nails,"[13] but these were probably unknown in Old Testament times, when the feet would be covered with the ordinary shoes or sandals.

[1] 1 Kings xi. 15. [2] 2 Sam. iii. 31, etc. [3] 1 Sam. xi. 7.
[4] Judg. iii. 27. [5] Jer. iv. 6. [6] 1 Kings ix. 19.
[7] 2 Sam. viii. 4. [8] 2 Chron. xxvi. 14. [9] 1 Sam. xvii. 7.
[10] Ibid. vers. 5, 38. [11] 1 Kings xxii. 34. [12] 1 Sam. xvii. 6.
[13] *Jewish Wars*, vi. 1, 8.

The offensive weapons generally employed by the Israelites were: first, the sword, of which several kinds are named. This was occasionally two-edged,[1] and from the figures on the Nineveh monuments seems to have been usually girt on the left side. It would, of course, be kept in a sheath.[2] Other weapons were the dagger;[3] the spear,[4] and lance; and the more formidable javelin,[5] which was hurled with the hand. The last were probably held by a wooden handle.[6] All these weapons are described under different names, some of which it is not easy now to render precisely. To continue: the "darts"[7] with which Absalom was slain were probably sharp-pointed wooden staves. The mace, or military hammer, rendered "maul" in Prov. xxv. 18, "battle-axe" in Jer. li. 20, and "slaughter-weapon" in Ezek. ix. 2,[8] seems to have been also frequently used; as was the "sling," for which, in the time of King Uzziah, stones were provided among the ammunition which he stored up.[9] And finally, the soldiers fought with the bow and arrows, the former generally made of hard wood, but sometimes, perhaps, even of steel,[10] requiring immense strength to draw. Some tribes are mentioned in the time of David as being famous for good archers; but previous to the accession of that King this weapon must have been almost unknown in Israel,[11] although from an early period both the Philistines[12] and the Elamites[13] seem to have been skilled in its use. The arrows would be probably made of reed, and kept in a quiver,[14] which was carried on the back. The bow, when not being used, was kept in a case—hence the expression "to make naked the bow."[15] To render the arrows more deadly, they were sometimes tipped with poison,[16] or wrapped in combustible material, so that, when shot, they would ignite, and set the object at which they were aimed on fire.

[1] Psa. cxlix. 6.
[2] 1 Sam. xvii. 51.
[3] Judg. iii. 16.
[4] 2 Sam. xxi. 16.
[5] 1 Sam. xviii. 11.
[6] Ibid. xvii. 7.
[7] 2 Sam. xviii. 14.
[8] Judg. xx. 16.
[9] 2 Chron. xxvi. 14.
[10] 2 Sam. xxii. 35.
[11] Ibid. i. 18.
[12] 1 Sam. xxxi. 3.
[13] Isa. xxii. 6.
[14] Lam. iii. 13.
[15] Hab. iii. 9.
[16] Job vi. 4.

Thus armed and equipped, the Israelites were wont to go forth to battle, and to conquer their enemies—when these were also God's. And in this earthly warfare also there was a higher meaning, as the sweet singer of Israel perceived. For the Lord Himself was a Man of War, mighty in battle,[1] and His weapons were thunder and lightnings, hailstones and coals of fire.[2] In His Name, then, might the righteous set up their banners,[3] while against the wicked the Lord would whet His sword and bend His bow.[4] But, finally, His enemies must be made His footstool,[5] and then would He make wars to cease unto the end of the earth, break the bow, cut the spear in sunder, and burn the chariot in the fire.[6] For when that time had come, in those days the God of heaven would set up a Kingdom which could never be destroyed.[7]

[1] Psa. xxiv. 8. [2] Ibid. xviii. 13, 14. [3] Ibid. xx. 5.
[4] Ibid. vii. 12. [5] Ibid. cx. 1. [6] Ibid. xlvi. 9.
[7] Dan. ii. 44.

CHAPTER VI.

TAXES AND TRIBUTES.

THE Pentateuch, contemplating a state in which all the members were to be brethren, and wherein the good of the whole community was to be the leading motive of conduct to each man, did not burden the Israelites with excessive taxes; in fact, did not provide for the payment of such at all, in the sense in which the term is now understood. It is quite in accordance with the spirit of that age, as well as with the fundamental principle of the Mosaic Code—the Theocracy—to find dues regarded as "gifts," and as such freely given, never to be exacted, but depending on the piety and liberality of each true Israelite. Such a view, of course, must be taken as indicative of the ideal state as designed by God Himself: the history of Israel will show how far the nation fell short of that for which it had been designed.

Under Moses, and till the introduction of royalty into Israel, the only taxes laid upon the people were ecclesiastical ones. These were not compulsory, but gifts, as the Hebrew original clearly shows, the words used being *terumoth*, offerings, *mattanoth*, gifts. The "gifts" and "offerings" were given to the priests and Levites, and consisted principally of the tithes, the first-fruits, etc. Besides these, the priests received other dues, partly from the sacrifices, partly from the booty which had been taken in war, as well as their own tithes from the Levites. Further, it would appear from Exodus xxx. 12-16 that, at least once in the lifetime of Moses, a poll-tax of half a shekel (about 1s. 4d. of our money) of the sanctuary was exacted from "every one that passeth among them that are numbered, from twenty years old and above." This tax, levied to supply funds for the building of the Tabernacle, does not seem to have been a regular due, but rather an extraordinary mode of obtaining money for special ecclesiastical—probably architectural—undertakings. Accordingly, King Joash, when about to repair the Temple, founded his appeal for the levying of this due on the example set by Moses,[1] and is described as making "a proclamation through Judah and Jerusalem, to bring in to the Lord the collection that Moses the servant of God laid upon Israel in the wilderness."[2] From these notices it would appear that the "redemption money," as it was termed, was a free-will offering; while from Nehemiah x. 32 it will further be gathered that the amount levied was not necessarily always the half-shekel of the sanctuary, since it is there recorded of Nehemiah and his companions that they made ordinances "to charge ourselves yearly with the third part of a shekel for the service of the house of our God." In later times, however, the payment yearly of the half-shekel of the sanctuary was rendered obligatory by the Rabbis, and levied on all Jews, whether residing within the Holy Land or outside Palestine.[3] The tax was then ordered to be paid between the fifteenth and the twenty-fifth of the month Adar, and as the sacred half-shekel alone might be given, the stalls of the money-changers were set up even within the Temple precincts,[4] and the ordinary coin was exchanged for the ecclesiastical one, which was double its value—the half-shekel of the sanctuary being worth one ordinary shekel. After the city of Jerusalem had been taken and destroyed by the Romans under Titus, Vespasian ordered the Jews to pay this "tribute-money" towards the building of the temple of Jupiter Capitolinus at Rome, a cruel command which was much resented by the Hebrews.

Civil taxes were not levied on the Israelites until after the establishment of royalty in that nation; and, indeed, up to that

---

[1] 2 Chron. xxiv. 6.
[2] Comp. 2 Kings xii. 7.
[3] Josephus, *Ant.* xviii. 9. 1.
[4] Comp. John ii. 14.

period had not been needed, since both the judges and the civil officers served without any salaries, and in most instances were persons of wealth and position. This explains how, appealing to the fact of his never having been paid, Samuel could acquit himself of having defrauded, oppressed, or taken anything from the people.[1] But matters were changed when a king was chosen to govern Israel. His expenses were, of obligation, considerable, and must be defrayed at the public cost. But as this part of the subject has already been alluded to, it need here only be remarked that the civil taxes levied during the reigns of Saul and David were, compared with those of later time, extremely light, as the court expenses were then very inconsiderable. On the other hand, the splendour of Solomon's surroundings, and his immense architectural undertakings, in which the chief part of the work was done by hired foreigners, laid a very heavy burden on the people, and, together with other causes, ultimately led to the separation of the ten tribes from the family of David under King Rehoboam's rule.[2] In fact, so enraged were the Israelites at the grievous exactions of King Solomon, which were, as they had been told, light as air in comparison with what they must now expect, that when Adoram, the chief of the tribute, was sent by King Rehoboam to act as mediator with them, they immediately stoned the envoy to death.[3]

Besides the regular revenues derived by the Israelitish kings from such sources as tithes, royal domains, taxes on articles of commerce, monopolies, and presents [4]—which were generally such only in name,—the custom seems to have obtained in the northern states that a tithe of the first crop of hay was royal property, called by the prophet Amos "the king's mowings."[5]

The Jews were evidently especially opposed to a royal poll-tax, which accordingly was only levied for urgent needs, such as when it became necessary that the king should buy off foreign invaders, or when it was exacted by heathen monarchs,

[1] 1 Sam. xii. 1-5.   [2] 1 Kings. xii. 4.   [3] Ibid. xii. 18.
[4] Ibid x. 25.   [5] Amos vii. 1.

to whom the Jewish king was tributary.[1] Exemption from taxes was offered as the reward for some great exploit,[2] and from this fact, as well as from the expression in Deut. xxiv. 5, "there shall not anything pass upon him"—in reference to dues—it has been argued by many that the taxes from which exemption was promised, and in some instances allowed, were those levied on the dwellers in a town, for the maintenance of its public and private buildings, walls, etc. At any rate, in later times, to pay these dues was held to be a sacred duty by the Rabbis.

All gifts and offerings were laid up in the Temple treasury till they might be required.[3] The funds there amassed were public property; but though confided to the custody of the priests, they were really entirely under the control of the king. In times of need this money, or the supply of precious things stored up in the Temple, was used to buy off threatened invaders, and this apparently without the consent of either priests or people having been obtained.[4] From 2 Kings xviii. 15, it would appear that there was another treasury besides that in the Temple, belonging to the king alone, the establishment of which is traced by many writers to the building by Solomon of "the house of the forest of Lebanon."[5]

In later times, during and after the exile, heavy taxes were paid by the Jews to their foreign masters—to the Babylonians, Persians, Syrians, and Romans. Under the Persian rule, at any rate, the priests and the Levites were exempted from taxes;[6] but when the Romans dominated the Holy Land the whole Jewish population groaned under the tyranny of the foreign exactors. The only poor consolation the sages could give their fellow countrymen could not ease their burdens, nor could the declaration that no publican had a share in the world to come make their taxes any lighter! So in the time of Christ we find His enemies putting to Him as a catch

---

[1] 2 Kings xv. 20; xxiii. 35.
[2] 1 Sam. xvii. 25.
[3] Num. xxxi. 48-54.
[4] 2 Chron. xvi. 2.
[5] 1 Kings x. 21.
[6] Ezra vii. 24.

question: "Is it lawful to give tribute unto Cæsar, or not?"[1] hoping that by any answer He might give, they "might entangle Him in His talk." For, if He answered in the negative, they would denounce Him to the Romans; but if in the affirmative, the devoutest Jews, who looked upon giving tribute to Cæsar as a real sin, would be scandalised. But by His answer our Lord not only exposed their wickedness, but elevated the political and social life of Israel in regard to their masters into the moral sphere—nay, placed it side by side with their duty to God. And even in this He fulfilled the law, by showing that though God was still King over Israel, His Kingship did not do away with earthly sovereignty, but rather that giving to God must involve keeping the rest of the law—honouring the King. No wonder then that "when they had heard these words, they marvelled; and left Him, and went their way."[2]

[1] Matt. xxii. 17.   [2] Ibid. ver. 22.

PART II.
Domestic Laws.

CHAPTER VII.

PROPERTY AND INHERITANCE.

AMONG all the regulations laid down in the law of Moses for the commonwealth and prosperity of Israel, none are so characteristic, nor so intimately connected with the fundamental principle underlying the whole, as the laws of property. Herein lies to a great extent the reason of their difference from those of other nations. They are not only political and social, but moral and religious, and as such they must now be very briefly sketched.

As has been before noticed, Israel was intended to be pre-eminently an agricultural nation. Not only did the provisions of the Mosaic law point to this, but throughout the whole Old Testament special favour is shown to those whose occupations seemed only to have fitted them for rural life. Elisha is called from following the plough to be a prophet of the Lord; David from the sheepfold to the throne.[1] Even Moses, learned as he was in all the wisdom of the Egyptians, had to keep the flock of his father-in-law for forty years.[2] And, besides the example thus furnished, Israel was reminded that husbandry and laborious work were things "which the Most High hath ordained."[3] It is no wonder, then, that not only should the land of Palestine have been most richly and lovingly cultivated, but that the pictures both of joy and sorrow[4] presented to us in the Old Testament should have been chiefly drawn from the agricultural life of Israel, and the types and prophecies pointing to the golden Messianic age to come be figured from the same source.[5]

[1] 1 Kings xix. 19; Ps. lxxviii. 70. [2] Acts vii. 22, 30.
[3] Ecclus. vii. 15.   [4] Psa. cxxvi. 5, 6, etc.   [5] Isa. xxxii.

Quite alien to the intention of Moses was it, nevertheless, to favour socialism on the one hand, or an aristocratic domination on the other. Such tendencies were impossible in his view, since the land of Israel really and finally belonged to God Himself, and all Israel were, so to speak, equally His tenants: "the land is Mine, for ye are strangers and sojourners with Me."[1] This land, to be held direct from God, Moses was commanded to divide among the tribes, Levi alone excepted. No partiality nor favour was to be shown to any family, but this qualification alone was to influence the division of the land: "To many thou shalt give the more inheritance, and to few thou shalt give the less inheritance: to every one shall his inheritance be given according to those that were numbered of him."[2] The land thus equally divided by lot was to be inalienable:[3] it might not be sold for cutting off, but was national property, of which the proprietor enjoyed the full benefit, though of course, as it was not *entirely* his own, not the absolute and unconditional control. Each Israelite, according to his tribe, was a small landed proprietor, free from all political or arbitrary interference, but responsible for the use to which he put his possession to his tribe and nation as a whole, and through them to his great Invisible King. Such laws must of necessity mark the ideal standpoint; but, to show that this ideal could be realized, Moses not only furnished ample directions, but hedged them round with the memory of Israel's bondage in and deliverance from Egypt, as well as of the fact that the land was "given," and therefore holy.[4]

The restrictions laid on each Israelitish proprietor were indeed few, but these most important. As enumerated in the 25th chapter of Leviticus, they are chiefly as follows:—

1. Every seventh year the land was to "keep a Sabbath unto the Lord."[5] For six years the owners might sow, reap, or prune, but in the seventh year neither might the field be sown, nor the vineyard pruned.[6] Nay, even what grew of itself might

---

[1] Lev. xxv. 23.   [2] Num. xxvi. 54, 55.   [3] Lev. xxv. 23.
[4] Ibid. xxv. 2.   [5] Ibid. xxv. 2.   [6] Ibid. ver. 3.

PROPERTY AND INHERITANCE.

not be reaped—to store up—but was public property, free not only to the owner and his household, but to the poor, as well as to cattle, both domestic and wild.[1] This seventh year of rest was called <u>the Sabbatical Year</u>. That its advantages would be great—that is, if Israel remained faithful to the character sketched out for them—can scarcely be doubted. An agricultural nation would not suffer from the intermission of trade; while famine was provided against by the special blessing of God, by which in the sixth year the land would bring forth fruit sufficient for three years.[2] On the other hand, not only would Israel feel how utterly dependent they were on their Heavenly King, but the land itself be benefited by being allowed to lie fallow, especially in an age when the system of rotation of crops was not understood. But, nevertheless, that the Sabbatical Year was not also without its disadvantages is obvious; and in fact there is record in the time of the Maccabees of an actual dearth of food, "it being a year of rest to the land," "the seventh year."[3] And Jewish tradition, following the notices in Leviticus xxvi. 34, 2 Chronicles xxxvi. 21, has it not only that this Sabbatical Year was neglected in pre-Exilian times, but that the Captivity was a Divine judgment on Israel for disobedience to the command. There is evidence, however, that the Sabbatical Year was observed after the return from Babylon,[4] while Josephus even goes so far as to assert that fighting was unlawful during its course.[5] Be this as it may, it is at least certain that the Rabbis insisted on a strict observance of this sacred year, even on the part of Jews not residing in the land of Palestine.

2. After a cycle of seven Sabbatical Years had been fulfilled, and forty-nine years had elapsed, the year following (the fiftieth) was to be hallowed, and proclaimed by blast of trumpet throughout the land as <u>the year of Jubilee</u>.[6] This sacred year, which was to begin on the tenth day of the seventh month—<u>the Day of Atonement</u>—was to be celebrated in memory of

---

[1] Lev. xxv. 4-7.   [2] Ibid. ver. 18-22.   [3] 1 Macc. vi. 49, 53.
[4] Neh. x. 31.   [5] *Ant.* xiii. 8. 1; comp. xi. 8. 6.   [6] Lev. xxv. 8, 9.

Israel's birth as a nation. Every fifty years, so to speak, Israel's national life was to begin anew; and to consecrate it wholly to God, not only was the land to be left fallow, as in the Sabbatical Year, but it was to be a year of universal liberty. "Ye shall return every man unto his possession, and ye shall return every man unto his family." "In the year of this Jubilee ye shall return every man unto his possession."[1] It follows from this command that it was an impossibility for a proprietor to sell his possession: it was his inalienably. But as obtaining money for present needs would in many cases necessitate, at some period or other, the owner's having the power of, at least temporarily, disposing of land, each Israelite possessed the right to let his property on a long lease, so to speak—that is, from Jubilee Year to Jubilee Year, these years marking the *limit* of tenancy. The system of disposing of land is thus explained in the Pentateuch: "According to the number of years after the Jubilee, thou shalt buy of thy neighbour; and according unto the number of years of the fruits" (that is, exclusive of Sabbatical Years), "he shall sell unto thee; according to the multitude of years thou shalt increase the price thereof, and according to the fewness of years thou shalt diminish the price of it: for according to the number of the years of the fruits doth he sell unto thee."[2] In this fiftieth or Jubilee Year, then, all landed property must return to its original owner, and this without any payment on his part, but as his right, understood and implied in the lease. The price of land would also vary according to the length of the lease; and so the mutual rights of both landlord and tenant would be respected, the moral principle underlying all such transactions being clearly set forth in these words: "Ye shall not therefore oppress one another; but thou shalt fear thy God."[3]

But as confusion might be engendered as to what was meant by "the possession," Moses further added some important particulars relative to the rights, both personal and substantial, of each Israelite.

[1] Lev. xxv. 10, 13.   [2] Ibid. vers. 15, 16.   [3] Ibid. ver. 17.

In reference to sale by reason of poverty, the land might be redeemed by the original owner, or by his kinsman for him, at any time when "his hand hath attained and found sufficiency." And in such case the then present occupier would only receive as compensation the "overplus" of "the years of the sale thereof"[1]—that is, not whatever he might choose to demand, nor the whole of the money he had before paid the original owner, but only the value of the years he would lose up to the next Jubilee. But should the poor seller be unable to redeem his land, it must remain in the purchaser's hands till the next Year of Jubilee.[2] This law applied to all landed property in the country, within a village,[3] and, according to the Rabbis, even to houses built on the walls of towns. But the law for houses sold within walled cities was of necessity different, since these must be inhabited by a non-agricultural population, and were therefore not so intimately connected with the inalienable soil of Palestine as were houses in the country.[4] A town house might be redeemed within a year after sale, but "if it be not redeemed within the space of a full year, then the house that is in the walled city shall be established for ever to him that bought it throughout his generations: it shall not go out in the Jubilee." This rule did not, however, apply to Levitical cities, which might be redeemed at any time, as might also their houses and fields.[5]

In the case of a man vowing to God either his house or his land, the law of redemption was somewhat different to that of disposal by sale.[6] Here the value of the house or land vowed must be estimated by the priest—in the case of land "according to the seed thereof"[7]—that is, according to its produce—and such money be paid to the priest, the owner holding the land or house as his tenant. Should this man wish to redeem his vow before the year of Jubilee, he might do so on payment of the estimated value, with the addition of one-fifth.[8] But

---

[1] Lev. xxv. 25–27. [2] Ibid. ver. 28. [3] Ibid. ver. 31.
[4] Ibid. vers. 29, 30. [5] Ibid. vers. 32–34. [6] Ibid. xxvii. 14.
[7] Ibid. ver. 16. [8] Ibid. ver. 19.

should he not do so before the next Jubilee Year, the property ceased to be his, and became the priest's possession, "holy unto the Lord."[1] If the possession vowed, however, had been purchased by the vower, and did not really belong to him, it must return in the Jubilee Year to its original owner, in the same manner as in ordinary sales.[2]

By this law of the Jubilee Year equality of possession would be secured to the Israelites, as well as each tribe settled in inalienable territory. By it pauperism would be rendered, as much as possible, non-existent, and all the great evils attendant on the richness of the few, and the moral and social abasement of the many, unheard of. Not that by it free trade would be cramped; rather would each one have an equal chance of success in life. And it seems not unlikely that the tradition may be correct, from which we learn that up to the Exile the Jubilee Year was regularly observed, but that after the return from Babylon it was neglected. In fact, its observance had then become well-nigh impossible, as the tribes had been so widely scattered, or intermixed, that family possessions could not be claimed, while the rule of foreign masters had swept away the ancient landmarks and boundaries.[3]

Thus viewed, both the Jubilee and Sabbatical Years were religious institutions, fulfilling for the land and cattle what the Sabbath Day was to do for man. Thus they were intimately connected with Israel's duty to God, and symbolic of their relation to Him—seven being the sacred covenant number. And more than this, the Jubilee Year pointed forward to the coming of Messiah, when the acceptable year of the Lord would be proclaimed, the old wastes built, the former desolations raised up; and while strangers stood and fed their

---

[1] Lev. xxvii. 21.   [2] Ibid. ver. 22-24.

[3] It has been contended that the Sabbatical and Jubilee Years were never intended to be observed at the same period of the nation's history, as this would imply two years' intermission of harvest. But the blessing by which three years' store was given in the sixth year evidently meets this objection. As a matter of fact, however, the Sabbatical and Jubilee Years were never both kept during one and the same period. Comp. Ezek. vii. 12; xlvi. 17.

flocks, and the sons of the alien were their ploughmen and vine-dressers, Israel would be named the Priests of the Lord, and the Ministers of their God.[1]

The landed possession of an Israelite might be parted with in various ways:

1. By *purchase*, or, rather, tenancy from Jubilee to Jubilee.
2. *Redemption*, either by the original owner or by his kinsman. This "redeemer," styled *Goel* (Hebrew: looser, redeemer), was bound to stand by his kinsman in all difficulties concerning his land. To him belonged the right to purchase property which otherwise might have been lost to the family, as well as the power of avenging his kinsman's blood upon the "manslayer" outside the city of refuge. Moreover, from the Book of Ruth it would appear that, at any rate in most instances, the nearest *Goel* was expected not only to purchase his deceased kinsman's inheritance, but, as part of it, also to marry his widow, if she were childless, in order "to raise up the name of the dead upon his inheritance."[2] Should he be unwilling or unable to do so, this duty would devolve upon a more distant kinsman. The reason of the importance attached to not letting a name be put out in Israel lay no doubt in the hope, cherished by every mother, that from her descendants might finally be born the Messiah. And so sacred a duty was it deemed for the nearest kinsman (the husband's brother) to take the widow, and raise up seed to his brother, that should he refuse to do so, he must openly announce his intention in the gate of his city to the elders, and "then shall his brother's wife come unto him in the presence of the elders, and loose his shoe from off his foot, and spit in his face, and shall answer and say, So shall it be done unto that man that will not build up his brother's house. And his name shall be called in Israel, The house of him that hath his shoe loosed."[3]

[1] Isa. lxi. 2, 4-6.   [2] Ruth iv.; Deut. xxv. 5-10.
[3] Deut. xxv. 9, 10. Every kinsman was considered a *Goel*, but the *privilege* of redeeming the deceased's land, and of marrying his widow, belonged first by right to the nearest kinsman. The right of redemption did not, of course, apply to movable property, which might be bought or sold as we do at the present time.

3. *Exchange.* This was perfectly lawful within the limits of the tribe; *i.e.* one family might exchange their possession for any other, provided the property thus disposed of remained in the tribe. The story of Naboth's vineyard furnishes a striking example of this. Ahab was doing nothing contrary to the letter of Moses' law when he offered an exchange; while at the same time he had no power to compel one, and could only succeed in his desire by the wholesale murder of Naboth and his sons. Such an exchange was termed *Temurah.*

4. *Giving.* This, though often for the person's lifetime only, might be for ever. Land thus settled was frequently given to a daughter upon her marriage, and was regarded as her property exclusively.[1]

5. *Marriage.* Property might be acquired by marriage with an heiress, usually within her tribe.[2] Should the husband belong to another tribe, or be a foreigner, his children must be called after their mother's name, and be reckoned as belonging to her family.

6. *Forfeiture.* Beyond the seizure of Naboth's vineyard, the only case of forfeiture mentioned in the Old Testament is that made in the time of Ezra, when proclamation was made "that whosoever would not come to Jerusalem within three days, according to the counsel of the princes and the elders, all his substance should be forfeited" (or devoted), "and himself separated from the congregation of those that had been carried away."[3]

When the purchase of some property had been decided on, no legal document was required to be produced, at least in the earliest times. The buyer and seller met in the gate of the city, and there, in presence of witnesses, completed the bargain by paying the sum named. Of such a transaction we have a truly Eastern account in Genesis xxiii. Ephron, in the proud Oriental manner, at first disdains Abraham's offer of purchase, but finally accepts the full price, which is weighed to him "in the audience of the children of Heth, even of all that went in

---

[1] Josh. xiv. 6-15; Judg. i. 12-15.
[2] Num. xxxii. 41; 1 Chron. ii. 21-23; Neh. vii. 63.
[3] Ezra x. 8.

at the gate of his city." Probably such a purchase would be accompanied by a symbolic act, as striking hands, or, as in the case of Naomi's land, loosing the shoe. Other modes of marking possession of property, acquired by gift, by purchase, or by force, were, setting apart seven sheep; or treading round the property; while casting out the shoe implied the subjugation and possession of a country.[1]

In later times, especially during the troublous years immediately preceding the Exile, a document or deed of sale seems to have been used, probably for extra security. This deed was sealed, and a copy of it, unsealed, given to some scribe in the presence of both buyer and seller and of witnesses. As such a document is described as "sealed according to the law and custom,"[2] it would appear that at that time this was the ordinary way of disposing of property.

The rights of property, acquired in any way, were most sacredly guarded. All boundaries were carefully marked out,[3] and a curse lay upon any one who dared to remove his neighbour's landmark.[4] These were probably stones; and while the punishment for removing them is not defined, it would, no doubt, be the same as that ordained for robbery.[5] Whenever injury had been done to a neighbour's field or vineyard by the wilful trespassing of cattle, the most ample recompense must be made. An incendiary, through whose mischief or malice corn, either standing or in stacks, had been destroyed, must also "surely make restitution."[6] A neighbour's grapes might be eaten to the full by a passer-by, but none might be carried away for future consumption: "thou shalt not put any in the vessel." The same rule held good with the neighbour's standing corn; ears might be plucked with the hand, "but thou shalt not move a sickle unto thy neighbour's standing corn."[7] To these few and simple directions as to the rights of property the Rabbis added many others, which of course cannot here be

---

[1] Gen. xxi. 28-30; Deut. xi. 24; Psa. lx. 8.   [2] Jer. xxxii. 11.
[3] Josh. xv. 1-12.   [4] Deut. xxvii. 17.   [5] Comp. Hosea v. 10.
[6] Exod. xxii. 5, 6.   [7] Deut. xxiii. 24, 25.

entered into. As an instance it may be mentioned that if land had been taken for seven years, it was forbidden to cut down sycamore wood, or to sow flax on it, except in the first year, since the cultivation of flax was bad for the soil, and the sycamore from which the wood had been cut would require all those years fully to recover.[1]

Not only were the rights and duties of landowners to be kept in mind, but the dignity of the land itself, and of cattle, was to be respected. Thus, it was forbidden to sow the fields or the vineyards with "mingled" or "divers" seed; probably in reference both to the idolatrous practices of the nations around, and also to the impossibility of giving an equal chance of development to plants differing in growth and height and in their time of perfection, as well as to prevent the mixing of poisonous with harmless plants, such an act being contrary to nature.[2] In regard to animals, all crossbreeds were forbidden,[3] and it was unlawful even to yoke an ass and an ox together to the plough.[4] The ox, when treading out the corn, must not be muzzled;[5] an animal and its young must not be killed on the same day;[6] nor might the young be taken from its mother till it was seven days old.[7] And the command is thrice repeated, as condemning a practice both idolatrous and unnatural, that a young animal must not be boiled in the milk of any other one.[8] All beasts of burden were to rest on the Sabbath Day.[9] Nay, further, no man might see his brother's ox or ass fall down, or lying under a burden, without helping or relieving the poor animal.[10] How important these stipulations would be to an agricultural people, which, from the constant use of domestic animals, might easily and unintentionally become cruel, and so forget man's dignity, and perhaps endanger life, is very evident. And this care for animals, so much insisted

---

[1] B. Mez. ix. 9. [2] Lev. xix. 19; Deut. xxii. 9; comp. Ant. iv. 8. 20.
[3] Lev. xix. 19. [4] Deut. xxii. 10. [5] Ibid. xxv. 4.
[6] Lev. xxii. 28. [7] Ibid. ver. 27.
[8] Exod. xxiii. 19; xxxiv. 26; Deut. xiv. 21. So according to the best authorities. [9] Exod. xx. 10; xxiii. 12; Deut. v. 14.
[10] Deut. xxii. 4; Exod. xxiii. 5.

upon in the Pentateuch, may well be, in the mouth of St. Paul, a figure of the Divine care for each one of God's children: "Doth God take care for oxen? or saith He it altogether for our sakes? For our sakes, no doubt, this is written: that he that plougheth should plough in hope, and that he that thresheth in hope should be partaker of his hope."[1]

Turning now to the laws of inheritance, it appears that, to a great extent, Moses adopted the lines followed by the Patriarchs. The family possession descended, after the death of the father, to his sons alone, as the natural heirs. All the property, both landed and personal, was divided equally amongst them; the firstborn, however, receiving a double portion, as the beginning of his father's strength.[2] This law, of course, only applied to legitimate sons, since such alone were contemplated by the Mosaic code.[3] The law of the firstborn was fixed and inalienable; even if a man had two wives, one beloved and another hated, the firstborn son, though his mother was the hated one, must receive the double portion. In addition to his double portion, the eldest son, as head of the family, had certain privileges—"the birthright"—eagerly sought after.[4] He it was who must support his father's widow, and act as guardian to his unmarried sisters; and it was probably in view of this that the double portion of goods and lands fell to him.

The privileges of an eldest son might be forfeited before the establishment of the Mosaic law (Reuben, whose double portion was given to the sons of Joseph);[5] but this was not possible or permissible after the entrance into Canaan. According to later Rabbinic explanations, the laws of inheritance were much more complicated, both in reference to what is called a firstborn son, or even what could be called hereditary property.

Daughters, unless by special favour of their father, had no claim to an inheritance if there were any sons. Should there

[1] 1 Cor. ix. 9, 10.   [2] Gen. xlix. 3; Deut. xxi. 17.
[3] The sons of concubines generally received only presents (Gen. xxv. 6), though by adoption they might be made co-heirs with the legitimate son (comp. Gen. xlix.).   [4] Gen. xxv. 31-34; Psa. cv. 36.
[5] Gen. xlix. 4; Lev. xx. 11; 1 Chron. v. 1.

be no male heirs, the father's possession went to his daughters, and after them to their male heirs, provided they themselves married within their tribe. The case of Zelophehad's daughters, which was brought before Moses for decision, furnished ample details concerning this and kindred points of the law of inheritance in the female line (Numb. xxvii.; xxxvi.; for the carrying out of the law for marriage of heiresses see 1 Chron. xxiii. 21, 22). Occasionally, and as a gift from their father, daughters inherited even when there were sons; as, for instance, did Caleb's daughter, and the three daughters of Job.[1]

Where both sons and daughters failed, the inheritance went to the owner's brothers, and, they failing, then to the nearest kinsman.[2] In any case the inheritance should not remove from one tribe to another;[3] and it seems a very doubtful thing how far it was allowable for a slave or a servant to inherit the property. Abraham certainly contemplated this, even to the exclusion of his nephew Lot;[4] but the general opinion on this subject after the Exodus seems well expressed in the words of Agur, that one of the four things for which "the earth is disquieted," and which "it cannot bear," is "an handmaid that is heir to her mistress."[5]

Wills, or any kindred documents, were unknown in Old Testament times, and the first trace we find of them is in the Epistle to the Galatians.[6] Nor were guardians deemed necessary, since it was a sacred duty to all to respect the widow and the fatherless,[7] and, at any rate during the time of the Maccabees, there was a fund laid up for their relief in the Temple.[8] And so St. James but acted out the spirit of the Mosaic law when he characterized as "pure religion and undefiled before God and the Father" "to visit the fatherless and widows in their affliction," as well as "to keep himself unspotted from the world."[9]

And so Israel's land, as well as its government, was to be

[1] Josh. xv. 16-20; Job xlii. 15. [2] Num. xxvii. 9-11. [3] Ibid. xxxvi .9.
[4] Gen. xv. 2, 3. [5] Prov. xxx. 21, 23. [6] Gal. iii. 15.
[7] Job xxix. 12. [8] 2 Macc. iii. 10. [9] James i. 27.

holy to the Lord. Thus, even in the darkest hours, when the husbandman went forth weeping, bearing precious seed,[1] he could look forward to the time, foretold with such gladness by the rapt prophet, when God would create new heavens and a new earth; and they should build houses and inhabit them, plant vineyards and eat the fruit of them; when they should not build and another inhabit, nor plant and another eat; nor labour in vain, nor bring forth for trouble; but in that glad Jubilee the wolf and the lamb should feed together, and the lion eat straw like the bullock, and even that old serpent, the Devil, be harmless, dust his meat: for "they shall not hurt nor destroy in all My holy mountain, saith the Lord."[2]

[1] Psa. cxxvi. 6. [2] Isa. lxv. 17-25.

CHAPTER VIII.

SLAVES AND SERVANTS.

AT first sight it may appear somewhat strange that the laws of a people intended to be so absolutely free, to have such equality of position and of possession, should have provided for the existence of a class of bondsmen, and taken it for granted that these were necessary in the domestic life of the nation. But, fairly examined, these objections will vanish. For Israel's laws were for *use*, as well as for the ideal standpoint up to which the nation must strive; and slavery being an evil then existing, and to such an extent that it was impossible to ignore its existence, the first work of the Divinely-directed lawgiver was to modify and soften what he could not efface, and, placing it on a different level, exalt it by making it symbolic of Israel's relationship to God Himself. This idea of slavery is without any parallel, even in modern history.

The Old Testament has but one designation for those in service, whether slaves or free; and this designation is peculiarly honourable, as existing among a nation so purely agricultural. It is that of *Eved*, most correctly translated labourer, or cultivator of the soil. And rightly was it counted honourable, when the title so often given to the expected King-Messiah was that of *Eved Jehovah*, the servant of the Lord, and when Abraham, the father of the faithful, Moses, the prophet and lawgiver, and even Israel itself, were all God's servants.[1] The names given to female servants were likewise full of signification. Such an one was *Shiphchah*, " she who joins herself" (to the house), one of the family; or, still more tender, *Ammah*, " bound " (more

---

[1] Isa. xlii. 1; Psa. cv. 26, 42; Isa. lxiii. 17.

closely united to the house). The same strain runs through all the provisions for service in Israel; and the very existence of these provisions, contrasting so vividly with the treatment of slaves in the civilized and intellectually advanced later state of society in the cities of Greece and in the Roman Empire, may well be regarded as further proofs of the Divine origin of the Pentateuch legislation.

Besides these considerations, slavery, though certainly originally a curse from God, bestowed by Noah on the descendants of his son Ham,[1] was not regarded in the East at that time as shameful. In fact, one of the greatest heroes of Old Testament history, Joseph, was sold by his brethren as a bondman,[2] and yet was able, even in the land of Egypt, to rise from his lowly position to that of ruler next to the king. The confidence placed in his chief slave by Abraham appears not only from the commission he gave to Eliezer of Damascus, which rendered him responsible for the choosing and bringing from a far country of a wife for Isaac, but from the fact, before noted, that he intended to make him his heir, exclusive of any near or distant relative.[3] In the same spirit it is recorded that Naaman's servants addressed him as "my father;"[4] so that St. Paul was speaking in true Old Testament terms when he pointed out to Philemon what position his runaway, but now repentant, slave Onesimus must in future occupy.[5] Only in this instance the Apostle spake of the relationship between master and slave in its higher and Christian aspect, when Onesimus was to be received "not now as a servant, but above a servant, a brother beloved, specially to me, but how much more unto thee, both in the flesh, and in the Lord."

Such being the position and meaning of service in Israel, as transmitted to the nation from patriarchal times, it can be understood how to be sold into Palestine was the best lot that could befall any foreign slave; and how the danger to be feared would be ofttimes, not over-severity, but over-leniency on

---

[1] Gen. ix. 18–27. [2] Ibid. xxxvii. 28. [3] Ibid. xxiv.; xv. 2, 3.
[4] 2 Kings v. 13.   [5] Philemon 16.

the part of the master. This foolish kindness is strongly censured by the son of Sirach, who found that in his days at least "bread, correction, and work" were "for a servant," for, "if thou set thy servant to labour, thou shalt find rest; but if thou let him go idle, he shall seek liberty."[1] More than this, he must be set to work "as it is fit for him," and "if he be not obedient, put on more heavy fetters." That rigorous control was needed may be gathered from the notice in the Book of Proverbs, where, as a thing "not seemly"—but evidently possible—it is characterized "for a servant to have rule over princes."[2]

The Pentateuch provisions for the protection and the rights of slaves contemplate two great divisions of the class—in the strict sense of the word, as meaning those hired without receiving regular wages, and who were under the entire control of their owners—viz. (1) Hebrew, and (2) non-Israelite slaves. Each class has again various grades, every several grade having its special rights and privileges.

Hebrew slaves. An Israelite might become a bondman either voluntarily—that is, by selling himself on account of poverty or debt—or be made a slave in punishment for the crime of stealing, when the amount stolen could not be replaced by the felon. As for the period during which he was to remain in slavery, that was thus fixed by the Pentateuch: "If thou buy an Hebrew servant, six years shall he serve, and in the seventh he shall go out free for nothing. If he came in by himself, he shall go out by himself; if he were married, then his wife shall go out with him."[3] This law is still further expanded on true Theocratic lines in the Book of Deuteronomy, where it is added: "And when thou sendest him out free from thee, thou shalt not let him go away empty; thou shalt furnish him liberally out of thy flock, and out of thy floor, and out of thy winepress; of that wherewith the Lord thy God hath blessed thee thou shalt give unto him."[4] Next, the master is reminded, as being the foundation stone, so to speak, whereon all these "brotherly" acts were

---

[1] Ecclus. xxxiii. 24, 25, 28. [2] Prov. xix. 10.
[3] Exod. xxi. 2, 3. [4] Deut. xv. 12-14.

SLAVES AND SERVANTS.   89

to be built, that "thou wast a bondman in the land of Egypt, and the Lord thy God redeemed thee; therefore I command thee this thing to-day."[1] In conclusion, the owner is bidden remember what benefit this six years' service had wrought him : " it shall not seem hard unto thee, when thou sendest him away free from thee; for he hath been worth a double hired servant to thee" (*i.e.*, he has worked twice as long as a hireling would have done—or, do not take it ill that he has cost thee twice as much as a hired servant, viz., his purchase and his support), " in serving thee six years; and the Lord thy God shall bless thee in all thou doest."[2]

Thus far the law has dealt with the term of bondage allowable for such Hebrews as found it impossible to remain free, and who, evidently, had sold themselves, and probably laid up the sum obtained by this transaction till their six years of service should be ended. And here attention must be called to the fact that this seventh year of "release," although kindred in meaning to the Sabbatical Year, was not necessarily identical with it, but dated from the period when each slave individually had entered into bondage. This oneness of Theocratic principle, manifested in the Sabbatical Year, the Year of Release, the Sabbath, and the Jubilee; this view of the slave as the "brother," and ample provision for supplying his needs when he should have regained his liberty, may well furnish subject of admiration, if not imitation, even in our days of freedom and much-boasted higher development—so called—of the laws of kindness and mutual responsibility.

The law for a thief "found breaking up," and who had nothing wherewith to "make full restitution," was that he should "be sold for his theft."[3] No doubt this sale would be, in most cases, to him from whom the property had been stolen; at any rate, certainly not into a foreign land. Josephus explains that the thief shall not be under perpetual slavery, but must be released after six years' bondage,[4] and relates it as

---

[1] Deut. xv. 15. [2] Ibid. ver. 18.
[3] Exod. xxii. 3. [4] *Ant.* iv. 8. 28.

one of the acts of Herod the Great, "not only grievous to be borne by the offenders," but "containing in it a dissolution of the customs of our forefathers," his making a law "to expose housebreakers to be ejected out of his kingdom," "for," he adds, "this slavery to foreigners, and such as did not live after the manner of the Jews, and this necessity that they were under to do whatsoever such men should command, was an offence against our religious settlement, rather than a punishment to such as were found to have offended, such a punishment being avoided in our original laws."[1] This tyrannical law, according to Josephus, "became a part of" Herod's "accusation, and an occasion of the hatred he lay under."

Other circumstances which might constrain a Hebrew to sell himself are provided for in Leviticus xxv., where the following laws are laid down:

1. Should "thy brother" be waxen poor, and be sold unto thee, he shall not be compelled to serve as a bondservant.[2] Rather must he be as a "hired servant," and as a "sojourner," and thus serve unto the Year of Jubilee, when, his land returning to him, he and his children shall again take possession of the property "of his fathers."[3] This manner of treatment of such a slave is explained to be necessary in a religious point of view, since "they are My servants, which I brought forth out of the land of Egypt; they shall not be sold with the sale of a bondman. Thou shalt not rule over him with rigour, but shalt fear thy God."[4] Further, such sale into bondage could hardly be termed slavery, since every distinctive feature of slavery was absent. Rather must the Hebrew slave be classed as a hired servant, or even as above that grade, the only difference between his condition and that of a freeman consisting in the fact that he received all his wages in a lump sum, and that at the beginning instead of at the end of his service. The term fixed for the year of bondage—the Year of Jubilee—shows us that these Hebrew bondmen were in

---

[1] *Ant.* xvi. 1. 1.
[2] Lev. xxv. 39.
[3] Ibid. vers. 40, 41.
[4] Ibid. vers. 42, 43.

different circumstances to those which are provided for in the Books of Exodus and Deuteronomy, who were to be released at the end of six years.[1] Many explanations of this difference have been offered, but the one which seems most satisfactory is that which, proceeding on the Theocratic basis on which the law of the Jubilee Year rests, fixes the *limit* of slavery at the six years prescribed in the Books of Exodus and Deuteronomy, but adds that, should the Jubilee Year intervene, all Hebrew slaves must, in accordance with the whole meaning and character of the glad time, be set free, and return each man to his possession.[2]

2. Should a "sojourner" or "stranger," dwelling in the land, become the owner, by his voluntary sale, of "thy brother," when waxen poor, this Hebrew slave might be redeemed at any time: "one of his brethren may redeem him: either his uncle, or his uncle's son, may redeem him; or any that is nigh of kin unto him of his family may redeem him; or, if he be able, he may redeem himself."[3] The price of this redemption would, of course, vary in proportion to the years between the time of sale and the next Jubilee, in the same manner as it was appointed in the case of the purchaser of land.[4] The Hebrew thus sold to the stranger must be treated by his master with all consideration and kindness: "as a yearly hired servant shall he be with him: and the other shall not rule with rigour over him in thy sight. And if he be not redeemed in these years, then he shall go out in the Year of Jubilee, both he, and his children with him."[5] And the grand reason for all these provisions, Israel's freedom from the yoke of man, Israel's renewal every fifty years of its existence as a nation, Israel's duty as between brother and brother, is once more given consistency and meaning by the summing up of the

---

[1] Exod. xxi. 2; Deut. xv. 12.

[2] The theory seems without solid basis which could explain that the poor Hebrew slave could *only* obtain freedom in the Year of Jubilee; for in that case it would only be a small percentage of bondmen which would survive to that time. The explanation given in the text is that supported by the best authorities.

[3] Lev. xxv. 47–49.   [4] Ibid. vers. 50–52.   [5] Ibid. vers. 53, 54.

Jubilee laws: "For unto Me the children of Israel are servants; they are My servants whom I brought forth out of the land of Egypt: I am the Lord your God."[1]

Thus viewed, all seeming inconsistencies must vanish. The Hebrew slave might not be in bondage more than six years—that was the limit of his time of service. These years might be shortened by the intervening of the Year of Jubilee; above all, he was no servant in any harsh sense of the word, but a poor brother. And rightly has it been remarked, by a most learned writer, that while the laws in the Books of Exodus and Deuteronomy deal with the *limit* and *time* of bondage, those in the Book of Leviticus deal with its *kind* and nature, and thus protect both master and servant from loss of self-respect, and from forgetfulness of the fact that all, both bondmen and freemen, were equally God's servants, and bound to obey Him.

To protect the right of the master, on the other hand, regulations were added providing for the marriage of slaves. They are thus briefly set forth in the Book of Exodus: "If his master have given him a wife" (*i.e.*, if he be married to a heathen slave after his six years of service have begun), "and she have borne him sons or daughters, the wife and her children shall be her master's" (*i.e.*, they all shall be reckoned as heathen slaves, and as such be perpetual bondservants), "and he shall go out by himself."[2]

But "if the servant shall plainly say, I love my master, my wife, and my children; I will not go out free: then his master shall bring him unto the judges" (*Elohim*: more correctly, to the Lord, *i.e.*, to the central Sanctuary, where the supreme court was to be); "he shall also bring him to the door, or unto the door-post; and his master shall bore his ear through with an awl; and he shall serve him for ever."[3] This

---

[1] Lev. xxv. 55. From the fact that no redemption is contemplated for those sold to Hebrew masters, it would appear that the law considered only those sold to heathens as needing special protection, probably chiefly on religious grounds.
[2] Exod. xxi. 4.   [3] Ibid. vers. 5, 6.

religious ceremony—for it was such—signified that the slave voluntarily surrendered his own liberty, and that for ever. For it seems extremely doubtful whether this voluntary slave would be set free in the Jubilee, although such certainly was the opinion of Josephus and the Rabbis. Boring the ears was, in other countries also, such as Mauritania, Libya, etc., a mark of obedience—not, as has been so often supposed, of degradation—since the slave was one from *love*, not from *compulsion*; and this practice, though not to be commended, was far from being censured by Moses. This tone is in accordance with the spirit of those archaic times; but at a later period, in the days of Christ and His Apostles, not only was all slavery held in abhorrence by both Essenes and Therapeutæ,[1] but even the learned Rabbi Jochanan ben Saccai taught that this boring of the ear was the punishment of that organ, since it had heard at Mount Sinai the words (Lev. xxv. 55), "For unto Me the children of Israel are servants; they are My servants," and, in spite of this, had taken upon itself the yoke of flesh and blood.

The second class of slaves consisted of *non-Israelites*. These would be chiefly acquired by purchase, or in war, or were those still surviving from the original inhabitants of the land of Canaan. This class of slaves belonged perpetually to their owners, as did also their descendants: "both thy bondmen and thy bondmaids which thou shalt have, shall be of the heathen that are round about you; of them shall ye buy bondmen and bondmaids. Moreover of the children of the strangers that do sojourn among you, of them shall ye buy, and of their families that are with you, which they begat in your land: and they shall be your possession. And ye shall take them as an inheritance for your children after you, to inherit them for a possession; they shall be your bondmen for ever."[2]

These non-Israelite slaves were, therefore, in bondage for ever, as were likewise their children. They constituted family

---

[1] Gemara to Kidd. i. 2. *Philo:* Quod omnis probus, lib. ii. 457; *De Vita Contempl.* ii. 482.   [2] Lev. xxv. 44-46.

property, which was to descend from father to son. But very different was their position from that of slaves in other countries. Treated with kindness and consideration, they became those "born in the house," "sons of the house,"[1] having in all things a regard for their master's interests, most faithful and trustworthy. And it is significant that, although a possession of their owners, we do not find among the presents given on great occasions—such as those sent forward by Jacob to propitiate his brother Esau—any slaves included. This marks a higher stage of domestic morality than had been reached in other countries. In Israel, moreover, heathen slaves were admitted to many religious rites, which would bestow on them special privileges. They were to be circumcised,[2] but, as afterwards explained by the Rabbis, this, in the case of adults, must be a voluntary act, which not consented to, would oblige the owner to sell his slave again, after he had patiently waited for a year, in the hope of his bondman then desiring the rite. Should a slave be circumcised, he must not be sold to a heathen. Further, this proselyte-slave was, according to the Pentateuch,[3] admitted to the Paschal Feast, and permitted, if belonging to a priest, to eat the sacred food. All slaves, whether circumcised or not, must rest on the Sabbath Day, according to the terms of the Fourth Commandment.[4]

The life and health of slaves were secure, and quite out of the master's power. "If a man smite his servant, or his maid, with a rod, and he die under his hand" (that is, if he smote with an intention to kill), "he shall be surely punished"[5]—that is, the master must suffer death, just as if the person thus slain had been free. But if the slave lingered for a day or two, "he shall not be punished, for he is his money;"[6] that is, the master evidently not having had the intention of taking his servant's life, would be sufficiently punished for his violence by the loss of his property. If a slave had been wantonly injured by his master (his eye or his tooth destroyed), he received his liberty

---

[1] Gen. xvii. 12; Eccl. ii. 7.   [2] Gen. xvii. 12, 13.
[3] Lev. xxii. 11.   [4] Exod. xx. 10.   [5] Ibid. xxi. 20.   [6] Ibid. ver. 21.

SLAVES AND SERVANTS.

"for his tooth's" or "for his eye's sake."[1] If a slave were injured by an ox, the owner of the animal was obliged to give to the slave's master thirty shekels of silver, while the ox itself "shall be stoned."[2] Improper conduct to a female slave necessitated the bringing of a ram as a trespass-offering.[3] By these laws the life and person, as well as the honour, of the bondservant were ranked on the same level as those of a free Israelite.

As concerned <u>female slaves</u>, the Pentateuch regarded those who were Hebrews by birth as divided into <u>two classes</u>: the first consisting of <u>ordinary slaves</u>, who served for six years, and were then sent away free, with presents;[4] the second consisting of those who had been sold by their fathers <u>for wives</u>. The last class of so-called slaves could hardly be regarded as such, but were rather the daughters of those poor Hebrews who, unable to give their children suitable marriage portions, received instead a sum of money for themselves, and also by this act secured the future of their maidens. The difference between these women and the ordinary female slaves appears from the words in which the rights of the former are secured: "If a man sell his daughter to be a maidservant, she shall not go out as the menservants do" (*i.e.*, if she has been purchased as a wife). "If she please not her master, who hath betrothed her to himself, then shall he let her be redeemed" (*i.e.*, her father may return the money he has received for her): "to sell her unto a strange nation he shall have no power, seeing he hath dealt deceitfully with her. And if he have betrothed her unto his son, he shall deal with her after the manner of daughters. If he take him another wife, her food, her raiment, and her duty of marriage, shall he not diminish. And if he do not these three unto her" (*i.e.*, neither let her be redeemed, nor marry her himself, nor marry her to his son), "then shall she go out free without money."[5] From these notices it will be gathered that such a "purchased" wife was no slave, but really free, and as such to be treated with due respect and courtesy.

[1] Lev. xxi. 26, 27.   [2] Ibid. ver. 32.   [3] Ibid. xix. 20-22.
[4] Deut. xv. 12-17.   [5] Exod. xxi. 7-11.

Female non-Israelite slaves would be chiefly captives of war, or descendants of such captives, or those who had been purchased for money. They were treated as ranking with the household servants, whether hired or bondmen.[1]

The price of a slave seems to have been fixed at, or about, thirty shekels of silver.[2] Notwithstanding the small encouragement slavery received from those at first in authority, it is evident, from the notices in the Books of Chronicles, that the slave class had greatly increased at the time of Solomon, since the entrance into Canaan. At that time this class probably included chiefly descendants of the Canaanites (since *Eved Cenaani* is a very ordinary term for a slave), or of that "mixed multitude" which followed Israel out of the land of Egypt.[3] These slaves were much employed by the Kings David and Solomon.[4] But, notwithstanding the large number of bondmen spoken of in the Book of Chronicles, it must be remembered that the proportion of slaves to free, even in the days of Ezra and Nehemiah,[5] goes far to establish the fact that Israel was far less tainted with this evil than was any other nation then existing. At any rate, there was never a revolt of the slaves, such as troubled the Spartan state; nor does the Israelitish nation appear to have taken any part, at least an active one, in the infamous slave trade, for which the Phœnicians were condemned at the mouth of such prophets as Obadiah, Amos, and Joel.[6]

Selling children into slavery for the debts of their father must have been an arbitrary and illegal proceeding, since it was condemned by the prophet Amos, and peremptorily forbidden by the governor Nehemiah.[7] After the Exile all the slaves purchased by the Jews seem to have been non-Israelites; while before that period it was ever regarded as a most sacred duty to redeem such Israelites as had fallen into the hands of foreign heathen masters. Further, while the punishment for

---

[1] Deut. xx. 14. [2] Exod. xxi. 32. [3] Ibid. xii. 38.
[4] 2 Chron. ii. 2, 17; viii. 7, 8; 1 Kings ix. 20, 21. [5] Ezra ii. 64; Neh. vii. 67.
[6] Obadiah 20; Amos i. 9; Joel iii. 4–6.
[7] 2 Kings iv. 1; Amos ii. 6; Neh. v. 5–8.

SLAVES AND SERVANTS.

man-stealing, according to the Mosaic law, was death,[1] an escaped slave might not be delivered to his master again, but "he shall dwell with thee, even among you, in that place which he shall choose in one of thy gates, where it liketh him best: thou shalt not oppress him."[2] All these considerations may well make us cautious in judging of this oft-maligned portion of the Pentateuch legislation.

The duties of the slaves, as noticed in the Bible, would be chiefly connected with agricultural labour, such as sowing, ploughing, reaping or keeping the flock.[3] Within the house the slave waited on his master at table; ground at the mill —considered hard labour, though often the task of female slaves;—unloosed his master's sandals when he went to the bath, etc.;[4] washed his feet;[5] opened and guarded the door;[6] or invited his master's guests to a feast.[7] Over each household was set a chief slave, termed "the steward" in Holy Scripture,[8] who was required to be faithful, since he often occupied the position of tutor or guardian[9] to his master's sons. In fact, so high could these head servants rise, that they might even be married to their masters' daughters.[10] Moreover, they could accumulate immense wealth, as it is, for instance, recorded of Ziba, Saul's servant, who being appointed by David sole guardian of the young Mephibosheth, had full control of all his possessions—of which power he did not fail to profit himself.[11]

The hireling, or free servant, generally hired for a year, might of course do service wherever he chose.[12] The law provided that he should not be defrauded of his wages, but that they should be paid him on the day that they were due, "lest he cry against thee unto the Lord, and it be sin unto thee."[13]

---

[1] Exod. xxi. 16.   [2] Deut. xxiii. 15, 16.   [3] Luke xvii. 7.
[4] Isa. xlvii. 2; Exod. xi. 5; Matt. xxiv. 41; iii. 11.   [5] 1 Sam. xxv. 41.
[6] John xviii. 16; *Ant.* xvii. 5. 2.   [7] Prov. ix. 3.   [8] Gen. xv. 2.
[9] Gal. iii. 24; παιδαγωγός.   [10] 1 Chron. ii. 35.
[11] 2 Sam. ix. 2, 9, 10; xvi. 4.   [12] Lev. xxv. 53.
[13] Lev. xix. 13; Deut. xxiv. 14, 15.

Lastly, the servants of the Sanctuary, and the Gibeonites were specially dedicated bondmen belonging to the priests, and bound to them in perpetual service.[1]

In this way, then, did the law of Moses modify and brighten the hard reality and stern necessity with which it had to deal. And more than this not even Christianity could do, till the very foundations of ancient social life had been done away with, and liberty of conscience had been found to necessitate liberty of speech, action, and person. And even now no man is free—bound, in every moral sense of the term; bound, above all, by the bonds of love to his Great King, to Whom he owes all good faith and obedience. And being so bound, the words of St. Paul, of such deep significance in the days of slavery, are still true and living in our days: "Let every man abide in the same calling wherein he was called. Art thou called being a servant? care not for it; but if thou mayest be made free, use it rather. For he that is called in the Lord, being a servant, is the Lord's freeman: likewise also he that is called, being free, is Christ's servant. Ye are bought with a price; be not ye the servants of men. Brethren, let every man, wherein he is called, therein abide with God."[2] And our Lord Jesus Christ has hallowed and beautified for ever all service, when, having taken upon Himself the form of a servant, He washed His disciples' feet, and then, while they watched Him in silent awe as, His service done, He again sat down with them as their Master and Lord at His Last Supper, He said unto them: "If I then, your Lord and Master, have washed your feet, ye also ought to wash one another's feet. For I have given you an example, that you should do as I have done to you."[3] And so, to all time, the highest life of Christianity is that of service, and the title most dear to Apostles and Martyrs that of servant of God, "for ye are bought with a price: therefore glorify God in your body, and in your spirit, which are God's."[4]

---

[1] 1 Sam. ii. 22; Josh. ix.
[3] John xiii. 14, 15.
[2] 1 Cor. vii. 20-24; Phil. ii. 7.
[4] Phil. i. 1, etc., ; 1 Cor. vi. 20.

CHAPTER IX.

WIVES AND CHILDREN.

FROM the beginning of the world's history has the union between God and man been shadowed forth and typified by the natural and social relationships we call family life. And, in truth, such union and fellowship are what still remain of the Divine in us; since the foundation of the first family was the work of God Himself. That this fact has been recognised by men in all ages, both Jew and Gentile, may even be gathered from the ancient Rabbinical saying, that one of the things which "the Lord of the world" "hath taught us" is "to unite the bridegroom and the bride in marriage, as He united Eve to Adam."[1] Marriage, then, was and is holy—the most sacred tie on earth, and as such it is viewed throughout the whole Bible, finally reaching its highest point as the greatest "mystery"—that symbolic of the union of Christ with His Church.[2] In like spirit the Revelation of St. John closes with a description of the "holy city, the new Jerusalem," whose beauty is so resplendent that it can only be compared to that of a "bride adorned for her husband;" while, finally, the greatest triumph and rejoicing since the world was created will be when, all Christ's enemies subdued, the Church of God reaches that blessedness seen in vision by God's "servant John:" "Let us be glad and rejoice, and give honour to Him: for the marriage of the Lamb is come, and His wife hath made herself ready. And to her was granted that she should be arrayed in fine linen, clean and white: for the fine linen is the righteousness of saints. And He saith unto

---

[1] Targum Pseudo-Jon. on Deut. xxxiv. 6. [2] Eph. v. 23, 32.

me, Write, Blessed are they which are called unto the marriage supper of the Lamb."[1]

This is marriage viewed ideally, as God intended it to be, and as He gave it, for the high point of family life up to which man must strive. Yet in no department of human life more than this does man's fall appear so great, nor the consequences of the first sin more dire; and this as regards both the relationship of husband and wife, of brother and brother, and of parent and child. Bearing this in mind, it must be perceived that many acts which we now see to be hateful to God and degrading to man, were, on account of the "hardness of heart" of Israel, suffered—not countenanced—by the Mosaic law. It is the glory of Christianity that it has helped to re-establish what had been to a great extent lost, and perfected what the Pentateuch code had only sketched as to be aimed after in regard to family life.

First, in regard to polygamy in general, the Mosaic code has nothing to say. The custom of having more than one wife appears first in antediluvian times, where Lamech, the first poet, addresses his Sword-song to his two wives, Adah and Zillah; the first war-song being thus associated with the first swerving from God's sanctioned law. Next, after the Flood, Esau, the son of the pious Isaac, marries two wives; and, yet again, Jacob, his brother, is deceived by Laban into marrying his cousin Leah, after which he marries his chosen Rachel also. These, and many other instances of polygamy, will readily occur to the mind. But nowhere can be found any praise, or even approbation, bestowed on the persons thus united for their act; but rather, on the contrary, sad family quarrels, endless jealousies, even cruel and wicked deeds are the outcome of such marriages. The reason for desiring many wives lay, no doubt, in the wish, natural to each Jew, to have a numerous family, as well as the fear of the name being "put out" in Israel. As the nation increased and became more civilized, polygamy gradually died out, or was

[1] Rev. xix. 7-9.

confined to the family of the king, or of the chief ruler, and this as part of his royal state. After the Exile it was a thing unknown among the Jews, and even when before that time it was "suffered," we may safely infer from the Old Testament that it was the exception, and not the rule.¹

The next point on which the Mosaic law is somewhat vague is that of divorce. From the wording of the provisions for it, it would appear that the lawgiver introduced nothing new, but restricted and more clearly defined laws already in use.² The reasons assigned for divorce were, however, to be true and just ones, and well considered, for such an act must be a final one: no more could the separated pair be united. To give the husband ample space and opportunity for reconsidering the matter, as well as to make divorce as difficult as possible, he must take three distinct steps to make it an entirely legal act. 1. He must write her a bill of divorcement—a matter in those days of limited education somewhat difficult, and probably requiring the aid of a third party. 2. He must give it in her hand—*i.e.*, see that she really has it; and 3. He must send her out of his house. Thus provided with documentary evidence that she was no longer a wife, the woman was at perfect liberty to marry again; only, after the second husband's death, she might not again be united to her first husband, "for that is abomination before the Lord." All improper conduct was most strongly condemned, and most severely punished, as violating the holiness of the nation, and as offensive to God, its great Head. How intimately all the domestic laws were connected with the religious duties of the nation may be clearly seen from the oft-repeated reminder which so frequently closes these admonitions, that Israel was God's peculiar people, "an holy nation unto the Lord thy God."

The perfect family life, then, was not found in the household where many wives, each desiring the supreme authority, had their miserable disputes and jealousies, but in the house

---

¹ The same may be said with regard to such unions as that of Abraham with Hagar. They are utterly ignored by the Mosaic law. ² Deut. xxiv. 1.

of such an one as Elisha's Shunammite patroness,[1] or even where the churlish Nabal was influenced and awed by the fair Abigail.[2] The Mosaic law strove indirectly to make such family life as universal as possible, by forbidding kings to have many wives, and by forbidding marriage with two sisters at the same time.[3] Further, marriage was forbidden with all near relatives, and disobedience to this law was punished, in some cases by death, in others by chastisement from God's hand, probably childlessness. These laws, in marked contrast to the unions sanctioned by other ancient states, are full of significance. For, not only was family life kept sacred, and the circle perpetually enlarged, but it was, as has been pointed out by St. Augustine, that so the whole world might be drawn into one family, and love reign supreme, to the banishment of self-concentration and isolation.[4]

Besides within the prohibited degrees, marriage was forbidden with the descendants of the seven nations formerly inhabiting the land of Canaan, and this on account of the idolatrous practices they would introduce into Israel.[5] But unions with other heathen nations were quite lawful, as is proved by the fact that one was entered into even by Moses himself.[6] At the same time, that these alliances were dangerous in a religious point of view, appears from the history of Solomon; [7] while after the return from the Exile, it is recorded that Ezra found *all* the marriage laws had been entirely set aside, and that unions had taken place between the Jews and the seven banned nations. This discovery caused deep sorrow to the zealous priest and to Nehemiah, and eventually led to a public renunciation of all these heathen wives, and to a "cleansing" of the whole nation, including the priesthood.[8] But even where allowed, marriage with a heathen was regarded with disfavour. So Samson's parents tried to dissuade their son from

[1] Comp. 1 Sam. i. ; [2] 2 Kings iv. 8.   [2] 1 Sam. xxv. 14.
[3] Deut. xvi. 17 ; Lev. xviii. 18.
[4] Quoted in Keil's *Archäologie*, vol. ii. pp. 56–61 (note).
[5] Deut. vii. 1–6.   [6] Exod. ii. 16, 21; Deut. xxi. 10–14.
[7] 1 Kings xi. 1–3.   [8] Ezra ix. 2 ; x. 3 ; Neh. xiii. 23–30.

taking "a wife of the uncircumcised Philistines."[1] And in truth, except in the case of the Moabitess Ruth, disaster seems to have followed nearly every foreign marriage after the settlement of Israel in Canaan.

The marriage formalities, as described in the Old Testament, are exceedingly primitive and simple. The choice of the bride, or at least the request for her hand, was usually made by the bridegroom's parents;[2] and although this was not necessary (see Esau's marriage),[3] yet in some cases the affianced pair had never even seen each other before they were united. Both parents would have an equal share in arranging the marriage; but where the father was either not alive, or else was absent, the mother alone had the power of choosing the wife.[4] The ceremony—if it deserved the name—was extremely simple. In the presence of witnesses the consent of the parents of the bride was asked—in many cases also of her brothers, chiefly of the eldest.[5] This being obtained, the maiden was next sent for, and her consent having been obtained in the presence of her family, the betrothal was said to be completed. On this occasion the bridegroom was accustomed to give the bride a present—of money, clothes, or ornaments.[6] Such bridal presents—termed *mohar*, translated "dowry" in Exod. xxii. 17—were not at all intended as the price of the wife, but rather as money to enable her to take her proper position in her husband's house. Quite different were the *mattanoth*, or gifts, presented by the bridegroom to the father and brothers of his bride (also termed *migdanoth*).[7] It is quite erroneous to regard these bridal gifts as placing the bride in an inferior position to her husband, and as implying that he had purchased her, and that she was as much his possession as any slave or personal property.[8] This

[1] Judg. xiv. 3. [2] Ibid. vers. 2-5. [3] Gen. xxvi. 34, 35.
[4] Ibid. xxi. 21. [5] Ibid. xxxiv. [6] Comp. Gen. xxiv. 53.
[7] Gen. xxxiv. 12; xxiv. 53.
[8] That receiving payment for a daughter specifically was an unusual thing appears from the complaint of Laban's daughter (Gen. xxxi. 15, 16). Yet even in later times the prophet Hosea buys a wife (Hosea iii. 1, 2). These, however, are exceptional cases.

is totally contrary to the whole spirit of the Mosaic economy, which places both husband and wife on the same footing—he *Ish*, she *Isshah*, his *Eser*, or help, bound to him by love, not by force.

The presents given, the maiden was now betrothed, and considered as solemnly bound to her future husband as though she were already his wife. The period of betrothal varied, and the damsel had no other bond but her pledged word, at least in the earliest times. In after ages a written document (*Shitrei-Erusin*) was signed, but in the primitive period of Israel's national life this was not considered necessary. The marriage day being at last fixed, the bridegroom, crowned and decked with ornaments, went, accompanied by companions, to the bride's house.[1] If this were in the same place as his own house, he simply brought her, beautifully attired, and covered with a mantle-like veil,[2] back to his home; but if she lived at a distance, the festivities were carried on in her father's house.[3] The marriage feasts and rejoicings lasted seven days,[4] sometimes even fourteen,[5] and were made occasions of great mirth and gladness.[6] No religious ceremony of marriage is spoken of in the Old Testament, although doubtless some such existed, of which the blessing pronounced in the Book of Ruth —" The Lord make the woman that is come into thine house like Rachel, and like Leah, which two did build the house of Israel: and do thou worthily in Ephratah, and be famous in Bethlehem. And let thy house be like the house of Pharez, whom Tamar bare unto Judah, of the seed which the Lord shall give thee of this young woman "[7]—may have formed a part. But this is mere conjecture, since the data requisite are not forthcoming.

From these notices it will appear that the marriage could not take place without the bride's full consent having been first obtained. This marks a true recognition of the rights and

---

[1] Cant. iii. 11 ; Isa. lxi. 10 ; Judg. xiv. 11. [2] Gen. xxiv. 65.
[3] Judg. xiv.   [4] Ibid.   [5] Tobit vii. 13.
[6] Jer. vii. 34.   [7] Ruth iv. 11, 12.

position of a wife. Certainly, wives were now and then bestowed, without any dowry or gift from the suitor, as rewards for valour.[1] But from the case of Saul's daughter Michal, it would appear that this was also with the full consent, and by the desire, of the bride herself. The age for marriage is not mentioned in the Bible. Isaac married at forty;[2] but the Rabbis laid it down that a man should marry at or about eighteen, a maiden at thirteen years of age.

The Books of Psalms and Proverbs give us many beautiful pictures of the wife and mother in Israel. She is the virtuous woman, whose price is far above rubies, who orders her household wisely and well, provides their meat and portions, looks well to their ways, and herself eateth not the bread of idleness.[3] Her children arise up, and call her blessed; her husband also, and he praiseth her. Such a husband is "blessed" in having her, "for the number of his days shall be double."[4] But, on the other hand, while a good wife was an unmixed blessing, an evil wife was a yoke shaken to and fro: " He that hath hold of her is as though he held a scorpion."[5] In accordance with this, it may be not without experience, Solomon taught: " It is better to dwell in the wilderness, than with a contentious and an angry woman."[6] Such power had the mistress of the house, and the mother of the family, to make her household either happy or else disunited. And it may fairly be argued, from the fact that the mother of each king is specially named, that the early training and teaching these queen-mothers gave their sons proved of the greatest import to the nation at large, as well as in moulding their sons' future lives and characters.

The wife had no power to separate herself from her husband, at least so long as he continued to support her. Josephus, however, relates of both Salome and Herodias that they divorced themselves from their husbands, adding that this "was not according to the Jewish laws, for with us it is lawful for a husband to do so; but a wife, if she departs from her husband,

---

[1] Josh. xv.; 1 Sam. xviii. 25.   [2] Gen. xxv. 20.   [3] Prov. xxxi.
[4] Ecclus. xxvi. 1.   [5] Ibid. ver. 7.   [6] Prov. xxi. 19.

DOMESTIC LAWS.

cannot of herself be married to another, unless her former husband put her away."[1] For such acts as these the Herodians were held in just abhorrence by all pious Jews.[2]

Among the Israelites rank and station were non-existent. Unequal marriages were therefore impossible, and the wife would be chosen for worth of character rather than for fortune. Widows were allowed to marry again, it being only provided that the high priest's wife should neither be one, nor a heathen; while ordinary priests might not marry a divorced wife, nor a woman of a bad character, although they might be united to a widow.[3]

The trial for a wife suspected of adultery, by means of the waters of jealousy, was a religious ceremony, the issue of which was left to a Divine vindication of the truth.[4]

Women were not only treated with great respect by the Jews, but their praise was much desired and sought after. They greeted the return of victorious heroes with triumphal processions, songs, and dances, and were also permitted to join in religious festivals.[5] Some were prophetesses (Miriam and Huldah);[6] another, Deborah, a judge.[7] They had full right to claim justice or to make complaints to the authorities;[8] and the Book of Proverbs over and over again chronicles the power and influence which the "wise" and "virtuous" mother may, and should, exercise over her son.[9]

Children, according to the Jewish opinion, were "an heritage of the Lord," "as arrows in the hand of a mighty man."[10] To be "written childless" was God's curse;[11] and no gift could an Elisha promise which would give more joy than the birth of a long-desired child.[12] The relationship between parents and children was especially tender and close, widely differing from

---

[1] *Ant.* xv. 7, 10 ; xviii. 5, 4.
[2] One of the main causes of dispute between the schools of the Rabbis Hillel and Shammai was the question as to what constituted the legal grounds for a divorce.   [3] Lev. xxi. 13, 7, 8 ; Ezek. xliv. 22.
[4] Num. v. 14.   [5] 1 Sam. xviii. 6–8 ; Psa. lxviii. 25.
[6] Exod. xv. 20 ; 2 Kings xxii. 14.   [7] Judg. iv. 4.
[8] 1 Kings iii. 16–28 ; 2 Kings vi. 26–29.   [9] Prov. i. 8; iv. 3, etc.
[10] Psa. cxxvii. 3, 4.   [11] Jer. xxii. 30.   [12] 2 Kings iv. 14.

WIVES AND CHILDREN.

that state of absolute possession as property, body, and soul, which marked the power of the father in the civilized states of Greece and Rome. No tender or delicate child was ever exposed, as not worth the trouble of rearing. The child, tended with loving care, was circumcised the eighth day, and on that same day named, often in commemoration of some great event or special answer to prayer.[1] Josephus mentions, with what accuracy it is doubtful, that "the law does not permit us to make festivals at the births of our children," adding, "and thereby afford occasion of drinking to excess; but it ordains that the very beginning of our education should be immediately directed to sobriety."[2] Forty days after the birth of a male child, eighty after that of a female, the mother was ceremonially purified,[3] while the first-born son must be redeemed by the payment of five shekels of the Sanctuary.[4] The next event in the child's life was his weaning, generally at the age of two years, or even three, which event would be often made the occasion for a great feast, as well as for offering a sacrifice, in token of joyful gratitude.[5]

The education of Jewish children in Old Testament times was chiefly entrusted to the mother. It would in most instances, no doubt, be a very limited one, especially in the early days of Israel's history, since schools were unheard of till post-Exilian times. Reading and writing would be rare accomplishments; and the main object striven after in teaching by the mother would be, no doubt, to impress upon the child the wonderful history of Israel's past, and the duties and obligations to which he, as partaker and member of the holy covenant, was bound.[6] Slaves sometimes served as tutors, while princes were taught by prophets.[7] The father himself was bound to teach his children "the commandments, the statutes, and the judgments, which the Lord your God commanded to teach you," and to speak "of them when thou sittest in thine house, and when

---

[1] 1 Sam. i. 20-28. [2] *Against Apion*, ii. 26. [3] Lev. xii.
[4] Num. xviii. 15, 16. [5] Gen. xxi. 8; 1 Sam. i. 24.
[6] Josephus, *Life*, 76. [7] 2 Sam. xii. 25.

thou walkest by the way," as well as "when thou liest down, and when thou risest up."[1] The religious ceremonies performed in the household were to be explained to the children by their parents,[2] while the child for his part was admonished (in the Book of Proverbs) to remember such commandment and law for ever; "bind them continually upon thine heart, and tie them about thy neck."[3] That these lessons were not forgotten is very evident, as may be gathered even from St. Paul's words to Timothy.[4]

When the children grew to years of discretion, the sons were made the father's care,[5] while the daughters remained with their mother till their marriage, which generally took place at a very early age.[6]

As regarded the mutual relationships of parents and children, the law required that parents should be treated with the greatest respect and courtesy by their children. "Every one that curseth his father or his mother shall be surely put to death; he hath cursed his father or his mother; his blood shall be upon him."[7] Even he that "set lightly by his father and his mother" was cursed[8]—in each case the offence to the mother being regarded as an equal crime with that to the father. Further, "if a man have a stubborn and rebellious son, which will not obey the voice of his father" or "mother," not even when he has been chastised, the father and mother were to "lay hold on him," and to bring him to the elders of the city in the gate, and to make their formal complaint of him. "And all the men of his city shall stone him with stones, that he die; so shalt thou put evil away from among you; and all Israel shall hear, and fear."[9] The parents, according to this provision, had only the power to complain; the punishment was not theirs to give. And it may well be imagined that this law would be but rarely put in force.

The love between parents and children is a beautiful feature

---

[1] Deut. vi. 1, 7, 20; xi. 19.   [2] Deut. xxxi. 11-13.   [3] Prov. vi. 20, 21.
[4] 2 Tim. iii. 15.   [5] 2 Kings iv. 18.   [6] 2 Macc. iii. 19.
[7] Lev. xx. 9.   [8] Deut. xxvii. 16.   [9] Ibid. xxi. 18-21.

in Jewish life. Isaac mourning for his mother,[1] David for his undutiful son Absalom,[2] are tender scenes familiar to all. Children were taught reverence and respect not only for their parents, but also for the aged, to "rise up before the hoary head, and honour the face of the old man,"[3] and the length of their days in the land which the Lord had given them depended on the honour shown their father and mother,[4] and, by implication, all those acting as such. On the other hand, the unnatural crimes sanctioned—nay, commanded—by heathenism were painted as "abomination to the Lord;" such as the burning of sons and daughters in the fire to heathen gods.[5] A right relationship, then, must exist between father and child, and in order to gain this, correction must not be spared; "the rod and reproof give wisdom, but a child left to himself bringeth his mother to shame."[6] Nay, the son of Sirach even esteems it better "to die without children than to have them that are ungodly."[7] But it is to be one of the gladnesses in the last days, a joy so great that to it nothing less than the Coming of the Great Forerunner is to be dedicated, that the hearts of the fathers shall be turned to the children, and the hearts of the children to the fathers"[8]—family union, a resolution of all domestic discord, a union of Jew and Gentile, a preparedness of the home for the coming Messiah.

Truly, then, was marriage God's covenant, and children are gotten from the Lord.[9] And on the earthly, as by Jacob's ladder, we ascend to the heavenly, and, with St. Paul, perceiving the unity of all in Christ, that great "mystery," bow our knees to the great "Father of our Lord Jesus Christ, of Whom the whole family"—once divided, now for ever united—"in heaven and earth is named."[10] For with God as Father, can the love that is to continue on earth be aught else but brotherly and eternal?

---

[1] Gen. xxiv. 67. [2] 2 Sam. xviii. 33. [3] Lev. xix. 32.
[4] Exod. xv. 12. [5] Deut. xii. 31. [6] Prov. xxix. 15.
[7] Ecclus. xvi. 3. [8] Mal. iv. 6. [9] Prov. ii. 17; Gen. iv. 1.
[10] Eph. iii. 14, 15.

CHAPTER X.

POOR LAWS: DEBTOR AND CREDITOR.

"THE poor shall never cease out of the land," was the truth proclaimed by Moses,[1] even in the days when Israel's obedience was owned and blessed by the Lord their God. And the words have been echoed in all ages since, both by Jew and Gentile, hallowed by our Lord Himself when He silenced the indignation of His disciples at "this waste" of precious ointment poured by loving hands on His feet: "Ye have the poor always with you, but Me ye have not always."[2] Poverty, then, the existence of which is a fact recognized by the God and Father of all, must have a higher meaning and purpose, and a wide bearing on the history of the Kingdom of God. And such, in truth, is the case. For not only does poverty—and by this not mere beggary is meant (that is, begging for alms), but a dearth of what is necessary for life—show what is in a man, of what stuff his character is made, but to others also it gives the grandest opportunities of exercising those Divine qualities of mercy and sympathy. So charity has ever been viewed as most God-like, from the time when the ancient Jewish view was immortalized in the words of the Targum: "Blessed be the Name of the Lord of the world, who hath taught us His righteous way. He hath taught us to clothe the naked, as He clothed Adam and Eve. . . . He hath taught us to feed the poor, as He sent Israel bread from heaven,"[3] to that period when Christianity could

---

[1] Deut. xv. 11.   [2] Matt. xxvi. 11.
[3] Targum Pseudo-Jonathan on Deut. xxxiv. 5.

find no better inscription to write over its hospitals than the words *Christo in pauperibus* (to Christ in His poor).

To the Mosaic ideal state, which had for its chief object and final goal the sovereignty of God over a nation of "brethren," and such not only in feeling, but in actual outward circumstances, the existence of poverty must have presented a great and ever-present difficulty. But, just as Moses did not, with respect to other difficulties, turn aside from, or ignore, what was and must be an imperfection, originally, no doubt, caused by imprudence or by sin, but rather softened and modified what he could not efface, thereby showing that the Divine code provided for these "rough places," as well as for the "smooth ones," thus in them also being able to "prepare a way for the Lord," so did he in regard to the poor.[1] This purpose he accomplished by framing several provisions, having mainly for their object: (1) To take away all the ideas of shame connected with necessary poverty; (2) To provide that all things needful for actual life should be freely given to him that needed; and (3) To lay down rules to be observed by those whose lot in life was a happier one.

(1) To begin with, no false poverty was contemplated as existing. There was no beggar, no importunate solicitor for alms, in the Old Testament. Begging—the demanding what may or may not be refused—was a judgment on God's enemies, a fate from which the righteous and his seed were and would ever be preserved.[2] But even of such vagabonds the Pentateuch knows nothing. The poor for whom the lawgiver provided were: the widow, the orphan, the stranger, the Levite, and "thy brother"—that is, the poor man in general, brought into poverty by some unforeseen circumstance, and made dependent for help, and even for support, on his more favoured compatriot. But yet the laws for the relief of such persons as constituted these five classes are cast in a form peculiar to themselves. For they are more *admonitions* than *commands*, as though Moses here touched a sacred chord,

[1] Isa. xl. 3, 4. [2] Psa. cix. 10; xxxvii. 25.

which must of necessity re-echo in each heart, and as if he felt it almost unnecessary, almost an insult to Israel's dignity, to do more than briefly indicate what was inborn and natural to each one, who had himself been rescued from the poverty and bondage of Egypt.

The Israelitish nation being designed for an agricultural people, the chief riches accumulated would, of course, be dependent on circumstances over which the landowner could have no control. A famine, or the incursions of some hostile nation or tribe, might be quite sufficient to reduce an opulent family to immediate want.[1] But as the Israelite's foundation of wealth—his inalienable property—would still remain, in many cases all such an one might require would be a temporary help from a more fortunate neighbour, to enable him to start again, and thus to tide over his then present difficulties. To such an impoverished proprietor one of two courses lay open : he might either voluntarily go into service (or slavery) for a time ; or, should he not wish to do so, he might borrow, either in money or in kind, sufficient to serve his present needs till, by God's blessing, his land should once more have yielded her fruit.

Borrowing was permitted—nay enjoined—by the Pentateuch code,[2] but had certain limits placed to it, mainly with the view of defending the debtor from the hardheartedness of his creditor. And here it must be noted, that the law never for one moment contemplated any dishonesty or nefarious dealings on the part of the debtor. He had every intention of restoring what he had borrowed; while the creditor for his part had made a distinct compact, and likewise had no wish to go beyond it, though up to that limit it may have been that he had sought his own advantage alone. He had the right and the power to demand payment at any time he chose to do so ; this law had come down from generation to generation, and was implied, though not expressed, in the Pentateuch. But on this arbitrary power the Pentateuch laid the restraint, that during

---

[1] Ruth i. 1 ; Job i.   [2] Deut. xv. 1.

POOR LAWS: DEBTOR AND CREDITOR.

the seventh or Sabbatical year the debtor should be free from molestation. For that year his creditor might not dare to demand payment, "because it is called the Lord's release."[1] "Of a foreigner," on the other hand, "thou mayest exact it again"[2]—since to him there is no sacred meaning in this year—"but that which is thine with thy brother thine hand shall release; save when there shall be no poor among you; for the Lord shall greatly bless thee in the land which the Lord thy God giveth thee for an inheritance to possess it: only if thou carefully hearken unto the voice of the Lord thy God, to observe to do all these commandments which I command thee this day. For the Lord thy God blesseth thee, as He promised thee: and thou shalt lend unto many nations, but thou shalt not borrow; and thou shalt reign over many nations, but they shall not reign over thee."[3] That is, *if* Israel kept God's commandments, such would be their position. But, as we know from Old Testament records, the nation never did fulfil its covenanted mission, so that these words, like a high-water mark, but served to indicate from what possible estate Israel had fallen.

Lest this "year of release" should furnish an excuse to the self-engrossed man for not befriending his poor "brother," the lawgiver straitly enjoined, and fully explained, the duty, in a *religious* point of view, of lending to the "poor man of one of thy brethren, within any of thy gates, in thy land which the Lord thy God giveth thee"—thus at the outset reminding the unwilling lender that all he had came from, and really belonged to, God.[4] The wording of this admonition is singularly concise and telling: "Thou shalt not harden thine heart, nor shut thine hand from thy poor brother: but thou shalt open thine hand wide unto him, and shalt surely lend him sufficient for his need, in that which he wanteth. Beware that there be not a thought in thy wicked (Belial) heart, saying, The seventh year, the year of release, is at hand; and thine

[1] Deut. xv. 2.   [2] Ibid. ver. 3.
[3] Ibid. vers. 4-6.   [4] Ibid. vers. 7, 8.

eye be evil against thy poor brother, and thou givest him nought; and he cry unto the Lord against thee, and it be sin unto thee. Thou shalt surely give him, and thine heart shall not be grieved when thou givest unto him: because that for this thing the Lord thy God shall bless thee in all thy works, and in all that thou puttest thine hand unto. For the poor shall never cease out of the land: therefore I command thee, saying, Thou shalt open thine hand wide unto thy brother, to thy poor, and to thy needy, in thy land."[1]

Such, then, was to be the attitude of the lender to the borrower; and this attitude is, as has been well noted by a learned modern writer,[2] quite in accordance with the spirit of the whole Israelitish code of laws, which allowed no place for self-aggrandisement—nay, actually forbade the "laying of house to house"—but which, on the contrary, was pre-eminently conservative in its tendency, and sought nothing further nor better than the keeping, and that entirely and for ever, of the hereditary possession of each family by that family. Herein lay the whole motive power of the Poor Laws; and it may be confidently asserted that had not this principle been definitely recognised, and not communism, but a feeling of brotherhood, aimed after, the laws for the relief of the deserving poor which were framed by Moses must have been defective, as well as fallen greatly short of what was needed.

Next, usury and interest must not be exacted from any Israelite. "If thou lend money to any of My people that is poor by thee, thou shalt not be to him as an usurer, neither shalt thou lay upon him usury."[3] "If thy brother be waxen poor, and fallen in decay with thee; then thou shalt relieve him: *yea though he be* a stranger or a sojourner; that he may live with thee. Take thou no usury of him, or increase: but fear thy God; that thy brother may live with thee. Thou shalt not give him thy money upon usury, nor lend him thy

---
[1] Deut. xv. 9–11.
[2] Comp. the article in Riehm's *Handwörterb. des Bibl. Alterthums*, p. 85.
[3] Exod. xxii. 25.

victuals for increase."[1] "Thou shalt not lend upon usury to thy brother: usury of money, usury of victuals, usury of anything that is lent upon usury."[2] From these passages it would appear that money-lending, as a trade, and means of accumulating wealth, was forbidden between Israelite and Israelite, and this on account of their "brotherhood;" as also, according to the interpretations of some of the ablest commentators, between Israelites and the strangers settled in the land of Canaan, even though these might not be worshippers of Jehovah.[3]

On the other hand, money-lending, not for immediate needs, but in trading, was permitted between Israelites and heathens. "Unto a stranger" (*nochri*, not a sojourner, but a stranger in the sense of a foreigner generally, probably a trader or hawker) "thou mayest lend upon usury."[4] Of course, money thus borrowed might be exacted in the seventh or Sabbatical Year, while no doubt the traffic would be carried on by means of money, the payments not being made in kind—a circumstance which the passage itself seems also to imply.

In Mosaic times, written bills of loan being unheard of, the property due to the creditor would be mainly secured to him by the "pledge," which he would hold from his debtor, till such time as the loan might be repaid. These "pledges," which it had been customary to use in patriarchal times[5] for the security of promises, etc., had been, and still often were, exacted in the most arbitrary manner; while in some instances even property absolutely essential to the very life and health of

---

[1] Lev. xxv. 35-37.   [2] Deut. xxiii. 19.

[3] Critics are much divided as to the distinction made by Moses between lending to an Israelite and lending to a stranger in Leviticus xxv. 35. The words inserted by our Authorized Version, "Yea though he be," are not to be found in the original, which would read, "a stranger and sojourner, and he shall live with thee." The probability is that the verse, though bearing the interpretation, either that the Israelite was *as* a stranger and sojourner, or that the law also included non-Israelites dwelling in the land, means what has been stated in the text, especially as we must bear in mind that Moses usually applied the specific terms, *toshav*, a sojourner, and *ger*, a stranger, to non-Israelites only.   [4] Deut. xxiii. 20.   [5] Gen. xxxviii. 17.

the debtor was taken possession of by his hard-hearted creditor. To limit and control such proceedings, Moses first laid it down that the "pledge" must be given and received in a manner consistent with the personal dignity of the debtor, with the object in particular to spare him any unnecessary disgrace or annoyance. "When thou dost lend thy brother anything, thou shalt not go into his house to fetch his pledge. Thou shalt stand abroad, and the man to whom thou dost lend shall bring out the pledge abroad unto thee."[1] Next, it was forbidden to take and to retain beyond the eventide the upper garment, which in the East serves the poor man also as a blanket. "If the man be poor, thou shalt not sleep with his pledge: in any case thou shalt deliver him the pledge again when the sun goeth down, that he may sleep in his own raiment, and bless thee: and it shall be righteousness unto thee before the Lord thy God."[2] The danger of sleeping in the open air without a covering in the East is, of course, obvious, the difference of temperature by night being very considerable, especially when it is remembered that in that climate it may be said even of the moon that it "smites."[3]

Further, neither a widow's raiment,[4] nor the "nether and the upper millstone"—(which last utensils, found in every house, were used for grinding the corn for each simple meal, and therefore absolutely essential to the preparation of daily food)—must be taken to pledge, it being added with regard to the millstone, "for he taketh a man's life (*i.e.* what is necessary for his existence) to pledge."[5]

In this manner, and by these provisions, Moses strove to alleviate the condition of the debtor, so lamentable in other countries, where ofttimes the creditor exacted the life-labour of the debtor, who thus became his bondman, body and soul. Yet, notwithstanding these laws, it is sad to mark how soon, in the history of Israel, these precepts fell into contempt.

---

[1] Deut. xxiv. 10, 11.   [2] Ibid. vers. 12, 13.
[3] Comp. Gen. xxxi. 40; Ps. cxxi. 6.   [4] Deut xxiv. 17.
[5] Deut. xxiv. 17

For already in the days of the prophet Elisha it is recorded that the creditor demanded the sons of his deceased debtor as bondmen in payment of the debt.[1] Nor did matters improve even in the days of trouble. In the time of Nehemiah the returned Jews came to him in utter despair because of their debts. Their more fortunate brethren had exacted of them usury (a hundredth part) for money lent "to pay the king's tribute, and "to buy corn, because of the dearth:" the consequence being that the family lands of the poor debtors had been mortgaged, and their sons and daughters brought into bondage. And all this was not the work of strangers, but of "their brethren the Jews." Such a state of affairs was more than the fiery Nehemiah could brook, and assembling "a great assembly," he sharply rebuked "the nobles and rulers" who had done this thing, and having shamed them thus publicly, exacted from them the promise, "We will restore and will require nothing of them; so will we do as thou sayest." "And," adds the sacred writer, "the people did according to this promise."[2] That such high-handed measures were only too necessary appears from such passages as Isaiah iv. 1; Ezekiel xviii. 7-17; xxxiii. 15.

But by the mass of the population, and by all the righteous in the land, usurers were ever regarded with abhorrence. So David makes it a characteristic of him "who shall abide in God's tabernacle" that "he putteth not out his money to usury;"[3] and Job's friend taunts him that he has "taken a pledge from thy brother for nought, and stripped the naked of their clothing;"[4] while finally the Book of Proverbs declares as the doom of such an "evil man," "He that by usury and unjust gain increaseth his substance, he shall gather it for him that will pity the poor."[5]

The law of Moses made no provision for those who by their own slothfulness, or other evil deeds, had brought themselves to poverty.[6] For such the only resource was, and must ever

---

[1] 2 Kings iv. 1. [2] Neh. v. 1-13. [3] Psa. xv. 1, 5.
[4] Job xxii. 6. [5] Prov. xxviii. 8. [6] Eccl. x. 18; Prov. vi. 9-11.

be, that labour which they had despised: "He that tilleth his land shall have plenty of bread: but he that followeth after vain persons shall have poverty enough;"[1] and, if necessary, avoidance of what might tempt to self-indulgence. "Love not sleep, lest thou come to poverty; open thine eyes, and thou shalt be satisfied with bread."[2]

As regarded the other classes of "poor"—the "widow," the "orphan," the "stranger," and the "Levite"—the Pentateuch code provided for their support and welfare by the following regulations:

1. As members of the one great family, they were to share equally in the great Feasts. "Thou shalt rejoice before the Lord thy God, thou, and thy son, and thy daughter, and thy manservant, and thy maidservant, and the Levite that is within thy gates, and the stranger, and the fatherless, and the widow, that are among you, in the place which the Lord thy God hath chosen to place His Name there."[3] This rejoicing in the neighbourhood of the Central Sanctuary of course implied sacred feasts and family gatherings; and it is most significant that even in matters of domestic joy and union those wider, all-embracing sentiments, so eminently Divine, should be inculcated, and that Israel's family circles should not be regarded as complete unless the poor found a place within them.

2. At the end of every three years the third year's tithes, instead of being, as usually, taken to the Central Sanctuary for the priests, were to be brought out and laid up "within thy gates"—that is, in each town where they had been collected throughout the land.[4] The store thus accumulated was to be reserved for the use of the poor of each neighbourhood. "And the Levite, because he hath no part nor inheritance with thee, and the stranger, and the fatherless, and the widow, which are within thy gates, shall come, and shall eat and be satisfied; that the Lord thy God may bless thee in all the work of thine

---

[1] Prov. xxviii. 19. [2] Prov. xx. 13.
[3] Deut. xvi. 11, 14. [4] Deut. xiv. 22-27.

hand which thou doest."[1] As the offerer brought in his third year's tithes, he was bidden utter this prayer and declaration "before the Lord thy God:" "I have brought away the hallowed things out of mine house, and also have given them unto the Levite, and unto the stranger, to the fatherless, and to the widow, according to all Thy commandments which Thou hast commanded me: I have not transgressed Thy commandments, neither have I forgotten them; I have not eaten thereof in my mourning, neither have I taken away ought thereof for any unclean use, nor given ought thereof for the dead: but I have hearkened to the voice of the Lord my God, and have done according to all that Thou hast commanded me. Look down from Thy holy habitation, from heaven, and bless Thy people Israel, and the land which Thou hast given us, as Thou swarest unto our fathers, a land that floweth with milk and honey."[2] The store laid up in each town was not consumed in one great feast, but kept against any emergency that might arise.

3. That which grew of itself in the seventh or Sabbatical Year was free to the poor and to the stranger, as well as to the owner's family and cattle. "The seventh year thou shalt let it" (thy land) "rest and lie still; that the poor of thy people may eat: and what they leave the beasts of the field shall eat. In like manner thou shalt deal with thy vineyard, and with thy olive-yard."[3] And as superscription to this command, as also to that concerning the seventh day's rest for "the stranger," as well as for the household and domestic animals, was set this admonition, peculiarly applicable and telling to the rescued Israelite: "Thou shalt not oppress a stranger: for ye know the heart of a stranger, seeing ye were strangers in the land of Egypt."[4]

4. "When ye reap the harvest of your land, thou shalt not wholly reap the corners of thy field, neither shalt thou gather the gleanings of thy harvest. And thou shalt not glean thy

[1] Deut. xiv. 29.
[2] Deut. xxvi. 13-15.
[3] Exod. xxiii. 11.
[4] Ibid. ver. 9.

vineyard, neither shalt thou gather every grape of thy vineyard; thou shalt leave them for the poor and stranger: I am the Lord your God." [1] Again, lest this command should in any way be defective, there is added to it this exposition in the Book of Deuteronomy: "When thou cuttest down thine harvest in thy field, and hast forgot a sheaf in the field, thou shalt not go again to fetch it: it shall be for the stranger, for the fatherless, and for the widow: that the Lord thy God may bless thee in all the work of thine hands. When thou beatest thine olive tree, thou shalt not go over the boughs again; . . . when thou gatherest the grapes of thy vineyard, thou shalt not glean it afterward;" both these after-gleanings were "for the stranger, the fatherless, and the widow." Here once more it is the same principle of conduct that underlies all: Israel is God's servant, rescued from the house of bondage. "And thou shalt remember that thou wast a bondman in the land of Egypt: therefore I command thee to do this thing." [2]

Kindred to these commands are those which have been already noticed in previous chapters: the prohibition to defraud the hired servant; the permission given to any passer-by to pluck grapes or ears of corn for his immediate need; the regulations for the proper treatment of Israelites reduced to slavery by reason of poverty; as well as the injunctions given to the elders to execute equal justice alike to rich and poor. But shutting the heart against the poor was not a sin ever characteristic of the Jewish nation as a whole, at least in the bright days when Israel served Jehovah. The lessons of the lawgiver were not neglected, and throughout the whole Old Testament, from the beautiful picture of Boaz's tender care for the reapers in the Book of Ruth onwards, charity and kindness to the poor and unfortunate were ever regarded as national virtues. It is in accordance with this manner of viewing almsgiving and sympathy for others that Job was able to plead for himself that: "I was a father to the poor. Did not I weep for him that was in trouble? Was not my soul

---

[1] Lev. xix. 9, 10. [2] Deut. xxiv. 19-22.

grieved for the poor?"[1] So it was a mark of spiritual degeneracy in the land, calling for the prophet's denunciation of judgment, when the needy were turned aside from judgment, the right of the poor taken away, when widows became a prey, and the fatherless were robbed.[2] But darker still was the hour when the true meaning and reason of almsgiving was lost, even to the religious in Israel, and charity became work-righteousness; when the angel Raphael could be supposed to have said, "Alms doth deliver from death, and shall purge away all sin. Those that exercise alms and righteousness shall be filled with life."[3] To those whose "alms" were *zedakah* (righteousness), well might it seem strange that she who gave her two mites was commended above all those who had cast much into the Temple Treasury.[4] And to the Pharisees truly it was a new thing, and to Christ's hearers a thing taught, "not as the scribes," when our Lord explained the true place for almsgiving in that kingdom of heaven which He had come to establish upon earth, as well as its real object and motive—not before, nor to be seen of, men, but "when thou doest alms, let not thy left hand know what thy right hand doeth: that thine alms may be in secret; and thy Father which seeth in secret Himself shall reward thee openly."[5]

---

[1] Job xxix. 16; xxx. 25. [2] Isa. x. 2. [3] Tobit xii. 9.
[4] Mark xii. 41-44. [5] Matt. vii. 29; vi. 1-4.

CHAPTER XI.

TRADE.

"As for ourselves, therefore, we neither inhabit a maritime country, nor do we delight in merchandise, nor in such a mixture with other men as arises from it; but the cities we dwell in are remote from the sea, and having a fruitful country for our habitation, we take pains in cultivating that only."[1]

So wrote Josephus after the destruction of Jerusalem: and what was true of the Israelitish state at the time of its downfall was still truer in the days when the people first took possession of the land. The whole occupation of the nation, that for which it was best fitted, and in which it took most delight, was agriculture; the cultivation of the rich and fertile land, as well as the tending and pasturing of flocks and herds. From patriarchal times onwards the wealth of the family, now expanding into a nation, had been derived from such possessions. Abraham had been "rich" and "great" in flocks and herds, menservants, maidservants, camels, and asses, as well as in silver and gold.[2] Isaac had been "envied" by the Philistines on account of his "possession of flocks, and possession of herds, and great store of servants;"[3] while Jacob's wives described "the cattle of their father," which had come into their husband's hands as "all the riches which God had taken from our father."[4] If further proof of the devotion of the people to agricultural pursuits were required, it might be found in the bitter complaints made by the children of Israel

---

[1] *Against Apion*, i. 12. [2] Gen. xxiv. 35; xiii. 2.
[3] Ibid. xxvi. 14. [4] Ibid. xxxi. 9, 16.

in Egypt at the uncongenial and burdensome work forced upon them, which "made their lives bitter with hard bondage in mortar, and in brick," as well as in "all manner of service in the field"[1] (*i.e.* irrigating and cultivating in the peculiar Egyptian manner).

It is not, therefore, surprising to find that the Mosaic law does not contemplate trade and bartering as occupations likely to be universally, or indeed to any extent, carried on by the Israelites. On the contrary, while the regulations to guard the holiness of the land, of the household, and of the individual are extremely minute and most explicit, those with regard to commerce and merchandise are not only very few in number, but calculated to restrict and limit, rather than extend, any desire for bargaining or commercial intercourse. This is especially the case in regard to the nations outside and around the land. There are, no doubt, higher reasons and purposes in this, both as regarded Israel itself, and the Kingdom of God, of which Israel was typical. For, not only were the nations around, with whom Israel would naturally have the most frequent intercourse, of world-wide infamy, as the professors of the most sunken and abject heathenism (the Phœnicians, with their worship of Baal and Ashtoreth); but it is a fact, as has been well noted,[2] that foreign trade would in this instance have been more prejudicial than beneficial to the real welfare of the state—*i.e.* the welfare considered apart from the accumulation of wealth—by taking out of the country some of the most able members of the community; and while, on the one hand, importing foreign luxury and splendour, on the other weakening and preventing that military training and service to be required from all the youth of the Israelitish nation. These and other considerations, illustrated by the suicidal desire of the Jews in Old Testament times to imitate every foreign vice, or any institution, without regarding whether such might be injurious to themselves or not, that they saw in the nations around, may well serve to show how

[1] Exod. i. 14.   [2] By Michaelis, *Mos. Recht.*, i. pp. 183-189.

wise was the lawgiver in trying to turn the attention of his "stiffnecked" countrymen to those pursuits which would offer them fewest temptations.

The first notice of "artificers," or of such as were instructed in the arts, furnished us by the Old Testament occurs in the Book of Genesis, wherein we read of Tubal-cain that he was "an instructor of every artificer in brass (or copper) and iron,"[1] while his half-brother Tubal was "the father of all such as handle the harp and organ."[2] But notwithstanding these notices, skilled labour seems to have been much neglected in the patriarchal and early ages. At any rate, such must have been the case as regarded the descendants of Israel. True, there is mention throughout the Pentateuch and the historical and prophetic books of the Old Testament of various workmen—the apothecary, who prepared curious spices, perfumes, and oils;[3] the founder,[4] the weaver,[5] and embroiderer,[6] the engraver,[7] the lapidary,[8] who cut and set precious stones; the wood-carver,[9] the gold and silversmith, who could not only make, but design "curious works;" the craftsman,[10] maker of idolatrous images; the smith,[11] the carpenter,[12] the potter,[13] the coppersmith,[14] the fuller,[15] the masons and hewers of stone,[16] the bakers,[17] the barbers,[18] etc. But although all these trades were carried on by Israelitish workmen, it is very evident that they can never have brought any of these works to very great perfection—that is, as compared with other ancient kingdoms. In fact, although the account of the fabrication of materials for the Tabernacle in the wilderness shows that it was eagerly undertaken by the whole nation, by "every wise-hearted man, in whose heart the Lord had put wisdom," it is at least very probable, from the circumstance that the two master-workers were entrusted with the devising and executing of several

---

[1] Gen. iv. 22.
[2] Ibid. ver. 21.
[3] Exod. xxx. 33-35.
[4] Judg. xvii. 4.
[5] Exod. xxxv. 35.
[6] Ibid.
[7] Ibid. xxxv. 33.
[8] Ibid.
[9] Ibid. vers. 32, 33.
[10] Deut. xxvii. 15.
[11] Isa. xliv. 12.
[12] Ibid. ver. 13.
[13] Ibid. xxix. 16.
[14] 1 Kings vii. 14.
[15] 2 Kings xviii. 17.
[16] Ibid. xii. 12.
[17] Hosea vii. 4.
[18] Ezek. v. 1.

works, and with the general supervision of all the labour, in which each department separately would require a life's experience to become skilled in, that the ornamentation and sculpturing of the Tabernacle must have been, though magnificent, somewhat different from what it is so often imagined to be, and that the assistance rendered the two wise men by the other Israelites was not very great. This is not so difficult to understand, when it is remembered that all representations of forms or figures in heaven, earth, or sea, were forbidden,[1] and that the only figures permitted were those of Cherubim. But even the little skill in mechanical arts possessed by the Israelites seems to have been lost, or unemployed, after the making of the Tabernacle. Reference may be made to the notice in the First Book of Samuel, that, during the wars between the Philistines and Israel there was "no smith found throughout all the land of Israel," and that all the weapons and instruments in common use had to be taken down to their enemies to sharpen.[2] Even in the days of Solomon all the important work connected with the building of the Temple had to be done by foreign artisans;[3] and before him King David's palace was built, not by Jewish, but by Tyrian workmen.[4] From these and kindred notices, it is evident that the artificers and mechanics among the Jews were far behind those of other nations, and it seems probable that at any rate most of their architectural undertakings were designed and carried out by such hired and foreign artisans.

As regarded, however, all the mechanical arts, the Pentateuch legislation by no means restricted or discountenanced such—that is, of course, where the tendency would not be to idolatry. On the contrary, the master-worker Bezaleel is described as "filled with the Spirit of God, in wisdom, and in understanding, and in knowledge, and in all manner of workmanship, to devise cunning works, to work in gold, and in silver, and in brass, and in cutting of stones, to set them, and

---

[1] Exod. xx. 4. [2] 1 Sam. xiii. 19-21.
[3] 1 Kings v. 6. [4] 1 Chron. xiv. 1.

in carving of timber, to work in all manner of workmanship." [1] The power thus Divinely given cannot, therefore, have been wrongly used; and we are correct in inferring that Moses approved of the development of the resources of the country, although he censured the carrying of these resources beyond the boundaries of the land. Besides—a circumstance most important in the development of the arts—skill in any branch of industry was not the monopoly of one tribe, nor exclusively the right or privilege of any one family.[2] Persons belonging to either sex might spin, while every man had an equal right, nay, obligation, to learn any trade he might choose. From the notice in Deuteronomy viii. 9, it would appear that Palestine was a country rich in minerals, and no doubt the mines would be worked, though whether this work was carried on by Egyptians, or by Israelites, is still matter of dispute.

As regards the limits set by the Mosaic Law to trade with foreign countries, the following particulars are especially noteworthy:—

1. The restrictions in regard to trading on the part of the king.[3]

2. The laws of the Jubilee and Sabbatical Years, which would cause a serious interruption in barter with those whose religious opinions differed from the Israelites.

On the other hand, there are several points in favour of foreign trade:—

1. The permission to exact interest from non-Israelites residing outside the land, and the fact that the money lent to such heathens might be demanded even during the Sabbatical Year.

2. The situation of Palestine, on the caravan high road, between all the great centres of ancient trade: Egypt, Tyre, and Damascus. But once more, as against this, must be set the fact that Palestine—so much of it as belonged to Israel—possessed a very limited sea-coast, while the only harbours along that coast—Joppa, Jamnia, Ascalon, Gaza, and Acco or Ptolemais—were always, in Old Testament times, in the hands

---

[1] Exod. xxxi. 2-5.   [2] Ibid. xxxv. 35, 36.   [3] See Chap. I.

of Israel's neighbours, the Phœnicians or the Philistines; while the principal towns on the great northern highway were also occupied, and carefully guarded, by the former of these two nations.

3. Those good roads, existing from early times, which were, by Divine command, to be kept in order, and always prepared, leading to the six cities of refuge from all the "coasts of thy land."[1]

Again, as regarded trade within the land—*i.e.* not trade with passing foreign merchants,[2] nor in foreign countries, but between Israelite and Israelite—the Pentateuch further provided:—

1. "If thou sell ought unto thy neighbour, or buyest ought of thy neighbour's hand, ye shall not oppress one another,"[3] which law is further extended to the "stranger," *i.e.* the non-Israelite sojourning in the land.[4]

2. "Ye shall not steal, neither deal falsely, neither lie one to another." "Thou shalt not defraud thy neighbour, neither rob him: the wages of him that is hired shall not abide with thee all night until the morning."[5]

3. "Ye shall do no unrighteousness in judgment, in meteyard, in weight, or in measure. Just balances, just weights, a just ephah, and a just hin, shall ye have."[6] "Thou shalt not have in thy bag divers weights, a great and a small. But thou shalt have a perfect and just weight, a perfect and just measure shalt thou have."[7] The reasons for such just dealings are: "I am the Lord your God, which brought you out of the land of Egypt," and the blessing and promise attached thereto: "that thy days may be lengthened in the land which the Lord thy God giveth thee." Further, it is added by way of explanation: "for all that do such things, and all that do unrighteously, are an abomination unto the Lord thy God."[8] These weights, carried usually in a bag,[9]

---

[1] Deut. xix. 3. [2] Gen. xxxvii. 25. [3] Lev. xxv. 14.
[4] Exod. xxii. 21. [5] Lev. xix. 11, 13. [6] Ibid. vers. 35, 36.
[7] Deut. xxv. 13–16. [8] Ibid. vers. 15, 16. [9] Prov. xvi. 11.

were originally stones, as the Hebrew of those two passages will show. The Pentateuch furnishes us with no details as to how the justness of these weights was to be ascertained, nor as to how the standard measures were to be kept equal; but from the fact that in 1 Chronicles xxiii. 29, David appointed as an office for some of the Levites the overseeing "for all manner of measure and size," it might very well be, as Michaelis supposes, that the standard measures were kept in the Sanctuary, and that all others used throughout the land were rectified by comparison with those.

Trade with foreign countries would be carried on, partly by land,[1] and partly by sea.[2] Of course some tribes, as especially Zebulun and Issachar, would be more exclusively engaged in trade than the others,[3] especially if these were such as dwelt on the borders of the land, or near the sea. Leaving aside the notices of King Solomon's commercial intercourse with Tyre and Egypt, it would appear that though the Phœnicians were regarded as the most opulent and important traders, yet the wealth of Israel was at all times not inconsiderable, so that even when the sovereign made heavy demands on his subjects, to enable himself to pay the tribute demanded by foreigners, he did not experience any difficulty in raising the sums required.

As regards the money used in trade during the early years of Israel's existence as a nation, it seems likely that coins would be either unknown, or very little used, and that the current money of the merchants[4] would consist of bars of gold or silver, probably stamped, and of fixed value according to their weight. The chief pieces of money mentioned in the Old Testament are: the *shekel*, which was worth twenty gerahs; the *minah*, worth fifty shekels; the *bekah*, worth half a shekel; and the *talent*, worth three thousand shekels. A table of these and other weights and measures of the Old Testament is subjoined. Their actual, though not their relative, value seems to have differed according to the various periods of Jewish history.

---

[1] Isa. lx. 5, 6.
[2] Psa. cvii. 23.
[3] Gen. xlix. 13; Deut. xxxiii. 18.
[4] Gen. xxiii. 16.

TRADE.

WEIGHTS.

10 Gerahs = 1 Bekah.
2 Bekahs = 1 Shekel.
50 Shekels = 1 Maneh.
3000 Shekels or 60 Manehs = 1 Talent.

MEASURES.

LENGTH.

4 Finger-breadths[1] = 1 Hand-breadth.[2]
3 Hand-breadths = 1 Span.[3]
2 Spans = 1 Cubit.[4]
6 Cubits = 1 Reed.[5]

DRY MEASURE.

6 Cabs[6] = 1 Seah.
3 Seahs or 10 Issaron or Omers = 1 Ephah.
10 Ephahs, or 2 Lethech[7] = 1 Chomer[8] or Cor.[9]

LIQUID MEASURE.

12 Logs = 1 Hin.
6 Hins or 3 Shalish = 1 Bath.[10]

---

[1] Jer. lii. 21.   [2] Exod. xxv. 25.   [3] Ibid. xxviii. 16.
[4] Comp. Exod. xxv. 10 (2½ cubits) with Jos. *Ant.* iii. 6. [5] (5 spans).
[5] Ezek. xli. 8.   [6] 2 Kings vi. 25.   [7] Hosea iii. 2.
[8] Lev. xxvii. 16.   [9] 1 Kings iv. 22.
[10] A Bath is equal to an Ephah, both the tenth part of a Chomer (Ezek. xlv. 11).

CHAPTER XII.

SICKNESS AND DEATH.

IT has ever been natural to man to regard sickness and death as judgments direct from God, brought upon the human race by reason of sin and evil deeds. And there is a broad foundation of truth in this; since it is self-evident that disease may be ultimately traced to causes specifically human—that is to say, to perversion of those laws intended by God for the maintenance of life. We cannot tell by what process man's body, as originally created by God, might have been raised from merely physical conditions to immortal life; we know that sickness and death are, in man, the result of the Fall, testimony to the evil wrought by sin.

Viewed, as it must be viewed, in the light of a necessity, disease, natural to every man, should and must be recognised and dealt with in the laws of a nation. But in regard to the Pentateuch Code, it should here be borne in mind that the lawgiver was forced to deal exclusively with those forms of disease prevalent among, and common to, the nation during the period when the laws were framed; but that he could not prescribe remedies, since such manifestly would belong to a medicinal work, not to a code of laws. Further, throughout this section of the Pentateuch it should be remembered that the land from which Israel had been brought out was Egypt, not only the home of some of the most loathsome forms of disease ever known, but especially famed for an extensive knowledge of the art of medicine, the chief seat of the "Black Art," and the land from which chemistry has derived its name.

These circumstances account for the fact that although Moses, who, no doubt, was acquainted with this branch of Egyptian learning, has furnished us with a most accurate diagnosis of all the symptoms of the disease most common there, he yet forbade the Israelites many practices connected intimately both with medicine and witchcraft, and stigmatized them as abominable to the Lord; and this on account of the very union of what, in a social point of view, might have been but frivolous and harmless, but in a religious one—and this is the all-important fact—was idolatrous and degrading.

There can exist no doubt, then, that Moses, skilled, as it is recorded he was, in all the learning of the Egyptians, understood medicine, and could practise the art when occasion required it. Should positive evidence of this be required, it might be traced in the sanitary laws which he laid down for the nation, and which to this day are the admiration of Biblical students. But there is another aspect of the matter which cannot be overlooked. For it may well be that, with his knowledge of Egyptian sickness, the brave heart of Moses should almost have died within him when he found himself the leader and director of that rebellious people Israel, whose hearts were already turning back to Egypt, and about to enter upon the difficult and dangerous journey through the wilderness. True, Israel had, by the mercy of God, escaped the terrible plagues of Egypt; but what guarantee could there be that, in attempting an entrance into Canaan, in undertaking an expedition altogether unparalleled in history, disease and death might not overtake them, and the whole nation perish miserably in the desert? But that faith which had led Moses to forsake the riches of Egypt also made him endure, as seeing Him Who is invisible;[1] and to Israel through him was given this promise, full of unspeakable consolation, at that Marah where God first "proved" them. "If thou wilt diligently hearken to the voice of the Lord thy God, and wilt do that which is right in His sight, and wilt give ear to His commandments, and keep all His statutes, I will put

[1] Heb. xi. 26, 27.

none of these diseases upon thee, which I have brought upon the Egyptians: for I am the Lord that healeth thee."[1]

What these diseases of the Egyptians were, between which and the children of Israel the Presence of God the Healer stood, like the pillar of fiery cloud, we can learn only too well. The Nile Valley, rich, smiling, and beautiful, is the home of some of the most terrible and loathsome forms of disease; and to them the children of Israel had, no doubt, been exposed during their sojourn in Egypt. It is a vexed question how far Israel may actually have brought sicknesses, similar to those enumerated in Deuteronomy xxviii. 27, 35, with them into the land of Canaan, and one which, from the absence of data, is not likely ever to be satisfactorily answered. Certain it is, however, that Israel were bidden know that such diseases would only come upon them as Divine punishments for disobeying God's laws; that they would be God's curse; and that when they came no human skill could cure them. Israel's immunity from these diseases, then, would only be secured by their obedience, for "if thou wilt not observe to do all the words of this law that are written in this book, that thou mayest fear this glorious and fearful Name, the Lord thy God; then the Lord will make thy plagues wonderful, and the plagues of thy seed, even great plagues, and of long continuance, and sore sicknesses, and of long continuance. Moreover He will bring upon thee all the diseases of Egypt, which thou wast afraid of; and they shall cleave unto thee. Also every sickness, and every plague, which is not written in the book of this law, them will the Lord bring upon thee, until thou be destroyed."[2]

Brought out of the rich and rank fertility of Egypt, where, as we now know it, even the diet of fish, so freely partaken of, and so bitterly lamented by, the Israelites,[3] might bring on disease, no land could have been found more suitable to God's chosen people, no climate more salubrious for them, than that of Palestine. There everything was beneficial to life and health —manner of living, daily occupations, natural productions,

---

[1] Exod. xv. 25, 26.   [2] Deut. xxviii. 58-61.   [3] Num. xi. 5.

situation, the abundance of fresh water, a temperature mild and equable, yet not enervating. But even in such a country, surrounded by all that heart could desire, the lawgiver knew full well that the slothfulness and want of cleanliness of his people might breed any disease. It would appear that the kind of sickness most prevalent among the Jews at that and at subsequent periods took the form generally not of fevers, but of skin diseases. Now, to prevent such illnesses, cleanliness would be an absolute necessity. Accordingly, we find baths and lustrations insisted upon as imperative, in a religious point of view also, in the ritual purifications from all sorts of diseases. Again, contagion had to be guarded against, as also the dangers attendant in the East on keeping a dead body in a human dwelling during the lengthened period of mourning. It by no means detracts from their sacred significance—for in Israel's law everything had its sacred, symbolic meaning—to find that in these circumstances of every-day life God the Healer had issued His commands, in obeying which the infected person had to be separated from all his brethren, while he or that thing which touched a dead body was unclean, defiled by it.

As a sanitary legislation, then, as might have been expected, the Mosaic Code was not only far in advance of that time, but on a level, if not in advance, of much of the knowledge of the present day. For, by placing the laws on a religious basis, they were made absolutely binding on Israel, and the legislator could enjoin and expect the strictest obedience to their very letter. The good results of the submission to the laws then inculcated appear, as regards the arresting of disease, throughout the whole Old Testament. For it may safely be asserted that, notwithstanding the fact that Israel had come out of a land so poisonous as Egypt, the terrible disease leprosy—to take one instance—was mastered and, to a great extent, kept under, so that, although throughout the Bible we every here and there may find traces of it, yet these are but isolated instances. This would even appear from the nature and the wording of the laws laid down concerning its treatment—impossible to have been observed, as has been well noted, had it been a national and widely extended sickness.

Besides leprosy, to which special attention must be directed, the disobedient Israelites were threatened, in punishment for their sins, with "terror, consumption, and the burning ague"[1] —the last probably a severe Eastern fever—if they refused to keep God's commandments; and with the diseases of Egypt, more specifically "the botch, emerods, scab, itch, madness, blindness, and astonishment of heart,"[2] as well as a sore disease "in the knees and in the legs, from the sole of thy foot unto the top of thy head."[3] A severe sunstroke was not only dangerous in the land of Palestine, but might even prove fatal;[4] while fevers, diseases both mental and nervous, together with such misfortunes as blindness and lameness, could, of course, only be expected. In sicknesses such as these, and others which will readily present themselves to the mind, the services of the physician would from an early period be found to be requisite. From the figures on the Egyptian monuments, as well as from the Biblical notice that the body of the patriarch Jacob was embalmed, at Joseph's command, by his private physician,[5] it is evident that at that time these officials were already employed, doubtless at first for surgical purposes. The sanitary arrangements made in the Mosaic law also seem to imply that the Jews had a previous acquaintance with the study of medicine; and from the circumstance that the man who has been wounded by another is to be "caused to be thoroughly healed,"[6] the cure must most probably have been effected by means of one skilled in surgery. Later on in the history of Israel, when the nation was under the rule of kings, the prophets were sometimes, doubtless under Divine direction, to be found acting as physicians (compare the account of Hezekiah's sickness, and the plaster of figs ordered by Isaiah).[7] Yet even well-meaning though self-confident kings

[1] Lev. xxvi. 14, 16. [2] Deut. xxviii. 27, 28. [3] Ibid. ver. 35.
[4] 2 Kings iv. 19. [5] Gen. l. 2. [6] Exod. xxi. 19.
[7] Isa. xxxviii. 21.

had to be taught, by sad experience, that it was God the Healer alone Who could make whole. For this was the sad end of King Asa, that he died from sore disease in his feet, "yet," significantly remarks the chronicler, "in his disease he sought not to the Lord, but to the physicians." [1]

The remedies resorted to by the Jewish physicians would be, doubtless, in accordance with the then generally received systems of medicine. Anointing with oils, especially with the far-famed Balm of Gilead, was regarded as an infallible remedy for wounds,[2] the leaves of certain trees possessing medicinal properties for sores and bruises,[3] plasters of fig leaves for boils,[4] and, of course, natural or mineral waters for more complicated complaints.[5] In the Mosaic Code it was the priest who acted as sanitary officer, and who decided as to the nature of the disease: it would therefore follow, as already noted, that the tribe of Levi were obliged to study the art of medicine. But this applies only to that early period when Israel first entered into the land of Canaan. In after ages the physician was quite distinct from the priest, and duly respected, with a reverence perhaps not unmixed with the superstitious awe of the ignorant. So the son of Sirach admonishes, "Honour a physician with the honour due unto him for the uses which ye may have of him: for the Lord hath created him;" for from the "apothecary is peace over all the earth."[6] Yet though the sick person was, to such an extent, dependent on man's skill, the wise-hearted could look still deeper. And so the admonition continues: "My son, in thy sickness be not negligent: but pray unto the Lord, and He will make thee whole. Leave off from sin, and order thine hands aright, and cleanse thy heart from all wickedness. Give a sweet savour, and a memorial of fine flour."[7]

The disease which, in the time of Moses, appears to have been most virulent was leprosy, which is described as that of men, of garments, and of houses.

[1] 2 Chron. xvi. 12. [2] Jer. viii. 22. [3] Ezek. xlvii. 12.
[4] 2 Kings xx. 7. [5] *Ant.* xvii. 6. 5. [6] Ecclus. xxxviii. 1.
[7] Ibid. vers. 9-11.

1. *Leprosy of men.* The thirteenth chapter of the Book of Leviticus deals exclusively with the various forms under which this terrible malady might appear, and according to which the sufferer was to be pronounced either clean or unclean. At the outset, it was commanded that should any man have contracted a skin disorder in any measure resembling leprosy, he was to be at once brought to the priest, who for his part would be obliged to examine his body carefully.[1] Should the priest feel doubtful as to the nature of the complaint, the infected man must be shut up for seven days, and after that period again examined. If during the interval the disease had not spread, nor gained any ground, the patient was once more to be shut up for seven days. If after that time the sore was in a fair way to be healed, the man might be pronounced clean, and was to "wash his clothes"—doubtless mainly with a view to remove any impurity he might have contracted. But if the disease had spread during the first seven days of confinement, the man was to be pronounced a leper, and unclean.[2]

It would be tedious, and altogether unnecessary, to follow in detail the minute description of the various symptoms of leprosy furnished us in this chapter. In general it may be noted:

1. That several kinds of leprosy are spoken of, and that one of them at any rate, the so-called white leprosy, which covered a man "from his head even to his foot,"[3] did not render a man Levitically unclean—*i.e.*, did not oblige him to separate himself from all human society.

2. That the most terrible form of leprosy, especially dreaded in Egypt, that now known as Elephantiasis, must have been unknown in Israel, since in Moses' view every leper, however seriously infected, may possibly be healed.

---

[1] Lev. xiii. 1-6.

[2] Ibid. vers. 7, 8. It has been made a matter of controversy by some, why the pestilence, so terrible in its ravages (comp. 2 Sam. xxiv.), is not commented upon in the Mosaic Code. But, as Michaelis so aptly remarks, it would have been highly unnecessary to insert provisions for such an unusual exigency in laws intended for ordinary every-day use. [3] 2 Kings v. 1, 27.

3. That although leprosy was a dire and dreadful disease, and, no doubt, to a certain degree infectious, it could not have been so to any great extent, since in each case the priest may, and in fact is commanded to, make most careful examination of the leper's person.

4. That many diseases, now known to us under very different names, are in the Pentateuch classed under the generic designation of leprosy.

When the leper had, after final examination, been pronounced unclean by the priest, he was obliged, for the sake of the whole community, to be separated from his brethren. This separation was twofold: his habitation must be "without the camp"[1]—that is, he must not live either in towns or in villages, but rove at large in the country; and secondly, his dress must mark his condition: "the leper in whom the plague is; his clothes shall be rent, and his head bare, and he shall put a covering upon his upper lip"—that is, cover his face to his upper lip, in fact, his attire must be that of a mourner —"and shall cry, Unclean, Unclean."[2] This was to be his condition "all the days wherein the plague shall be in him." No wonder, then, that the leper was "as one dead," and that leprosy was viewed as a punishment direct from God Himself, and has ever been regarded as a type of sin.[3] It was also designed to be a terrible warning to Israel, a dread evil from which the only way of escape lay in obeying implicitly God's commands, and in following out the injunctions of His servants the priests. "Take heed in the plague of leprosy, that thou observe diligently, and do according to all that the priests the Levites shall teach you: as I command them, so ye shall observe to do. Remember"—that solitary instance standing out like a danger light—"what the Lord thy God did unto Miriam by the way, after that ye were come forth out of Egypt."[4]

Leprosy seems in many instances to have been an inherited

[1] Lev. xiii. 46.
[2] Ibid. ver. 45.
[3] Num. xii. 12; 2 Kings v. 27.
[4] Deut. xxiv. 8, 9.

disease,[1] and accordingly some writers have supposed that the warning which is attached to the Second Commandment[2] may apply to it. Be this as it may, it is very evident that the *lepra Mosaica*—a term given in distinction from the other forms of this disease—was not utterly incurable. However, the ritual prescribed for the purification of the leper, though very interesting, does not properly belong to our province, more particularly as the Pentateuch does not furnish any particulars as to *how* this terrible disease had been healed.

It is still a matter of grave dispute as to what Moses contemplated as leprosy of garments.[3] Some writers have imagined that it was an infection imparted by the body of the leper to his garment; others that it was due to the burrowing of innumerable animalculæ; others, again, that the stuffs thus rendered unclean were those that had been woven from the fleece of, or made from the skins of, animals which had died from some foul disease. Another theory, equally ingenious, has it that leprosy of garments was due to damp, and to the owners neglecting to have them properly aired. In the absence of all data it is impossible to decide the question satisfactorily; but it may be added that the first view has the support of Talmudical authority.

2. *Leprosy on houses* is also a matter that cannot now be determined with any satisfaction.[4] At any rate, even although it may or may not have been, as Michaelis, Saalschütz, and others have supposed, due to some nitrous acid corroding and gradually eating away or loosening the walls; or, as other writers have conjectured, to be traced to the action of some minute insects, it is evident that this was not a disease which could be contracted by man, since the priest was able to enter and examine the infected house without fear, while before his entrance into the dwelling nothing in it could be pronounced unclean.

Viewed religiously, these regulations were to provide for the

[1] 2 Kings v. 27.
[2] Exod. xx. 5.
[3] Lev. xiii. 47-59.
[4] Lev. xiv. 33-57

holiness of person of each Israelite. In this light, of course, those laws respecting contact with the dead are kindred in signification. It would be deemed in Israel, no doubt, as in the present day, an act of filial piety to kiss the lips and to close the eyes of the dead.[1] The mourning for such would be truly Oriental, accompanied by the most vehement gestures and expressions of grief, such as beating or "tabering upon" the breast,[2] covering the upper lip—*i.e.*, the face to the upper lip—putting off the shoes and walking barefoot, crying aloud,[3] cutting one's self or making one's self bald,[4] tearing, dishevelling, or shaving the hair,[5] fasting and lying prostrate on the ground, in a sack-like garment without sleeves.[6] Most of these expressions of grief were tolerated by the Mosaic Law, which did not seek to destroy or suppress the natural feelings of each true mourner. But "cuttings in the flesh for the dead,"[7] either on the body or "between the eyes," were sternly forbidden, the reason for this prohibition being thus furnished: "Ye are the children of the Lord your God"[8]—therefore these practices, eminently heathen in origin and use, must be avoided and detested.

Further, no doubt mainly as a sanitary precaution, to oblige the Israelites to bury corpses speedily—a very important matter in Eastern countries—it was declared that all contact with a dead body defiled the toucher for the space of seven days, and required two purifications—on the third and on the seventh days. Nay, all that came into the tent, and all that was in the tent, even down to open vessels, were by the presence of the dead rendered unclean—all this, no doubt, with a view to preventing the display of affection by keeping a corpse unburied, and thus polluting the atmosphere.[9] And the punishment for the man who, having touched the dead, had refused to purify himself, was that of being "cut off" from

---

[1] Gen. l. 1. [2] Nahum ii. 7. [3] Ezek. xxiv. 17.
[4] Jer. xvi. 6. [5] Job i. 20.
[6] 2 Sam. xii. 16; 2 Kings vi. 30. [7] Lev. xix. 28.
[8] Deut. xiv. 1. [9] Num. xix. 11–16.

among the congregation, " because he hath defiled the Sanctuary of the Lord." [1]

The dead man, in the days before the Exodus embalmed by the physicians,[2] but in later times simply washed, and attired in plain linen garments, or wrapped in a shroud, was carried to his burying on an open bier, and deposited in a grave far apart from any human habitation, usually hewn out in the rock.[3] To the Israelite of the time of Moses and of the Kings the grave was something mysterious—to the wicked the king of terrors, to man his eternal home (*beth olamo*).[4] But not so utterly dark, as though beyond it there was no hope, for beyond the grave and gate of death Moses could see Him who is Invisible; and he and all the patriarchs looked for that city which hath foundation, whose maker and builder is God.[5] And we also, to whom through the Death and Resurrection of our Lord, death has been abolished, and life and immortality brought to light, may well believe that, as in the appearing of the great Lawgiver on the Mount of Transfiguration,[6] so it is but the overshadowing cloud of death that hides from us the great army of witnesses;[7] but that finally, at the last day, all will be done away in Christ, and the chant sung by the ransomed of earth be, " Death is swallowed up in victory: O death, where is thy sting? O grave, where is thy victory?"[8]

[1] Num. xix. 20. For the laws for the mourning of the priests see Chapter ii.
[2] Gen. l. 2.
[3] 2 Sam. iii. 31.
[4] Job xviii. 14; Eccles. xii. 5.
[5] Heb. xi. 10.
[6] Matt. xvii. 3.
[7] Heb. xii. 1.
[8] 1 Cor. xv. 54, 55.

PART III.

The Ten Words: Moral Laws in Daily Life.

CHAPTER XIII.

THE "TEN WORDS": IDOLATRY.

THE laws of Moses differ from those of other nations of the same period in so many respects, that it seems almost unnecessary to repeat the fact in regard to the Moral Code. But whereas many of the other provisions of the Pentateuch Code were evidently designed for the use of the Jewish nation alone at that time, the moral laws are as binding to this day on all men as they were to the Israelite who, standing in the plain below the Mount Sinai, saw it "altogether on a smoke, because the Lord descended upon it in fire: and the smoke thereof ascended as the smoke of a furnace, and the whole mount quaked greatly,"[1] and heard the voice of God Almighty, speaking the Ten Words, ushered in by the sublimest Prologue ever heard on earth : "I am the Lord thy God, which have brought thee out of the land of Egypt, out of the house of bondage."[2] A Prologue this befitting such a law, given in that magnificent desert solitude by God the Deliverer, by the Covenant—God of Israel in His revealed Name of Jehovah.

The "Ten Words"—as they should more properly be called—were written, or graven, by the finger of God on two tables of stone, on both sides, and delivered to Moses upon his descending from the mountain, to be laid up in the Ark of the Covenant before the Lord. These two tables of stone were also styled "the testimony," and are rightly to be regarded as containing the whole sum and substance of the Pentateuch Code. For it is capable of abundant proof, that all the

[1] Exod. xix. 18.   [2] Ibid xx. 1, 2.

other laws which have been briefly alluded to are, in one way or another, intimately connected with either one, or even more, of the Ten Commandments. From the moral power of these was it that the religious life of Israel could be fed, so that the Book of Ecclesiastes could aptly sum up as the "conclusion of the whole matter," the bounden "duty of man," "Fear God, and keep His commandments,"[1] to which the Apostle St. John adds, by way of consolation, "His commandments are not grievous."[2] In the Ten Commandments, then, lie the foundations of all that may become God-like in man, reaching as they do from his outward to his innermost life, to the thoughts and imaginations of his heart—from his bounden duty to God to those unuttered desires which are, as one has so beautifully remarked, words in the ears of God.

The division of the Ten Words on the Two Tables at present most usually made—that of distinguishing the first four as man's duty to God, while the last six commands teach man's duty towards his neighbour—is not altogether to be preferred. The most ancient division—for our present one cannot lay claim to any great antiquity—was that into two Pentads, or sections consisting of five each. According to this, the First Table would include: (1) the command concerning the worship of other, false gods; (2) the prohibition to worship graven images; (3) that forbidding blasphemy; (4) the command to observe the rest of the Sabbath Day; (5) that enjoining respect to parents. The Second Table would contain: (1) the command to guard the preservation of life; (2) that concerning adultery; (3) the prohibition to steal; (4) that forbidding false witness; (5) and that concerning covetousness. A third division of the Ten Words was first proposed by St. Augustine, who would divide the sections into two, the first containing three, the second seven commandments. In this, however, the two first commandments were united into one, while the last was divided into two, the ninth commandment in this way treating of the desire of houses, the tenth of coveting the

---

[1] Eccles. xii. 13.   [2] 1 John v. 3.

neighbour's wife, etc. For many reasons, however, the division into the two Pentads seems preferable. For instance, it is to the first five commandments that an admonition or a blessing is attached, while the last five are given without any comment.[1] Again, the suggestion that the Ten Words should be summarised rather as embodying man's duty towards his superiors, towards God, and towards those whom Luther aptly designates as God's vicars; and his duty towards his equals—in other words, as setting forth his *religious* and his *social* obligations—seems to enable us to perceive more clearly the beautiful gradation from man's highest, purest form of worship to his deepest thoughts, as well as the intimate connection between each link of this glorious chain.

The Ten Words are repeated, with a few additional remarks by the lawgiver, in the Book of Deuteronomy. It is not intended here to enter into any discussions concerning the nature of these laws, but, simply viewing the Decalogue as the essence of the whole Mosaic economy, to offer a few remarks on the connection between its several parts.

THE FIRST PENTAD.

Reverence is, as has been often noted, the true foundation of all society. This is the connecting line which runs through the whole of the first Pentad: beginning, as its key-note, with man's acknowledgment of the One True God; then, flowing from this as its centre and spring, prescribing what sort of worship he is to pay to his Creator. Next, it is this same principle which guards that by which Israel was alone to know God: His Name; it is this once more which is his motive power in consecrating to God of his time—in this reflecting and following the Divine example; and, finally, reaching to

[1] It must, however, be remembered that the writing on the Two Tables may not have been exactly the words given from Mount Sinai, since the admonitions are more likely to be the additions, or comments upon the Words by the inspired Lawgiver. If such be the case, the division into Pentads would be that most equal.

the sources of life, acknowledging in God's vicars not the love that was owed them, *that* required no command, but the respect and reverence already become part of his nature, of his outward deed, of his speech, and of his time. Actuated by such motives, each Israelite might well be holy in whatsoever his hand found to do, and bow before authority, knowing, as St. Paul afterwards taught his Roman brethren, that "the powers which be are ordained of God."[1]

The First Word. "Thou shalt have no other gods before Me."[2] More correctly, perhaps, it should be rendered: " besides " or " except me " (Hebrew : *alpĕnei*, literally, before the face of). This command is couched in a negative form, as are so many of the "Words," probably with reference to what in former ages man had done unreproved by God. The sin here forbidden is not necessarily the forsaking of the True God, but rather the worshipping of other gods as well as Jehovah, so that instead of the whole of man's energy and service being devoted to the Lord, it is shared, or even altogether set aside by, some false god. Positively viewed, therefore, the First Word commands the service and acknowledgment of Jehovah as the One True God, and this from motives of love and gratitude, since He is the Deliverer, as well as from the fear of punishment.[3] If Israel, then, neglected or disobeyed this command, they would sin against knowledge and understanding, and a curse would be brought down upon the nation, followed by vexation and rebuke, and, finally, terrible destruction.[4]

The Second Word. If the First Commandment had taught Israel what God they might alone worship, the Second Word was designed to show them what kind of worship was in accordance with God's will.[5] Here two dangers must have presented themselves before the mind of the Lawgiver. In the first place, Israel was to stand alone in the midst of the blackest darkness of heathen worship, to occupy a land stained with

[1] Rom. xiii. 1. [2] Exod. xx. 3. [3] Deut. iv. 32-39.
[4] Deut. xxviii. 20. [5] Exod. xx. 4-6.

the blood of human sacrifices, to be surrounded by nations practising the most abominable and degrading idolatry. Secondly, by the very essence of their laws, so eminently agricultural, Israel would be brought into constant contact with that Nature in which they had been taught to recognise the Hand of their Creator. How easily from acknowledging the Divine Power and Wisdom in Nature could they, if they once forgot Jehovah, sink into the worship of the Creator through and in the creature; and how small the step between this worship, and the losing sight of the Divine altogether, and so falling, through Pantheism, into actual idolatry and the worship of Nature! So, on the one hand, Israel might altogether forsake the worship of Jehovah for that of graven images; or, worshipping God through Nature, might mistake the shadow and symbol for the real and actual. Therefore, next to the command to serve the Lord, came, as most appropriate, that which defined the way in which God must *not* be worshipped. He must not be worshipped through or in a graven image, nor through anything in heaven (*i.e.*, birds, or flying creatures), on earth, or in the sea, nor by any representation of any of these things. Such images or likenesses were not to be made (for idolatrous purposes), nor bowed down to, nor served. God was a Spirit, and must be worshipped spiritually. And with the twofold danger to Israel, the "stiff-necked" nation always in view, the Lawgiver entreated them further as regarded this in the Book of Deuteronomy. "Take ye therefore good heed unto yourselves; for ye saw no manner of similitude on the day that the Lord spake unto you in Horeb out of the midst of the fire: lest ye corrupt yourselves, and make you a graven image, the similitude of any figure. . . . And lest thou lift up thine eyes unto heaven, and when thou seest the sun, and the moon, and the stars, even all the host of heaven, shouldest be driven to worship them, and serve them, which the Lord thy God hath divided unto all nations under the whole heaven."[1] If, then, Israel sinned, and worshipped God

[1] Deut. iv. 15-19.

through images, they could only have themselves to blame. Repeatedly had they been warned of their danger; before them had been set God's wrath and judgments as the certain wages for their sin. Yet, strange as it may seem, this law, more definite and more elaborated than any other, was the earliest to be disobeyed;[1] and throughout the whole of Israel's history prior to the Exile, in spite of warning, threatening, and judgment, idolatry continued to be the national sin: perhaps, as we remember the words of St. John, it is not conquered even in our days.[2]

To both of these two commandments belongs equally the admonition attached to the second, since it refers to what is necessarily connected in man's mind—the *object* and the *manner* of his worship. The exhortation and the warning read thus: "For I the Lord thy God am a jealous God"—not only *zealous* but *jealous*, in the sense of demanding for Himself alone the glory sinful man so often desires to give to another —"visiting the iniquity of the fathers upon the children, unto the third and fourth generation of them that hate Me; and showing mercy unto thousands of them that love Me, and keep My commandments."[3] The explanation of this "visiting the sins of the fathers upon the children" is not difficult to find. For, in God's sight Israel was one—not an aggregate of individuals, but a community in the truest sense of the word. History teaches us by experience how terribly the sins of the fathers are visited on their descendants; Revelation declares that this extends to the *third* generation—thus seeming to limit the penal consequences, as one writer thinks, to those who are alive during the lifetime of the first offender. Thus far reaches God's justice. But His mercy is unlimited, it is to the *thousandth* generation [4]—infinite, God-like. Or, if we take the other interpretation, His mercy is to thousands: whereas the punishment of the offence is limited to the one family. God's mercy is like an ever-widening circle, including more

---

[1] Exod. xxxii.   [2] 1 John v. 21.
[3] Exod. xx. 5, 6.   [4] So according to the best commentators.

and more; and those who fear Him are like the salt of the earth, or the leaven, leavening the whole lump.[1]

Not only was Israel warned against the danger, folly, and sin of idolatry, and the forsaking of Jehovah in a general sense in these two words, but these commands were particularised and applied to their own special dangers and temptations in many other parts of the Pentateuch. It can scarcely be doubted that many of the heathen rites forbidden by Moses had been brought by Israel with them from Egypt, notably the worship of animals, or of images fashioned like them, as, for example, the Golden Calf.[2] Other idols, in particular the Teraphim, or household gods,[3] were Chaldean; while others, again, were Canaanitish or Phœnician—the Baalim and Asheroth. Connected with all these forms of heathen worship were the mysterious incantations, magic, and soothsaying by which the heathen priest or prophet strove to awe and govern the unenlightened. For all such things the Mosaic Code could find no place; they were utterly incompatible with its fundamental ideas, the Sovereignty of God alone, and the Holiness of His people. Again and again Israel was warned or threatened, entreated or expostulated with, as though Moses could already see in prophetic vision how his people would be altogether joined to idols, as if the Lawgiver would not "let him alone," till he was clear before heaven and earth of all blood-guiltiness.

There was but one punishment for an idolater, whether Israelite or non-Israelite—death by stoning.[4] An idolatrous city, also, must be utterly destroyed.[5] But when the worship of images should have become national, and no man could be found, himself blameless, to administer this punishment, God Himself would be the Avenger of "the quarrel of His covenant," and would scatter and disperse the people among the heathen, till they that were left pined away in their own iniquities, and in those of their fathers, in their enemies' land.[6]

[1] Matt. v. 13; xiii. 33.   [2] Exod. xxxii.   [3] Gen. xxxi. 19-42.
[4] Deut. xvii. 2-5.   [5] Ibid. xiii. 12-18.   [6] Lev. xxvi. 25, 39.

But what were the practices for which Israel was to be so direly punished? This question will best be answered by the Pentateuch itself.

In general, it should first be noted that the worship of the ancient heathens consisted chiefly, not in prayers—for, in truth, they could not pray to their deities in any real sense of the term—but in sacrifices, propitiatory, or offered in thanksgiving. These sacrifices were usually followed by a sacred feast; and as friendly intercourse thus begun might lead Israel to closer relationships, and so into idolatry, the Jews were forbidden to take any part, either in the sacrifices or in the feasts of their heathen neighbours.[1]

Next, Israel was warned against introducing into the worship of the True God any of the abominable rites practised by the Canaanites—notably human sacrifices.[2]

But beyond these limits of half-hearted allegiance to, and worship of, Jehovah, lay the black darkness of hideous idolatry itself. Each step Israel would take into this would be a deadly one. First came the inciter to idolatry—a brother, son, daughter, or even wife—who it mattered not, for one doom must be his: death at the hands of all the people, the first stone unpityingly cast by him who had been tempted.[3] With such an one ranked the false prophet, who had tried to induce the nation to sin, and in his case also must "the evil be put away" by his death.[4] But Moses knew full well that, not only as a negative, but as a positive and actual evil, must he condemn idolatry. In the land of Canaan, Israel would find graven images set up, and altars on the high mountains, upon the hills, and under every green tree. All these were to be ruthlessly destroyed.[5] Terribly cursed was the man who should make a graven or molten image, to be set in a secret place.[6] Again, the *Maskith*-stones (rendered "standing image" in our Authorised Version), or mysterious pillars, probably covered with hieroglyphics, erected on so many high

---

[1] Exod. xxxiv. 15-17. [2] Deut. xii. 29-31. [3] Ibid. xiii. 1-11.
[4] Ibid. ver. 2-5. [5] Ibid. xii. 2, 3. [6] Ibid. xxvii. 15.

FIRST PENTAD: IDOLATRY.

places in the land of Canaan, were forbidden to be set up, or bowed down unto, as utterly unbefitting and degrading to those of whom God should say, "I am Jehovah your God."[1]

Leaving aside the minor idolatrous practices forbidden by Moses, such as men and women wearing each others' garments;[2] mixing linen and woollen cloth together;[3] tonsuring the head; cutting the corners of the beard; or making incisions in the flesh for the dead,[4] the most horrible feature of ancient heathenism was human sacrifices. These bloody sacrifices consisted mostly of children, who were first slain, and then burnt to Moloch, Milcom, or Malcam, "the abomination of the Ammonites,"[5] a deity originally Phoenician, and worshipped with most terrible rites. Any Israelite found sacrificing to Moloch must surely be put to death by the whole nation; and should Israel fail to do so, God Himself would set His face against that idolater, and his whole family, and cut him off, him and his fellow-sinners.[6] In face of all these threats, the reader of the Old Testament may well marvel at the list of heathen deities worshipped during the yet early ages by Israel. In the wilderness they worshipped the star Chiun or Chevan— probably Saturn[7]—and the Golden Calf.[8] Having reached Canaan, they served the gods of the seven nations and of the Phoenicians—the Baalim and Asheroth: Baal-berith, the "covenant Baal;"[9] Baal-peor, the Moabitish Chemosh;[10] and Baal-zebul, the Fly-God of Ekron;[11] the terrible Moloch; and Astarte, the Phoenician moon-goddess.[12] Later on, we read of the women weeping for Tammuz, the Phoenician Adonis.[13] What wonder, then, that in the ears of the prophet sounded the voice of God's righteous anger: "Therefore will I also deal in fury: Mine eye shall not spare, neither will I have pity: and though they cry in Mine ears with a loud voice, yet will I not hear them."[14]

[1] Lev. xxvi. 1.　　[2] Deut. xxii. 5.　　[3] Lev. xix. 19; Deut. xxii. 11.
[4] Lev. xix. 27, 28.　　[5] 1 Kings xi. 5.　　[6] Lev. xx. 1-5.
[7] Amos v. 26.　　[8] Exod. xxxii. 4.　　[9] Judg. viii. 33.
[10] Num. xxv. 1; 1 Kings xi. 7.　　[11] 2 Kings i. 2.
[12] 1 Kings xi. 5.　　[13] Ezek. viii. 14.　　[14] Ibid. ver. 18.

The dark picture will not be complete without notice of another feature of ancient heathenism—magic, soothsaying, and the consulting of oracles. Israel was provided with prophets to warn or to foretell, and the mystic Urim and Thummim for any special emergency. And therefore, since they were permitted such a knowledge of the Divine will, they were without excuse concerning this. Accordingly, the law directed that a witch—and by inference, a wizard—must not be suffered to live;[1] nor were such to be sought after; nor enchantment used, nor were "times"—probably by this is meant astrology—to be observed.[2] All those who used divination, or were observers of times, enchanters, witches, charmers, consulters with familiar spirits, wizards, or necromancers, were "an abomination unto the Lord;" for these abominations had God driven out before Israel the seven nations of Canaan— "but as for thee, the Lord thy God hath not suffered thee so to do."[3]

Guarded, then, from all idolatry, whether of imagination or of deed, must Israel keep alive in the earth the knowledge of the One True God. But to the Church of Christ, which is to shine as the light of the world,[4] are the warnings and dangers less real than they were to Israel of old? Surely she also must watch, and keep her lamp burning,[5] that when her Lord returns she may not be found wanting, but hear the words: "Well done, good and faithful, enter thou into the joy of thy Lord."[6]

[1] Exod. xxii. 18.   [2] Lev. xix. 31, 26.
[3] Deut. xviii. 10-14.   [4] Matt. v. 14.   [5] Luke xii. 35, etc.
[6] Matt. xxv. 21. Space will not permit us to enter upon many interesting questions, such as the worship of demons referred to in Lev. xvii. 7; dreams, and the divination by means of a goblet, practised in Egypt (Gen. xliv. 5), etc.

CHAPTER XIV.

THE "TEN WORDS."

THE FIRST PENTAD (*continued*).

WHILE the nation, considered as a whole, was to be God's Servant in worship and in public obedience, it equally befitted each family and individual apart to be the Servant of Jehovah. In accordance with this sublime underlying idea, the next Word to that forbidding idolatry, and, by inference, commanding the true and fitting worship of Jehovah, runs thus : "Thou shalt not take" (*nasa*, uplift) "the Name of the Lord thy God in vain" (*lasshav*, to vanity), with the warning attached, more terrible than any threatened punishment from the hand of man—"for the Lord will not hold him guiltless that taketh His Name in vain."

Closely connected with the two preceding commands, as indicative of man's relationship to the Divine, this Word provided for the keeping holy of that by which alone God had revealed Himself. Not by another deity, nor by any similitude or likeness of Himself, would He be known and worshipped, but in His Ineffable Name of Jehovah.[1] What, then, was to Israel the manifestation of the Divine, that by which He was known, must be kept holy, guarded from all profanity. By its very indefiniteness the command not only overlapped, so to speak, the two preceding, but formed a suitable connecting link between them and the following Word. For, it not only forbade swearing falsely by the Divine Name, but all profanation of it, or blasphemy either by word or deed—*i.e.*, any wicked,

[1] Exod. iii. 14.

false oath in God's Name; or its improper, profane use, either in daily life or, still more, for heathen, magical, or any other purposes.[1]

This command was both right and suitable. For, as has been well noted, for what purpose had God revealed Himself in His Name but that it should be used in prayers,[2] invocations,[3] praises,[4] and thanksgivings?[5] How, then, could it be used for vanity, or, still worse, in the service of devils?[6] For the blasphemer there could be but the same punishment as for the idolater: death by stoning, in the presence, and by the act of the whole congregation. Were he Israelite or stranger it mattered not, he must bear his own sin,[7] whoever it might be who cursed what to him was God,[8] his Deity.

According to Philo[9] and Josephus,[10] it was "expressly forbidden" to the Jews "to laugh at and revile those that are esteemed gods by other people." But this forced interpretation of Exod. xxii. 28, where the word "elohim" evidently stands for "judges" or "rulers" (comp. the use of the same word in verse 9), was undoubtedly not the ordinary view, but rather prompted by the peculiar circumstances connected with the political dangers to these writers in the then troubled state of Jewish affairs.

To the Jew of our Lord's time blasphemy included much more than the uttering profanely of the Divine Name. For, in their view, Christ was "a blasphemer," for making Himself equal to God; and it was in token of lamentation for this supposed sin, considered the most awful blasphemy, that the High Priest Caiaphas rent his clothes.[11]

The *Fourth Word*, which opened with the word "Re-

[1] Lev. xix. 12.   [2] Psa. xxv. 11.   [3] Ibid. lxxvi. 6.
[4] Ibid. lxxiv. 21.   [5] 1 Chron. xxix. 13.   [6] Comp. Deut. xxxii. 17.
[7] Lev. xxiv. 10–16. From these verses, read by the ancient Jews as meaning a prohibition to utter the Divine Name at all, originated the practice, still in use by the Synagogue, of substituting for the Name Jehovah that of *Adonai*, rendered *the Lord* by the LXX.
[8] So according to some of the best authorities.
[9] *Opp.* ii. 166. 219.   [10] *Against Apion*, ii. 34.   [11] Matt. xxvi. 65.

FIRST PENTAD: THE SABBATH.

member," looked back to the Creation, and to God's rest after it, as well as reminded Israel that this Sabbath institution was not a new and arbitrary limit to their freedom of action, but a hallowing and sanctifying of that which they had already acknowledged. What was new in the Sabbath command was not its existence, but the element of holy joy, the making it a festival. Nor could this rejoicing be isolated, in each family apart, without consideration of the social duties binding on every Israelite. It was to be pre-eminently a day of rest to, and for, all, Israelite or heathen: "in it thou shalt not do any work, thou, nor thy son, nor thy daughter, thy man-servant, nor thy maid-servant, nor thy cattle, nor thy stranger that is within thy gates"—*i.e.*, not the door of thy house, but of thy city; therefore, by inference, this festival must be kept throughout thy whole land. The work to be rested from was any and all labour, and is expressed by a different word from that used in reference to labour forbidden during the days of the great festivals (rendered " servile work" in our Authorised Version, Lev. xxiii. 7). What manner of work was thus to be laid aside on the Sabbath Day, for all alike, free or slaves, man and beast, it is not hard to trace. In the wilderness on that day no manna was to be gathered,[1] while he that collected sticks on it was punished by death.[2] It therefore follows, from these instances, that everything required for domestic use must be in readiness before the Sabbath Day. Further, no fire must be kindled throughout Israel's habitations upon the Seventh Day, and this on pain of death.[3] It is even added, as providing for what concerned every part of Israel's life work—that on this day Israel must rest "in earing-time and in harvest"—*i.e.*, from agricultural labour.

Positively viewed, Israel should every seventh day consecrate to God their time, and this not of necessity, but gladly. For had they not before them the highest motive for obedience, that on the seventh day God Himself had rested; and that on this account to this day His blessing and hallowing attached?

[1] Exod. xvi. 22, 23.   [2] Num. xv. 32-36.   [3] Exod. xxxv. 3.

And beyond this, as the Book of Deuteronomy reminded them, they were bound to show their gratitude to God, their Deliverer from Egypt, by keeping this commandment, since, delivered from their service to man, they were bound to a higher service, that of Jehovah Himself, and that love should be the source of this obedience.[1] It is not possible to do more than indicate these leading ideas, nor can the necessity of the Sabbath rest be here demonstrated. Vindicated by judgments in the Exile, then made a burden by Pharisaical punctiliousness, this weekly acknowledgment of the Creator by rest in labour is now, since our Lord Himself has rested from His life-work on it in the rock-hewn tomb, been converted for us to all time into a memorial of His Resurrection, till we reach at last the final and eternal rest that remaineth for the people of God.[2]

Fitting is it that, after the owning of God's sovereignty in man's time, He should be reverenced in those put in authority under Him. Love need not be commanded, that is natural to man; but the honour due to age and position might easily have been withheld by the Israelite. Accordingly, in Leviticus xix. 3, fearing "his mother and his father" is commanded to every man in connection with keeping the Sabbaths, that in this, as each one's first social duty, the Jew might show himself holy, "for I the Lord your God am holy." It is remarkable also that to this fifth Word, and to it only, a promise attaches of long life in the God-given land, a promise which may be interpreted as implying both a long natural life (comp. 1 Kings iii. 14) and long possession of the land (Deut. iv. 25, 26). Of course, this command applied not merely to honouring of parents, but to meet reverence to any God-separated or man-appointed authority, which authority in things temporal and spiritual was, and served as, a father, and to which, therefore, Israel must submit with due obedience.[3]

[1] Deut. v. 12-15.   [2] Heb. iv. 9.   [3] 2 Kings ii. 12.

THE SECOND PENTAD.

As the first Pentad had closed with the beginning of man's existence, so the second Pentad opens with the possible end of man's natural life. The *Sixth Word*, "Thou shalt not kill," by its indefinite width included every kind of, or intention to, destroy life, from the deed of violence to another, or to oneself, to the sinful anger against a brother. Life was God's gift, and he who despised it showed himself unworthy to be its possessor. So, negatively viewed, murder is ever a deadly sin; while taking this command as meaning still more, and reading it by the light thrown on it by our Lord Himself, the life is not only more than meat, raiment, or any such thing,[1] but Christ is its Prince,[2] the Life itself,[3] and through Him shall we finally receive that whereof it is but the foretaste: eternal life.

But dear to the man as his own being is his family life; and he who would be pure in God's sight must be pure also in the eyes of all men. So from the command to preserve life, man's "only one,"[4] the transition is but short to "Thou shalt not commit adultery." Equally wide is this Word, applying not only to outward deed, but to secret desire;[5] so that, like as Israel as a family must keep the Sabbaths holy, so also to each circle apart came the command to be holy in daily life, even as their God was holy.

Passing from the family possession to the individual's property, "Thou shalt not steal," presupposes the banishment of self-seeking, the presence and influence of love to, and sympathy for, one's neighbours, and all those acts of kindliness which draw men together. As further expanding this command should here be included those laws for the preservation of another's property,[6] for restitution where injury had been inflicted,[7] as well as the commands and injunctions to deal justly and truly in weights and measures, etc.[8] In view of all

[1] Matt. vi. 25. [2] Acts iii. 15. [3] John xiv. 6.
[4] Psa. xxii. 20. [5] Matt. v. 27-32. [6] Exod. xxi. 33, 34.
[7] Exod. xxii. [8] Lev. xix. 35-37.

this, the Apostle St. Paul rightly characterises that love which "worketh no ill to his neighbour" as "the fulfilling of the law."[1]

The ninth Word, rendered in our Authorised Version: "Thou shalt not bear false witness against thy neighbour," or, as it is in the original: "Thou shalt not answer against thy neighbour as false (or lying) witness," marks the next stage in the searching out of man's conduct and motives, and guards what to each is dearer even than life, family, or possession— his good name. Such false witness-bearing in judicial proceedings would, of course, be punished by death (comp. Chapter v.). But the command is not limited to public slander or perjury. It goes far deeper, and includes all lying reports, and anything whereby a brother might suffer in honour or in public estimation.[2] By inference, therefore, this command lays down truthfulness as essential in all communications between man and man, and since a "good name is rather to be chosen than great riches,"[3] would have all "keep far from a false matter,"[4] nor be among those whom the Psalmist knew the Lord would cut off, "whoso privily slandereth his neighbour."[5]

Lastly, the searching light of God's holy law brings to view the innermost thoughts and desires of the heart, that so no part of man may be left impure, but he be altogether holy and pure. With self as centre, man's desires must necessarily move in an ever-narrowing circle; and to the Israelite was the command as needful to beware of, and to flee from, covetousness as to the Jewish world in the days of Christ. St. Paul rightly names covetousness idolatry;[6] and with this light uniting the first and the last we can perceive how the Ten Words have a higher union and connection between themselves, so that each overlaps the other, forming, so to speak, a circle round man, within which he may walk with safety, God's Servant and representative on earth. The terms of the Tenth Word are very explicit, and cover all that the imagination of man may

---

[1] Rom. xiii. 10. [2] Exod. xxiii. 1. [3] Prov. xxii. 1.
[4] Exod. xxiii. 7. [5] Psa. ci. 5. [6] Col. iii. 5.

desire, as possessed by another. The danger is all the greater, since this other is "thy neighbour," and most likely unconscious of thy coveting.[1] This last Word, therefore, reaches down to, and guards the whole foundation of, social life, and forms a most fitting close to such a Moral Code.

Viewed in their higher meaning, these Words were, in all senses of the term, a testimony to Israel. First, they bore witness of God's relationship to them: that He was their Deliverer, the One True God, to be worshipped in spirit and in truth, Who had revealed Himself to them in His sacred Name. And next, therefore, as most fitting, the Israelites for their part owed Him such service, and should consecrate to Him their time, and bow before the authorities He had ordained. And their obedience to God must manifest itself not only in this manner, but in care for what He had given each, in the most tender regard for the family life, property, and good name of others, and, lastly, in preferring the good and happiness of that other rather than his own. And so, finally, in his religious, social, and moral life each Israelite should "diligently keep the commandments of the Lord your God, and His testimonies, and His statutes, which He hath commanded thee, and do that which is right and good in the sight of the Lord: that it may be well with thee."[2]

[1] In Exod. xx. 17, the wife is put after the house, evidently as included in it; in Deut. v. before, more in accordance with the manner in which women were viewed by the ancient Jews. [2] Deut. vi. 17, 18.

PENTATEUCH CODE AS SUMMARISED IN THE TEN WORDS.
FIRST TABLE.

	Exod.	Lev.	Num.	Deut.
I. First Word: What God is to be worshipped	xx. 3	... ...	... ...	v. 7.
Not through images	{ xx. 23; xxiii. 13.			
II. Second Word: How God is to be worshipped	xx. 4-6	... ...	... ...	v. 8-10.
1. At the Altar	xx. 24-26.			
2. In His Sanctuary	{ xxiv.; xxvii.; xxx.	... ...	xviii.	xii. 26, 27.
3. By Sacrifices	{ xxiii. 18; xxix.	{ i.-vii.; xvi.; xvii.	{ xv. 1-29; xix. 1-10; xxviii.; xxix.	xvii. 1.
4. Firstfruits are to be brought	xxiii. 19	... ...	... ...	xxvi. 1-11.
5. Vows to be paid	... ...	xxvii.	xxx.	xxiii. 21-23.
6. Nazarites	... ...	... ...	vi. 1-21.	
7. Through the priests and Levites	xxviii.	{ x. 9, 10; xxi.; xxii.		
8. Their tithes and portions	... ...	... ...	... ...	{ xiv. 22-29; xviii. 1-8; xxvi. 12-15.
9. By a holy people	... ...	xii.	{ xix. 11-22; xxxi. 21-24	xxiii. 1-14.
10. Holy in their food	{ xxii. 31; xxiii. 19; xxxiv. 26	{ vii. 22-27; xi.; xvii. 10-16; xix. 23-26; xx. 25	... ...	{ xii. 15-26; xiv. 3-21.
11. Holy in their dress	... ...	... ...	... ...	xxii. 5, 11, 12.
12. In a holy land	... ...	... ...	... ...	xxi. 22, 23.
God will not be worshipped by a people				
1. Following witchcraft	xxii. 18	{ xix. 26, 31; xx. 6, 27	... ...	xviii. 10-12.
2. Following idolatry	{ xxii. 20; xxiii. 24, 32; xxxiv. 17	{ xix. 4, 27, 28; xx. 1-5; xxvi. 1	... ...	{ vi. 14; xii. 2; xiii.; xiv. 1; xvi. 21, 22; xvii. 2-7; xviii. 10.
3. But idolaters are to be exterminated	... ...	... ...	... ...	xx.
III. Third Word: How God has revealed Himself: in His Name	xx. 7	... ...	... ...	v. 11.
Blasphemy	... ...	xxiv. 10-16.		
IV. Fourth Word: Times to be consecrated to God	xx. 8-11	... ...	... ...	v. 12-15.
1. Sabbaths	{ xxiii. 12; xxxi. 12-17; xxxiv. 21; xxxv. 2, 3	{ xix. 3, 30; xxiii. 3; xxvi. 2.		
2. Sabbatical Year	xxiii. 10, 11	xxv. 1-7.		
3. Jubilee Year	... ...	xxv. 8-54.		
4. Year of Release	... ...	... ...	... ...	xv.
5. Festivals and Fasts	xxiii. 14-17	xxiii.	... ...	xvi. 1-17.
V. Fifth Word: Duties of superiors and inferiors	xx. 12	... ...	... ...	v. 16.
1. Rulers and subjects	xxii. 28	... ...	... ...	xvii. 15-20.
2. Judges and magistrates	... ...	... ...	... ...	{ xvi. 18-20; xvii. 8-13; xxv. 1-3.
3. Parents and children	xxi. 15, 17	xix. 3.	... ...	xxi. 15-21.
4. Servants and masters	xxi. 1-11	... ...	... ...	xv. 12-18.
5. Young and old	... ...	xix. 32.		
6. Ill-treating the defenceless (blind and deaf)	... ...	xix. 14.		

SECOND TABLE.

	Exod.	Lev.	Num.	Deut.
I. Sixth Word: Preservation of life and health	xx. 13	... ...	... ...	v. 17.
1. Murder	xxi. 12,14	... ...	xxxv. 30-33	xix. 11-13; xxi. 1-9.
2. Injuries, mortal or otherwise, to and from man or beast	xxi. 18-36	xxiv. 17-21.		
3. Manslaughter	xxi. 13	... ...	xxxv. 9-29	xix. 2-10.
4. Precautions to be taken in building	... ...	... ...	... ...	xxii. 8.
5. Hatred and grudging	... ...	xix. 17, 18.		
6. Diseases and sicknesses	... ...	xiii.-xv.	v. 2, 3	xxiv. 8, 9.
II. Seventh Word: Holiness in domestic life	xx. 14	... ...	... ...	v. 18.
1. Sins against this holiness	xxii. 16, 17, 19	xviii.; xix. 20-22, 29	v. 11-31	xxi. 10-14; xxii. 13-30; xxiii. 17, 18; xxv. 11, 12.
2. Divorce	... ...	... ...	... ...	xxiv. 1-4.
3. Privileges of a newly-married man	... ...	... ...	... ...	xxiv. 5.
4. Marriage with deceased brother's wife	... ...	... ...	... ...	xxv. 5-10.
5. Marriage portions of heiresses	... ...	... ...	xxvii.; xxxvi.	
III. Eighth Word: Just dealings between man and man	xx. 15	... ...	... ...	v. 19.
1. Man-stealing	xxi. 16	... ...	... ...	xxiv. 7.
2. Defrauding of wages	... ...	xix. 13	... ...	xxiv. 14, 15.
3. Kindness to poor and strangers	xxii. 21; xxiii. 9	xix. 9, 10, 33; 34; xxiii. 22	... ...	xxiv. 17.
4. Kindness to widows and orphans	xxii. 22-24	... ...	... ...	xxiv. 19-22.
5. Kindness to debtors	xxii. 25-27	... ...	... ...	xxiii. 19, 20; xxiv. 6, 10-13, 17.
6. Kindness to runaway slaves	... ...	... ...	... ...	xxiii. 15, 16.
7. Restoring lost property	xxiii. 4	... ...	... ...	xxii. 1-3.
8. Helping another's cattle	xxiii. 5	... ...	... ...	xxii. 4.
9. Kindness to birds and beasts of burden	... ...	... ...	... ...	xxii. 6, 7; xxv. 4.
10. Gathering another's fruits	... ...	... ...	... ...	xxiii. 24, 25.
11. Just weights and measures	... ...	xix. 35, 36	... ...	xxv. 13-16.
12. Theft	xxii. 1-4	xix. 11, 13.		
13. Removing landmarks	... ...	... ...	... ...	xix. 14.
14. Injury to another's property, wilful or otherwise	xxii. 5-15.			
IV. Ninth Word: Truthfulness	xx. 16	... ...	... ...	v. 20.
1. Evil reports	xxiii. 1	xix. 16.		
2. Falsehood, by word or deed	... ...	xix. 11.		
3. Partial or prejudiced decisions	xxiii. 2-8	xix. 15	... ...	xvi. 18-20.
4. Witness-bearing	xxiii. 1	xix. 16	... ...	xix. 15-20.
V. Tenth Word: Covetous and greedy desires	xx. 17	... ...	... ...	v. 21

CHAPTER XV.

THE CLEAN AND THE UNCLEAN.

FIRST and foremost in that list of purifications by which Israel was to show to all the world that they were a "peculiar people," holy, even as their God was holy, stand the laws marking "a difference between the unclean and the clean, and between the beast that may be eaten and the beast that may not be eaten."[1] This arrangement is both true and just. For one of the broadest lines of distinction between nations is traced by their food, and one of the first effects of civilisation, and we may add of religion, must and does appear in this respect. Thus much is true of every race. But in regard to Israel the distinction is far more marked and far more weighty. For it is a religious one, even as Israel itself was a typical and holy nation. These laws, then, are not arbitrary, nor are they unreasonable; they are an essential part of the whole Theocratic Code, and as such full of meaning even now to the Israel of God. For, although no longer binding, their underlying principle must still be ours: "I am the Lord your God, which have separated you from other people. Ye shall therefore put difference between clean beasts and unclean, and between unclean fowls and clean: and ye shall not make your souls abominable. . . . And ye shall be holy unto Me : for I the Lord am holy, and have severed you from other people, that ye should be Mine."[2]

With this principle of national holiness in that which was most common, as well as in that which was most sacred,

[1] Lev. xi. 47.   [2] Ibid. xx. 24-26.

always in view, Moses framed his laws concerning the clean and the unclean, partly from what had been handed down from father to son, from the days of the Flood, or even before that, and partly with the object of more effectually severing Israel from the nations around. Many and ingenious are the suggestions as to the *rationale* of these laws, and doubtless the majority of these suggestions are not without weight. It is very possible, for example, that Moses not only contemplated that the complete separation of Israel from other nations was to be partially effected by their food, but that his motives for rejecting certain kinds of animal food as "unclean," and *vice versâ*, may have been influenced by such reasons as the peculiarities of the climate, the traditional habits and modes of thinking of the people, supposed sanitary dangers, or their uses for idolatrous purposes. But the Pentateuch, though by no means militating against such reasons, does not place them in the foreground; but, building upon ancient customs and traditions, elevates man's common life into relationship with God, by thus putting under His rule that in which man might so easily forget his Maker.[1]

The first food of the human race was, undoubtedly, vegetable; but how long this continued after the Fall is a matter of some doubt. Most likely the flocks kept by Abel[2] and Jabal[3] were not simply pastured for their fleeces and for their milk, but were also used for food. However, the first mention of animal food does not occur till after the Flood, when among the so-called Noachic commands is inserted one forbidding the eating of "flesh with the life thereof, which is the blood thereof."[4] Already had the line of distinction been drawn between "clean beasts" and "beasts that are not clean," in the words by which God directed Noah to preserve in the ark "of every living thing of all flesh." But at the outset it must be remembered that these terms, "clean" and "unclean," were not at all intended to convey the ideas now

[1] Hosea iv. 10, 11.
[3] Ibid. ver. 20.
[2] Gen. iv.
[4] Ibid. ix. 4.

attaching to them. Nothing created by God could be called of itself common or unclean. Nor did the ancient Jew by any means despise that which to him was forbidden as food. It was simply *as food* that he might not use thereof, and to him (as Michaelis has pointed out) an unclean animal meant nothing more nor less than one whose flesh might not serve him for food. Here, no doubt, national tastes and inherited likes and dislikes had originally helped to mark the difference now completed by the Lawgiver. Perhaps this inherited aversion is what is expressed in such words as "they are an abomination," so often introduced. Whatever these words may imply, it is evident that from the very beginning man's daily food was under the Creator's rule. Thus, in the garden of Eden, although Adam might freely eat of every tree in the garden, yet he might not take of the Tree of Knowledge of Good and Evil. And as here the sin of the body was punished by death, so in the Mosaic Law disobedience to these commands was to be punished by God Himself, by cutting off, or by the offender bearing his own iniquity.

With regard to vegetable food, no restriction whatever was laid on Israel by Moses.[1] The reason probably was that an agricultural people would be able readily to distinguish between what was good and what hurtful in these natural productions. Nor could a limit be conveniently put to their use; such must be learnt by experience. On the other hand, not only the hurtfulness or the usefulness of the animals used for food had to be considered, but religious questions here came up, as well as those relating to the dignity alike of man and beast. For example, beasts of burden, such as the ass or the camel, were forbidden food, on account of their service to man, as also were serpents or creeping things, probably as being objects of adoration to the heathen, or with reference to the Fall. Nor must it be supposed that these distinctions in animal food were confined to the Jewish Code. They appear among the

---

[1] Except the prohibition to eat of any tree that had been planted till it was three years old (Lev. xix. 23).

Egyptians, among the Mahometans, and in many other ancient religious systems (such as the Zend); only the *rationale* of these is far different from that of Israel's law.[1] And again, even in later times, the mysticism of Philo and of some of the Fathers saw in the Jewish laws of food an allegorical meaning, in some animals the Logos, or Divine Word, in others again evil deeds, vices, or even faulty exegesis.

But to return. Two limits hedged in the Israelites in regard to food. They must not eat certain things, because they were holy and consecrated; nor again others, because they were abominable. Within these limits they were allowed to partake freely:

1. Of quadrupeds: whatsoever "parteth the hoof," and is cloven-footed, "cleaveth the cleft into two claws and cheweth the cud;" or more particularly: "the ox, the sheep, and the goat, the hart, and the roebuck, and the fallow deer, and the wild goat, and the pygarg, and the wild ox, and the chamois."[2]

2. Of fishes—*i.e.*, " of all that are in the waters": all "that have fins and scales in the waters, in the seas, and in the rivers."[3]

3. Of birds and winged fowls: "all clean birds," and "all clean fowls."[4]

4. Of insects, or any "flying, creeping thing that goeth upon all four, which have legs above their feet, to leap withal upon the earth"[5]: four different kinds of locusts.

These animals were all clean, and might be eaten under certain conditions, with the following limitations:

1. The beasts must be killed in a particular manner—*i.e.*, the blood must be allowed to pour out freely, "as water,"[6] and be then covered with dust.

2. Certain portions of the fat of the ox, of the sheep, and of the goat, viz., that portion of it "of which men offer an offering

---

[1] For example, some of the heathens supposed that the two classes were different creations, or due to the good and the evil principle, etc.

[2] Deut. xiv. 4–6. The identification of many of the animals enumerated in this part of the Mosaic Law is much in dispute. It would appear that the four last-mentioned animals were species of antelope. [3] Lev. xi. 9.

[4] Deut. xiv. 11, 20. [5] Lev. xi. 21. [6] Lev. xvii. 13; Deut. xii. 16.

MORAL LAWS IN DAILY LIFE.

made by fire unto the Lord,"[1] might in no wise be eaten, as being the Lord's, and therefore "most holy,"[2] too holy for any common use. If any Israelite ate of this sacred fat, his punishment would be terrible, for he would "be cut off from his people."[3]

3. No Israelite might eat the blood of either beast or fowl, nor might any stranger do so.[4] Against the man who did so God would "set His face," and would "cut him off from among his people." Two reasons are furnished for this command. In the first place, "the life of the flesh is in the blood;" *i.e.*, blood possessing "the mysterious sacredness which belongs to life," was withheld from common use as food. And further, secondly, "I have given it to you upon the altar to make an atonement for your souls: for it is the blood that maketh an atonement for the soul."[5] That is, what had been set apart for the most solemn sacrifice, that which before God made atonement, must to the Israelite be always consecrated; and as belonging to God, must not be touched as food even by a stranger. Another reason may have been that blood was drunk by some of the idolatrous nations in their heathen orgies.[6]

4. The flesh of no animal, clean as well as unclean, which had "died of itself, or had been torn with beasts,"[7] might be eaten, but must be cast to the dogs.[8] Not only so, but whosoever touched the carcase of such an animal was "unclean until the even," and must "wash his clothes."[9] If he neglected to do so, he would bear his own iniquity.[10] The same law applied, of course, to the carcases of unclean animals, and was kindred in meaning to that which declared that touching the corpse of a man contracted defilement.[11]

By far the larger proportion of animals were to be "unclean,"

---

[1] Comp. Lev. vii. 1–5; iii. 17. [2] Lev. vii. 1. [3] Ibid. vers. 25, 27.
[4] Ibid. vers. 26, 27; iii. 17; xvii. 10. [5] Lev. xvii 10–14.
[6] Comp. Psa xvi. 4. [7] Lev. xvii. 15. [8] Exod. xxii. 31.
[9] Lev. xi. 39, 40.
[10] Lev. xvii. 16. By many critics this kind of food is supposed to be the "strangled "—*i.e.*, not properly bled-food forbidden the Gentile converts in Acts xv. [11] See Chap. xii.

THE CLEAN AND THE UNCLEAN. 167

and, as such, forbidden food to the Israelites, and "abominable to them." Many of these, however, cannot with certainty now be identified, partly by reason of the lack of sufficient knowledge of the natural history of Palestine, partly on account of linguistic difficulties. Following the same division as has been made use of in regard to "clean beasts," it would appear that—

1. Of quadrupeds were forbidden: those that chewed the cud, but did not divide the hoof, and those who divided the hoof and did not chew the cud; or, more specifically, the camel, the hare, the coney, and the swine.[1] Their carcases, of course, must not be touched: "they are unclean unto you."

2. Of fishes: "all that have not fins and scales in the seas, and in the rivers, of all that move in the waters;" "but ye shall have their carcases in abomination."[2]

3. Of birds might not be eaten: "the eagle, the ossifrage, the ospray, the vulture, the kite, every raven after its kind"—*i.e.*, all birds feeding on carrion, or preying on it; "the owl and the night hawk"—*i.e.*, birds loving darkness; "the cuckoo," which deserts its eggs; "the hawk after his kind;" "the little owl, the cormorant, the great owl"—*i.e.*, birds of prey and of darkness; "the swan" (*tinshemeth*, "probably a species of owl"); "the pelican,"[3] the type of desolation; "the gier-eagle, the stork" (*pia avis*, whose love for its young is so great), the "heron after her kind," which preys upon fish; "the lapwing" (*duchiphath, hoopoo*, whose smell and nest are most foul); "and the bat," as being something between fowl and reptile.

4. All fowls or "flying things that creep,"[4] or insects, might not be eaten, with the exception of the locust; nor might their carcases be touched or borne, for whosoever did so was unclean until even.

5. Of reptiles, those creeping things, including the smaller quadrupeds, were unclean, which were most commonly found

---

[1] Lev. xi. 4-8; Deut. xiv. 7, 8. Swine were also forbidden the Egyptian priests. They were likewise used in heathen worship. Comp. Isa. lxvi. 17, etc.
[2] Lev. xi. 10-12; Deut. xiv. 10.   [3] Comp. Psa. cii. 6.
[4] Lev. xi. 20; Deut. xiv. 19.

near human habitation, viz., "the weasel, and the mouse, and the tortoise (?) after his kind, and the ferret, and the chameleon, and the lizard, and the snail, and the mole."[1] These reptiles not only defiled any man who touched their dead bodies, but "any vessel of wood, or raiment, or skin, or sack, whatsoever vessel it be, wherein any work is done" would be rendered unclean by the dead body of one of these creatures falling upon it, so that for its cleansing it was necessary to put it into water till the even. An earthen vessel so rendered unclean must be broken, and meat or drink on which, or in which, their dead bodies had fallen could not be used. Ovens or "ranges for pots" (cauldrons, LXX.), "whereupon any part of their carcase" fell must be broken down as unclean, and seed whereon water had been put was defiled by the same thing. But if the seed were dry, no defilement was contracted. Fountains or pits (*i.e.*, cisterns) "wherein there is plenty of water" were not rendered unclean by these dead bodies; only that part which touched their carcase was defiled.[2]

Besides these "unclean beasts," the Israelites were likewise forbidden to eat a kid boiled in milk.[3] This has been supposed by some to mean the forbidding to prepare any meat in milk, as being a practice inhuman and idolatrous. Further, no Israelite might partake of food offered in sacrifice to idols,[4] nor of the "sinew which shrank, which is upon the hollow of the thigh."[5] This last observance, though not noticed in the Mosaic Code, dated from the time of Jacob.

No person who had touched any unclean thing or animal might partake of sacrificial food, on pain of being cut off.[6] Even the meat of the offering itself might be defiled by contact with an unclean thing, and in that case would have to be burnt.[7] At any rate, whether defiled or not, no portion of the flesh of the sacrifice of peace-offering must be left till next day;

---

[1] Lev. xi. 29, etc.   [2] Ibid. xi 29–38.   [3] Exod. xxiii. 19.
[4] Ibid. xxxiv. 15.   [5] Gen. xxxii. 32.   [6] Lev. vii. 21.
[7] Ibid. ver. 19.

only if the sacrifice had been for a vow, or a voluntary offering, might part be left till the morrow.[1] From these and other ritual ordinances, such as the command not to leave the Paschal lamb, and the rapid decay of the manna, it has been inferred by some writers, perhaps on hardly sufficient grounds, that the Lawgiver intended animal food to be eaten as soon as possible after the beast had been killed.

What the punishment from the hand of man for disobeying these commands was, the Pentateuch does not define. The Rabbis held that the offender should be scourged, and laid great stress on obedience in this respect. How earnest such Jews as Daniel and his three companions were in not defiling themselves with forbidden food, is well known.[2] Thus the prophet Ezekiel could boast that, even in exile, his soul had not been polluted, for that from his youth up he had not eaten of that which died of itself, or was torn in pieces, and that "abominable flesh" had not come into his mouth.[3]

The principal meals of the Israelites were, besides a light breakfast, the midday and the evening meals.[4] At these, in early days,[5] men sat, and, of course, partook of food according to their means;[6] the poor subsisting mostly on grain and fruit, the rich having their tables covered with many dainties. The staple drinks were: water, *chomes*—rendered "vinegar" in Ruth ii. 14—the drink of the poor, milk,[7] clotted cream,[8] wine, generally mixed with water (comp. Isaiah i. 22) or flavoured with aromatic herbs,[9] and "strong drink"—an intoxicating liquor (perhaps date wine, as Keil suggests). Besides animal food, and various kinds of grain, we find mention in the Old Testament of cheese,[10] butter,[11] honey,[12] figs,[13] date cakes,[14] and of course locusts. Meat might be roasted, or "seethed," *i.e.*, boiled.[15]

To the Jewish nation, which, after long centuries of training

[1] Lev. vii. 15, 16.   [2] Dan. i. 8.   [3] Ezek. iv. 14.
[4] John xxi. 12.   [5] Gen. xviii. 1; xix. 1.   [6] Ibid. xxvii. 19.
[7] Deut. xxxii. 14.   [8] Judges v. 25.   [9] Song Sol. viii. 2.
[10] Job x. 10.   [11] Prov. xxx. 33.   [12] 1 Sam. xiv. 25.
[13] Jer. xxiv. 1-3.   [14] 2 Sam. xvi. 1.   [15] 1 Sam. ii. 13.

by their teachers, had learnt to make such distinctions between the clean and the unclean, to whom eating with men uncircumcised was a thing beyond possibility, the words of our Lord, that "whatsoever thing from without entereth into the man, it cannot defile him,"[1] must have been utterly mysterious. His "making all meats clean" by this saying opened up to His disciples a new point of sight, that by which not Israel as a peculiar people, but the Gentiles as equally God's children, were to be united to their Father by purity of heart and life. Yet, strange to say, it was round this same question of what was lawful and unlawful in food and in eating that much of the first difference of opinion in the early Church centred,[2] and it was this difficulty which would almost have prevented St. Peter from going to Cornelius, had he not received Divine command to do so.[3] Eating and not eating with the Gentile brethren was again the cause of St. Peter's "condemnation" by St. Paul at Antioch.[4] But whether for Jew or Gentile, the same principle must underlie all our daily life, if it is to be such as is worthy of its Giver. The principle is that with which St. Paul sums up all his teaching on this point to the Corinthians: "Whether therefore ye eat, or drink, or whatsoever ye do, do all to the glory of God."[5]

[1] Mark vii. 18.   [2] Acts xv.   [3] Ibid. x. 9-23.
[4] Gal. ii. 11-13.   [5] 1 Cor. x. 31.

CHAPTER XVI.

HOSPITALITY: THE STRANGER.

To an Israelite the admonition given in the Epistle to the Hebrews, "Be not forgetful to entertain strangers, for thereby some have entertained angels unawares,"[1] would not have sounded either novel or strange. Dwelling as he did in a land where, at least in the early ages, inns were either non-existent or little better than four rough walls, perhaps roofless, it would have been a sin to the Jew to have left a traveller unprotected, or even to have entertained the man and to have left his animals shelterless. Like Job, each righteous man could say, "The stranger did not lodge in the street: but I opened my doors to the traveller."[2] Nor did the stranger need to seek hospitality; neither would he have insulted his host by offering him payment for it. Rather did the householder deem it a privilege to press and entreat the travellers to partake of his hospitality, to wait on his guests himself, and afterwards to accompany them a little on their way.[3] Simple, yet most true to the manners and customs of the patriarchal times, is the account of the entertainment "unawares" of the angels by Abraham and by Lot, and dire the contrast presented by the conduct of the Sodomites.[4] But the "sinners before the Lord," the Sodomites, were not solitary in their behaviour towards strangers. Ancient history furnishes us with many instances of oppression, and of ill-treatment of foreigners, from

---

[1] Heb. xiii. 2.
[2] Job xxxi. 32.
[3] Gen. xviii. 1, 2, 8, 16.
[4] Ibid. xix.

the unjust and excessive taxes and tributes demanded of the sojourner in Greece, to secure him, as the natives declared, in being protected by the laws of the states, from the treatment of such a conquered race as the Helots by the Spartans, to the general contempt on the part of the world's conquerors for all that was not Roman, expressed in the word "barbarian." And it must be added, modern history, with the persecutions and expulsions of the Jews, with the treatment by Christian countries of the coloured races, cannot be said to have even yet thoroughly learned the lesson taught by the Pentateuch.

The hospitality of the Israelite was not to be confined to his fellow-countrymen, but was to be extended to all strangers, whether Jews or heathens. And this was in order that that "love which is the fulfilling of the law"[1] should not only be lavished on the kinsman, but embrace in one family all the dwellers upon earth. Two reasons, and these based upon those which gave meaning to Israel's existence as a nation, were put forward as the ground of the clauses in the Mosaic Code which provided for the equal rights of the stranger and sojourner. The first was: God's relationship and frame of mind (if the term may be permitted) towards the stranger: "He loveth the stranger, in giving him food and raiment;"[2] and the second, Israel's own relationship to God, their Deliverer: "Love ye therefore the stranger, for ye were strangers in the land of Egypt;"[3] "thou shalt remember that thou wast a bondman in Egypt, and the Lord thy God redeemed thee thence."[4] It is, as one has beautifully remarked, as though Moses would say, "He is a stranger to you, his fellow-man, but he is not such to God, for in God's sight both you and he are equally strangers." And so the Psalmist, to whom life was a journey, could speak of himself as "a stranger"—a guest—"with Thee, and a sojourner, as all my fathers were."[5] He that showed hospitality, then, was doing that which God did for the whole world;[6] and what wonder if, viewed in such a light, hospitality

---

[1] Rom. xiii. 10. [2] Deut. x. 18. [3] Ibid. ver. 19.
[4] Deut. xxiv. 18. [5] Psa. xxxix. 12. [6] Ibid. civ. 27, 28.

HOSPITALITY: THE STRANGER.   173

was a grace to be cultivated by all, and therefore set forward, and strongly insisted upon, in the Mosaic Code?

The word rendered in our Authorised Version "stranger" has several Hebrew equivalents, marking degrees of distinction between the "foreigner," speaking generally, as signifying him who is without; and the "stranger," more particularly, in the sense of one who, though really belonging to another nationality, is residing in a country not his own. The most ordinary term given by the Jew to the stranger was *ger*, which might be used either for a non-Israelite residing in Palestine, or for one living outside the land. This was the general name. More specific was *toshav*, a sojourner, a dweller, one who had come to settle in Canaan. Such an one might either himself be the first of his family to settle in the land, or else be the descendant of a family which only by birth—and perhaps religion—differed from the ordinary Israelite. Again, the sojourner might be a hired servant (*sachir*), or he might be a slave purchased with money (*eved*). Another class of "strangers" comprises the *nochri*, or *ben nochri*, a foreigner, probably a trader or hawker, who had not come to settle in the land, but to barter for, and to exchange goods. The *nochri* was distinguished from the *toshav* in this respect, that from the former the Israelite was allowed to take interest. But in none of these names was there implied anything either contemptuous or yet degrading. The stranger in the eyes of the Israelite was not one of a conquered race, nor was he one whom the laws of property or of personal security could not protect. He was simply a non-Israelite, whose liberty must not be interfered with—that is, so long as he kept within the bounds prescribed to him—and he was one for whom each Jew ought to have a lively sympathy: "for ye know the heart of a stranger, seeing ye were strangers in the land of Egypt."[1]

Under circumstances of such unusual large-heartedness, it is not surprising to find that, from a very early period, Palestine was continually resorted to by strangers anxious to settle there.

[1] Exod. xxiii. 9.

These were always made heartily welcome, and frequently rose to positions of great honour and usefulness. Mention may here be made of the descendants of the father-in-law of Moses, the Kenites, afterwards better known as the Rechabites;[1] of Uriah the Hittite, in the days of King David;[2] of Ittai the Gittite, captain over one-third of David's army;[3] and of Araunah the Jebusite.[4] The dependence of the Israelites on foreign workmen and artisans has already been alluded to.

As regarded Israel's conduct to those who were not of their own nationality, the only exceptions they were commanded to make to the law of brotherly kindness towards all men were to be in the cases of the seven idolatrous nations of Canaan, and their descendants to all generations, as well as in that of the Amalekites, Ammonites, and Moabites (see chapter v.). On the other hand, the Egyptian and the Edomite must not be abhorred—the former, "because thou wast a stranger in his land;" the latter, "for he is thy brother." Nevertheless, it might not be till, in the third generation, the memory of the evil-doing of those Egyptians and Edomites who had vexed and oppressed Israel at the time of the Exodus, had been blotted out, that "the children that are begotten of them" would be permitted to "enter into the congregation of the Lord."[5]

From this last verse it will be gathered that it was possible for an ordinary stranger—for one who did not belong to any of the accursed nations, nor was a bastard, nor had any serious personal defect—to enter into the congregation of the Lord; that is, to become, outwardly at least, a member of the holy nation, and thereby a partaker of all their benefits. The road to this entrance was through circumcision, by virtue of which a stranger obtained the privilege of being allowed to celebrate the Paschal Feast. "When a stranger shall sojourn with thee, and will keep the passover to the Lord, let all his males be circumcised, and then let him come near and keep it; and he shall be as one that is born in the land: for no uncircumcised person shall eat

---

[1] Judg. i. 16; v. 24; Jer. xxxv. [2] 2 Sam. xi. 6.
[3] Ibid. xviii. 2.   [4] Ibid. xxiv. 18.   [5] Deut. xxiii. 7, 8.

thereof."[1] Did a stranger, then, desire to own Israel's God as his, and to become an Israelite in religion, he might do so by being circumcised. By this act Israel's distinctive institution was opened to him, and by it Israel's duties and responsibilities as regarded the world at large would be laid upon him.

But also, as regarded a stranger who was not circumcised, his privileges were not few, and in proportion to them were his duties and responsibilities. In the first place, he was protected by the law which classed him along with the poor, the Levite, the widow, and the orphan; and if he were really in poverty, he had a right to the corners of the harvest field, free use of anything that grew of itself in the Sabbatical or Jubilee Years, and an equal share in the third year's tithes. As a dweller in the land of Canaan, the judge must show him impartial justice, for the charge given by Moses to the elders had been, "Judge righteously between every man and his brother, and the stranger that is with him."[2] Further, "if a stranger sojourn with you, or whosoever be among you in your generations, and will offer an offering made by fire, of a sweet savour unto the Lord; as ye do, so he shall do"—he, the stranger, may offer a burnt-offering as freely as may any Israelite—for "one ordinance shall be both for you of the congregation, and also for the stranger that sojourneth with you; . . . as ye are, so shall the stranger be before the Lord. One law and one manner shall be for you, and for the stranger that sojourneth with you."[3] Again, as regarded his social standing, the stranger was as safe within the city of refuge after an unintentional deed of manslaughter as was any Israelite.[4] In the matter of food, his liberty was greater than was that of the Jew, for he might eat the flesh of an animal that had died a natural death, or which had been torn.[5] He might become owner of Israelitish slaves;[6] and, if he were a hired servant, he must not be defrauded of his wages.[7]

[1] Exod. xii. 48.
[2] Deut. i. 16.
[3] Num. xv. 14-16.
[4] Ibid. xxxv. 15.
[5] Deut. xiv. 21.
[6] Lev. xxv. 47.
[7] Deut. xxiv. 15.

Upon him, as well as upon the Israelite, lay the prohibition not to offer to God anything that was "bruised, or crushed, or broken, or cut."[1] If he disobeyed any of the laws of God, his punishment would be the same in kind and in degree as that which would overtake the Jew.[2] Even though the stranger had not been circumcised, he must not eat the consecrated portions of the fat of certain animals, nor the blood of any beast.[3] The Sabbath rest was equally for him throughout the whole land;[4] and while he made Palestine his dwelling-place, he might not, on pain of death, offer any of his seed in sacrifice to Moloch,[5] nor commit any of the "abominations" practised by any of the seven nations cast out before Israel.[6] These, and many other regulations, go far to show that the stranger sojourning in the land of Canaan was no outlaw, no person suffered, barely tolerated, but a member of the state, subject to all the social and domestic laws, and in matters of religion bound to reverence Jehovah, and to obey the seven Noachic commandments.[7]

The only respects in which the law for the sojourner and stranger differed from that of Israel were—(1) that the heathen owner of an Israelitish slave was bound to let his servant go free as soon as his *Goel* could redeem him;[8] and (2) that although a stranger might rise to a very high position in Israel, yet he could never become king.[9] A third restriction would seem to be that forbidding the marriage of any Israelite maiden with an uncircumcised heathen.[10]

The curse laid by Moses on him "that perverteth the judgment of the stranger,"[11] as well as the whole spirit of the Pentateuch, must have been strangely overlooked or misunderstood by those post-Exilian Jews, according to whom it was lawful to neglect every brotherly act towards the so much despised Gentile. Strangely also must they have forgotten the word of

---

[1] Lev. xxii. 25. [2] Ibid. xxiv. 22. [3] Ibid. xvii. 10.
[4] Exod. xx. 10. [5] Lev. xx. 2. [6] Ibid. xviii. 26, etc.
[7] Comp. Acts xv. 19, 20. [8] Lev. xxv. 47–52. [9] Deut. xvii. 15.
[10] Comp. Gen. xxxiv. 14. [11] Deut. xxvii. 19.

HOSPITALITY: THE STRANGER.

God revealed to the prophet Ezekiel, when, in the vision of the Holy Land once more divided among the tribes, he was told that not to the Israelite alone would all be given, but "it shall come to pass, that ye shall divide it by lot for an inheritance unto you, and to the strangers that sojourn among you, which shall beget children among you: and they shall be unto you as born in the country among the children of Israel; they shall have inheritance with you among the tribes of Israel. And it shall come to pass, that in what tribe the stranger sojourneth, there shall ye give him his inheritance, saith the Lord God."[1] Such sojourners would be those who, in the words of the prophet Isaiah, "join themselves to the Lord, to serve Him, and to love the Name of the Lord, to be His servants; every one that keepeth the Sabbath from polluting it, and taketh hold of My covenant"[2]—*i.e.*, those who had joined themselves to the Lord when there was nothing earthly to attract them. These would not be such self-seekers, aptly called "strange children," from whom Nehemiah separated the seed of Israel after the return from the Exile;[3] nor those who, like the "enemies," would only seek to hinder that good work in which they had not been allowed to help.[4] In those days it had been a necessity that Israel should be separated from all idolaters; but what had been to Nehemiah and to Ezra merely acts of security became grievous wrong when carried out to the bitter end by the Rabbis and their disciples. Into all this mutual antagonism did Christianity come with a teaching certainly not as the scribes. For the Lord Jesus Christ brake down the middle wall of partition between Jew and Gentile, and made what were called Uncircumcision "no more strangers and foreigners, but fellow-citizens with the saints, and of the household of God."[5] And therefore now all alike, both Jew and Gentile, one flock under one shepherd,[6] walking by faith, not by sight, confessing they are strangers and pilgrims upon earth, look "for the city which hath the foundations, whose builder and maker is God."[7]

[1] Ezek. xlvii. 22, 23. [2] Isa. lvi. 6. [3] Neh. ix. 2; xiii. 3. [4] Ezra iv.
[5] Eph. ii. 11, 14, 19. [6] John x. 16. [7] Heb. xi. 10, 13.

CHAPTER XVII.

MUTUAL RIGHTS AND OBLIGATIONS.

A SKETCH of the Jewish social laws would scarcely be complete without brief notice of those provisions by which not only equal justice between man and man, but between man and beast was secured, while at the same time this justice was made voluntary, to be willingly done, not grudgingly eked out. Of course this applies to the laws themselves, and does not necessarily imply that the nation possessing that code kept strictly by its provisions. On the contrary, often and grievously were they departed from, yet, it must be added, never without loss. For Israel's existence was, so to speak, bound up in these laws, and when untrue and disobedient to them the great *raison d'être* of the nation—to show that even amidst the darkest idolatry it was possible for a people to be holy and obedient to their God—was lost; and with this loss of a higher motive for conduct, even love to, and fear of, God, its outward manifestation in love to, and reverence for, what was another's, must also vanish.

But granted that Israel firmly intended to serve and obey God in all things which concerned each individually, there must be further some connecting link between every member of the community, exclusive of family ties or of tribal alliances. This connecting link would be that "love which worketh no ill to his neighbour;" the neighbour being not, as some would fain have it, one's own self, but, according to the teaching of our Lord, any and every one.[1] Fitly this royal law[2] is put in contrast with those evil feelings and actions which are the

[1] Luke x. 29-37. [2] James ii. 8.

result of long-cherished ill-will: "Thou shalt not avenge, nor bear any grudge against the children of thy people; but thou shalt love thy neighbour as thyself."[1] And not only is "the neighbour" "the child of thy people" to be so loved, "but the stranger that dwelleth with you shall be unto you as one born among you, and thou shalt love him as thyself."[2] Yet, after all, this love must have a higher origin than mere natural inclination, or even the desire to make others happy; for it is an impossibility unless associated with, and flowing from, that love to God which is to be the all-absorbing, all-constraining motive for obedience: "Thou shalt love the Lord thy God with all thine heart, and with all thy soul, and with all thy might."[3] So, entering by the door of the affections, penetrating into the secrets of life and thought, and diffusing itself through the powers and energies, would the all-pervading love drive out self-seeking and selfish isolation, making each "esteem other better than himself," and look upon the things of others as well as, or rather than, on his own things.[4]

To put this principle of neighbourly love into force in all respects and aspects would have been beyond the power and the limits of the Mosaic Code. The more ordinary and frequently recurring circumstances were, however, provided for, while the remainder of instances can easily be dealt with by comparison with these. As fitting among laws destined for a nation purely agricultural, these provisions concern, with few exceptions, pastoral and agricultural pursuits, the neighbour's cattle and the neighbour's land. The laws are not detailed, but briefly indicate the boundary between mischance and misdemeanour, between what was punishable and what not.

Putting aside each man's religious obligations, every Israelite was liable, as member of the state, to be called upon to fight for his country, after he had attained the age of twenty, or after he had been married more than one year.[5] Next, he was bound to provide for the succour of the poor, the widow, the

[1] Lev. xix. 18. [2] Ibid. ver. 34. [3] Deut. vi. 5.
[4] Phil. ii. 3, 4. [5] See chap. v.

orphan, the Levite, and the stranger, as well as to protect them all from every injustice and cruelty. This protection of the weak extended beyond human beings to animals, and even to trees and inanimate objects. These objects might either concern the man himself particularly, or his neighbour, or might again be what, though belonging to another, had been entrusted to his care. Injury in each case might be due either to carelessness or else to wilful neglect.

1. In the first category should be reckoned the injuries done by masters to their slaves, which were to be punished either by fines, or by the loss to the owner of the slave's life, or by the forfeiture of his service.[1]

2. The second category would include most of the laws which have hitherto been noted; but as particular instances, beyond the commands against murder, injustice, and false witness, and as specially applicable to an agricultural people, we would enumerate :—

(*a*) In regard to domestic animals. Should any Israelite be the owner of an ox which, without previously being in the habit of doing so, of a sudden so gored a man or a woman that the injury resulted in death, the animal must at once be killed, while its flesh might not be used for food. But if, knowing that his ox was "wont to push with his horn in time past," the owner had neglected to secure him, he must pay for the injury done a fine, varying according to whether the person killed or wounded was free or a bond-servant.[2]

From harm done to a person the Lawgiver proceeded to harm done to an ox or to an ass by reason of the carelessness of some one not the owner of the animal. Here it was provided that if, through want of attention, the man who owned a pit had left it open, either after first digging it or at a later period, and an ox or an ass had fallen therein and been killed, a fine was to be paid by the owner of the pit to the master of the animal; but, as part compensation for this fine, the former was allowed to keep "the dead beast."[3]

[1] See chap. viii.   [2] Exod. xxi. 28-32.   [3] Ibid. vers. 33, 34.

To protect further the life of animals from the cruelty of man, and to show that it also was as precious in *kind* as that of man, the punishment for him "that killeth a beast" follows in Lev. xxiv. that prescribed for him "that killeth any man." The word used to express the life of the man and of the beast is the same in both verses—*nephesh;* the distinction between the two crimes being marked by the *degree* of punishment to be meted out: in the case of killing a man, death; in that of killing a beast, "life for life"[1]—that is, an animal was to be restored equal in value to that which had been destroyed.

Beyond these acts of wanton or unintentional cruelty on the part of man, it was very possible that the ox or beast might come to harm through no fault of its owner; as, for instance, when two oxen, belonging to different owners, had been fighting, till, from the hurt done by the one, the other had died. If the ox that caused the death of the other had been known by his owner "to push in former years," and yet had not been kept in, the living animal must be given as recompense for the loss sustained; but that an undue punishment might not be borne by the offending party, he was permitted to retain the dead ox. But if the animal inflicting the injury had hitherto been perfectly inoffensive, both parties shared the loss equally— the offending ox was sold, and his purchase money divided between the two owners, while the dead ox was also divided.[2]

Through carelessness, the field of a neighbour might be seriously injured, if the owner who had turned out his "beast" to graze in his own vineyard or field had not properly watched his animal, which, accordingly, had broken through into the neighbour's property and fed there.[3] For such thoughtlessness, and want of consideration for his neighbour, the owner of the "beast" must make restitution, in proportion to the amount of injury done.[4]

Fire kindled by the heedlessness of any one, which, spread-

[1] Lev. xxiv. 18, 21.   [2] Exod. xxi. 35, 36.   [3] Ibid. xxii. 5.
[4] So according to some of the best authorities, as well as the LXX, and the Samaritan Pentateuch.

ing to the thorns that made the hedge or boundary, destroyed corn, either standing or in stacks, or the field itself with all the herbage it contained, must be recompensed—not too heavily—by him who had caused it.[1]

Within the boundaries of the house also the safety of each person must be secured. It was a possibility that from the flat-topped roof some one might fall and be killed. Accordingly, it was commanded that, when a new house was built, a "battlement," or railing, should be put round this part, in order "that thou bring not blood upon thine house, if any man fall from thence."[2]

From carelessness in regard to the good or safety of others, the step is but short to wilful neglect of their interests. To guard against this, Moses commanded that if the ox, the sheep, or the ass of the "brother" or the "enemy"[3] were met with going astray, he who found them must not hide himself from them, but must either, if he knew the owner, and he was at no great distance, bring them back to him again, or if he lived at a distance, or was unknown, keep the animals in his (the finder's) own house till they were claimed by their rightful owner.[4] The same law applied to raiment, or anything belonging to another which might be found. Should this duty have been neglected, and perchance the sin added to by lying, a trespass offering must be brought by the offender.[5]

An overburdened animal, found lying helpless by the way, was not to be passed by, but, whether belonging to a friend or to an enemy, was to be lifted up again, or at least help was to be given to him who was endeavouring to raise it up.[6]

Finally, as regarded the moral character of another, no secret injury was to be done by word, which might lead to terrible consequences, even to imperilling the life of another. "Thou shalt not go up and down as a talebearer"—more exactly, as a calumniator, a slanderer—"among thy people : neither shalt

---

[1] Exod. xxii. 6. Comp. Isa. v. 5.   [2] Deut. xxii. 8.
[3] Exod. xxiii. 4.   [4] Deut. xxii. 1–3.
[5] Lev. vi. 2–7.   [6] Exod. xxiii. 5 ; Deut. xxii. 4.

thou stand against the blood of thy neighbour"—*i.e.*, compass his death in any way : " I am the Lord." [1]

3. When to the charge of another, money or any "stuff"— household or personal—had been confided, and this thing had been stolen, but yet the thief afterwards discovered, double its value must be paid by the felon to the owner of the goods.[2] But if the thief could not be found, the owner of the lost property and he to whom it had been entrusted must both appear before the supreme court [3] (*elohim*, judges). Here the party blamed would protest by an oath that the thing confided to him, whether ox, ass, sheep, raiment, or anything else, had not been abstracted by himself, and the cause be fairly judged of by the elders. In general, if the owner of the lost property had been unfairly used by him whom he had trusted, the latter was considered the thief, and as such paid him double.

Another case was possible. Most probably for money, a man had undertaken the charge of another's cattle, whether ox, ass, sheep, or any other animal, it mattered not. From some unavoidable mishap the "beast" had died, or had been hurt, or driven away by a robber horde, without any one's seeing it. These disasters the keeper being unable to prevent, "an oath of the Lord" was reckoned sufficient to be required of him, "that he had not put his hand unto his neighbour's goods." If from the "torn" animal a piece could be bought as witness to his word, this was considered a sufficient testimony to his honesty.[4] But if, through his carelessness, he had suffered a thief to steal the animal, he must make the owner restitution thereof: for while, if the goods had simply been deposited in his house to be kept free from charge, he might not have been judged responsible, in this case, when probably paid, and in the field well able to guard his trust, he deserved due censure and punishment.[5]

An animal borrowed from a neighbour, and injured in the absence of its owner, must be made good; but had the owner

[1] Lev. xix. 16. [2] Exod. xxii. 7. [3] Ibid. vers. 7-9.
[4] Ibid. ver. 13. [5] Ibid. ver. 12.

been present, and so might have prevented the accident, the borrower was not held responsible. Had the animal been hired, the amount of damage was reckoned with the price of hiring, and the whole sum paid together.[1]

Perhaps no more beautiful instance of the care of the Jewish law for what was weak and defenceless, is the command which provides that if a bird sitting on its young, or upon eggs, be found, not the old bird, which could never accustom itself to captivity, but only the young or the eggs, might be taken. Appropriately is the explanation of this that also attaching to the Fifth Commandment : "that it may be well with thee, and that thou mayest prolong thy days."[2] No act of cruelty could be thought of in a code where love, shown in reverence alike to the greater and the weaker, was the sum and substance.

A law so exactly fitted to the wants of those for whom it was intended, embracing all circumstances and conditions of life, searching all things, from unspoken desire to criminal deed, dealing with sin sternly, yet full of mercy to the repentant ; in which unity of will and purpose was aimed after, and in all things the fear and love of God set forth ; in which self was lost in the desire to serve another's good, in which, in short, holiness, of the land, the people, of life and of death, was the one great object, might truly be the delight of the righteous, to be kept by them for ever, under the Old Covenant.[3] And though some things in it were written by Moses for the hardness of heart of Israel,[4] and though by it was "the knowledge of sin,"[5] still it was and is the Law of God, the spiritual, holy, just, and good commandment;[6] best of all, "our schoolmaster to bring us unto Christ,"[7] "who has redeemed us from the curse of the law,"[8] that being so delivered from that curse, we may "serve God in newness of spirit, and not in the oldness of the letter."[9]

---

[1] Exod. xxii. 14, 15. This is probably the meaning of the words rendered in the Authorised Version, " If it be an hired thing, it came for his hire."
[2] Deut. xxii. 6, 7.   [3] Psa. cxix. 44, 92.   [4] Matt. xix. 8.
[5] Rom. iii. 20.   [6] Ibid. vii. 12, 14.   [7] Gal. iii. 24.
[8] Ibid. ver. 13.   [9] Rom. vii. 6.

INDEX.

AARON, family of. See *Priesthood*.
Agriculture, how regarded in Israel, 73, 112, 122.
Amalekites, 55, 56.
Ammonites, 56; later wars with, 57, 58.
Animals, how treated, 82; beasts of burden, 164; how protected, 180; punishments for injuries to or by, 180, 181; those met going astray, 182; those overburdened, 182.
Armour, portions of, 63.
Arms, 64.
Army, organization of, 59; officers, 59; pay, 60; share of booty given to, 60; of what troops composed, 63.
Artificers, earliest notices of, 124; trades practised by, 124; mainly foreigners, 125; arts permitted to Israel, 125; skill in trade not limited to tribes, 126.
Atonement, Day of, 21, 24.

Begging, how viewed, 111.
Betrothal, ceremony of, 103; documents used in later times, 104.
Birds, protection of, 184.
Blasphemy, 154.
Borrowing, 112. See *Debtor*.
Burial, 140.

Camp, form of, 61; holiness in, 62.

Canaan, religious and political state before Joshua, 53-55; its nations to be destroyed, 55; climate very salubrious, 132; forms of idolatry in, 150, 151.
Census, military, in time of David, 59.
Children, how regarded, 106; relation to parents, 107; education and training of, 107, 108; punishment for illtreating parents, 108; love between parents and children, 108, 109.
Clean and unclean, Jewish views concerning, 164.
Code, Mosaic, general principles of, 178, 179; how universally applicable, 184.
Cohen. See *Priesthood*.
Courts of Law, supreme, 39; local, 40.
Criminal Code, apparent severity of, 44; law of retaliation, 44, 45; general meaning of laws, 51. See also *Punishments*.

Dead, laws forbidding contact with, 139; corpses to be speedily buried, 139; resurrection, of, 140.
Debtor and creditor, honesty of both, 112; laws for, if a foreigner, 113; religious duty of lending, 113, 114; usury and interest not exacted from an Israelite, 114; such permitted

186 INDEX.

from heathens, 115; Pledges, 115, 116; later treatment of debtors, 117.
Deuteronomy, antiquity and authority of, 1.
Disease, specially loathsome forms in Egypt 130-132; sent to Israel in punishment, 132; what kind most prevalent among the Jews, 133; forms of sickness common in the East, 134. See also *Leprosy.*
Divorce, steps in obtaining a, 101.

Edomites, 56, 58.
Egypt, later relations with Israel, 5; Priesthood in, 13; knowledge of medicine in, 130.
Elders. See *Legal Judges.*

Family Life, meaning in, 109; holiness in, 157.
Food, laws of, their religious bearing, 162; suggestions as to their rationale, 163; food of earliest races, 163; distinctions drawn between forbidden and permitted, 163, 164; not confined to Jewish code, 164, 165; animal food permitted to Jews, 165; how killed, 165; portions not eaten, 165, 166; unclean food, 166-168; defilement by touching such, 168; sacrificial food, 168, 169; punishments for disobedience in regard to, 169; principal articles of food, 169; meals, 169; questions concerning food in early Church, 170; general principle in, 170.

Goel, as avenger, 47, 50; family duties of, 79.
Government, principle of, in Israel, 1.

Hananiah, judgment on, 29, 30.
Hospitality. See *Strangers.*
Houses, precautions for safety in, 182.

Idolatry, forms specially dangerous to Israel, 149, 151; punishment for, 149; human sacrifices, 150; inciters to, 150; magic and soothsaying, 152.
Inheritance, laws of, 83; privileges and duties of eldest son, 83; daughters as heiresses, 83, 84; next of kin, 84.

Joshua, government by, 2.
Jubilee Year, 75; its meaning, 76; bearing on landed property, 76; on slavery, 91, 92; its advantages and disadvantages, 78.
Judah, the royal tribe, 4.
Judges, the, Israel under, 2.
Judges, legal, how termed, 37; institution of, 37; character of, 38; powers, 39; obligations laid on, 40.
Justice, character of, 38; how administered, 39, 40; in later times, 41; officers of, 41; various modes of obtaining it, 42-44.

King, appointment of, 3; an Israelite, 4; not to have intercourse with Egypt, 4, 5; riches, 6; to observe the laws, 6, 7; supreme ruler, 7; his heirs, 8; later history of, 9; not a despot, 9; revenues, 9, 10, 68, 69; officers, 10; enthronement, 10; respect shown him, 11; insignia, 11, 12.
Kingdom in Israel, meaning of, 12.
Korah, rebellion of, 19.

Land, dignity of, 82. See *Property.*
Leprosy, mastered, 133; various kinds of, 135; of men, 136-138; of garments, 138; of houses, 138.
Levites, separation of, 15; duties of, 16; time of service, 16; families, 17; general influence of, 17; position in Israel, 17; cities and landed property, 18; revenues, 18; historical notices of, 18, 19; consecration of, 19.
Lot, the, 43.

INDEX. 187

Marriage, how viewed, 99-101;
polygamy in Israel, 100, 101;
with whom forbidden, 102, 103;
formalities of, 103; gifts and
dowry, 103; ceremony of, 104.
Midian, priesthood in, 14.
Military laws, how regarded, 52;
meaning of, 65.
Moabites, 56, 58.
Money, 128.
Moses, rule by, 2.

Neighbours, love to, 178; how
manifested, 179; talebearing
among, 182, 183; injury to property
confided by, or borrowed
from, such, 183, 184.

Oaths, legal, kinds of, 43.

Physicians, in early times, 134;
remedies used by, 135; how
regarded, 135.
Poor, necessary existence of, 110;
provisions for, 111, 120, 179;
classes of, 111: such by their
own fault, 117, 118; deserving
poor to share in the feasts, 118;
given third year's tithes, 118,
119; privileges in Sabbatical
year, 119; in harvest, 119, 120.
Priesthood, meaning and need of,
13; Israel intended to be such,
14; typical, 15, 26; selection
of, 20.
Priests, Hebrew name for, 20;
duties, 20, 21; revenues, 22;
food, 22; holiness of, 22, 23;
garments of, 23; consecration
of, 25; history of, 25.
Priest, High, special duties of, 21;
dress, 23, 24.
Prisons, 49.
Property, significance of laws of,
73; landed, how apportioned,
74; restrictions laid on, 74;
sale and redemption of, 77;
vowing to God of, 77, 78; manner
of disposing of, 79, 80; of
purchasing, 80, 81; deeds of sale,
81; rights of property guarded,
81, 82; injuries to, 181, 182.

Prophets, Hebrew names for, 27;
kinds of, 28; meaning of their
mission, 28; how secured, 29;
punishment of false, 29, 30;
historical activity of, 30, 34;
character of, 31, 33; form of
their message, 32; signs attending,
33; manner of call, 33, 35;
dress, 34; enemies of, 35; list
of, 36.
Prophets, schools of, 30, 31.
Punishments, legal, who borne by,
45; their benefit to the community,
46; moral element in,
46; classes and kinds of penalties,
46-49; offences thus punished,
50.

Release, Year of, 89.

Sabbatical Year, 74, 75; its advantages
and disadvantages, 75;
debts not claimed during, 113.
Sabbath, positive and negative observance
of, 155.
Samuel, rule by, 2, 3.
Saul, rule by, 3.
Servants, poor Hebrew, 90; hirelings,
97; of the Sanctuary, 98.
Service in Israel, meaning of, 98.
See *Slaves*.
Shoterim, duties of, 41, 42, 58.
Sieges, how conducted, 61.
Slaves, why permitted, 86;
hebrew designations for, 86, 87;
how regarded in Palestine, 87,
88; *Hebrew*, how become so, 88;
release of such, 89; legally so
made, 89, 90; under foreign
masters, 91; marriage of, 92;
voluntary perpetual, 93; *Non-
Israelite*, 93; how regarded, 94;
privileges of, 94; injuries to
slaves, 94; *Female* slaves, grades
of, 95; price of slaves, 96; sale
of children as, 96; runaway
slaves, 97; duties of servants, 97.
Strangers, how treated, 171;
reasons for kindness to, 172;
Hebrew names for, 173; how
viewed by Jews, 173, 174; exceptions
in regard to some, 174;

INDEX.

received into congregation of Israel, 174; privileges of, 175; their religious duties, 176; slaves belonging to such, 176; later views and treatment of foreigners, 176, 177; Prophetic utterances concerning, 177.

Taxes and Tributes, how regarded, 66; Ecclesiastical, 66, 67; Civil, 67, 68; for necessary purposes, 68; Royal dues and taxes, 68; poll tax, 69; foreign taxation, 69.
Theocracy, the, 1.
Trade, not encouraged, 123; limits to trade with other countries, 126; points in favour of, 126, 127; provisions for trade within the land, 127; how carried on by the Jews, 128.
Treasury, Temple, 69; royal, 69.
Trial of Christ, 50, 51.

Wars, actual necessity of, 52; character of those on entering Canaan, 53, 54; conditions of, 55; with whom waged, 55, 56; Israel not the aggressor in, 58; to be strictly religious, 58; manner of waging it, 58, 59, 62; age for, 59, 179; prisoners of, how treated, 60, 61. See also *Army*, *Camp*, *Military Laws*, *Sieges*.
Weights and Measures, to be just 127; officers inspecting, 128; Tables of, 129.
Widows, 106, 179.
Wills, 84.
Witnesses, number and necessity of, 42; punishment of false, 42; 158; responsibility of, 42, 43.
Wives, position of, 104, 105; not to separate themselves, 105, 106; suspected, 106.
Women, how treated, 106.
Words, the Ten, contains substance of Pentateuch Code, 143, 144, 160, 161; division of the Tables, 144, 145; higher meaning of, 159; division into Pentads, 145, 157. *First Word*, meaning and practical application of, 146; *Second Word*, dangers guarded against by, 147; admonition attaching to two first, 148; *Third Word*, for what provided, 153; *Fourth Word*, 154-156; *Fifth Word*, honour to authority, 156; *Sixth Word*, negatively and positively, 157; *Seventh Word*, 157; *Eighth Word*, what included in, 157; *Ninth Word*, truthfulness insisted upon, 158; *Tenth Word*, covetousness, 158; dangers guarded against by, 158, 159.

STANDARD WORKS

PUBLISHED BY THE

RELIGIOUS TRACT SOCIETY.

Sketches of Jewish Social Life in the Days of Christ. By the Rev. Dr. Edersheim. 5s. cloth boards, gilt edges.

The Temple: its Ministry and Services at the Time of Jesus Christ. By the Rev. Dr. Edersheim. Imp. 16mo. 5s. cloth boards.

Bible History. By the Rev. Dr. Edersheim. Each vol. in Crown 8vo. 2s. 6d. cloth boards.
Vol. 1.—*The World before the Flood, and the History of the Patriarchs.* With Map.
Vol. 2.—*The Exodus and the Wanderings in the Wilderness.*
Vol. 3.—*Israel in Canaan under Joshua and the Judges.*
Vol. 4.—*Israel under Samuel, Saul, and David, to the Birth of Solomon.*
Vol. 5.—*History of Judah and Israel, from the Birth of Solomon to the Reign of Ahab.*
Vol. 6.—*Elisha the Prophet: the Lessons of his History and Times.*

New Pocket Paragraph Bible. Being the Authorized Version arranged in PARAGRAPHS instead of in verses. By this arrangement sentences are preserved in their completeness, and the meaning, which is sometimes obscured by the arbitrary division into verses, is more plainly seen. This Bible is an exceedingly useful one for the minister or Sunday School teacher. It contains a preface, references, marginal notes containing improved renderings of many words and passages, chronological tables, and coloured maps, carefully printed on fine paper.

	s.	d.		s.	d.
Cloth boards, sprinkled edges	4	0	Best morocco, limp, with flaps to cover edges.........	10	6
Roan, with gilt edges.........	5	0	Morocco, plain sides, gilt edges.....................	7	6
Persian, calf grained, gilt edges.....................	6	6	Morocco, extra, medium quality, gilt edges	9	0
Morocco, limp, with flaps to cover edges	7	0	Best morocco, full gilt	10	0

The Annotated Paragraph Bible. Containing the Old and New Testaments, according to the Authorized Version, arranged in Paragraphs and Parallelisms; with Explanatory Notes, Prefaces, and an entirely New Selection of References. With Maps and Plans. Super-royal 8vo.
Old Testament, cloth boards, 14s. New Testament, ditto, 7s.
Old and New Testament, complete in 1 vol., cloth boards, 20s. Also kept in superior bindings, suited for presents.
Large Paper Ed., in 1 vol., cloth boards, 28s.

Standard Works.

The Holy Bible, according to the Authorized Version. In Paragraphs and Sections; *with Emendations of the Text*; also Maps, Chronological Tables, and Marginal References. Royal 4to, large type.
Old and New Testaments complete, 35s. bevelled boards. Also in superior bindings.
The New Testament, 10s. 6d. cloth boards.

Paragraph Bible. 12mo edition. 6s. cloth boards; 10s. calf; 15s. morocco.

The New Biblical Atlas and Scripture Gazetteer. With 16 finely engraved Coloured Maps by W. and A. K. Johnston. 5s. cloth boards.

The Bible Handbook. An Introduction to the Study of Sacred Scriptures. By Joseph Angus, D.D. 12mo. Map. 5s. cloth; 7s. half-bound; 8s. 6d. calf.

Lectures on the Lord's Prayer. By the Rev Richard Glover, of Bristol. Crown 8vo. 1s. 6d. cloth boards.

What do I Believe? By Rev. S. G. Green, D.D., Author of "Bible Sketches and their Teachings," etc. Fcap 8vo. 1s. cloth bds.

Why do I Believe? or, The Bible Historically True and Divinely Inspired. By Mrs. J. B. Patterson. 1s. cloth.

Jesus of Nazareth: Who was He? and What is He now? By the Rev. Dr. Patton. Crown 8vo. 2s. 6d. cloth boards.

The Trades and Industrial Occupations of the Bible. By the Rev. W. G. Lewis. Crown 8vo. 3s. cloth boards.

Meditations on the Miracles of Christ. By the Very Rev. J. S. Howson, D.D., Dean of Chester. First and Second Series Crown 8vo. Each, 3s. cloth boards.

The Parables of our Lord Explained and Applied. By the Rev. F. Bourdillon, M.A. Crown 8vo. 3s. 6d. cloth boards.

Handbook to the Grammar of the Greek New Testament. Together with complete Vocabulary, and an Explanation of the chief New Testament Synonyms. By the Rev. S. G. Green, D.D. 8vo. 7s. 6d.

The Philosophy of Prayer, and other Essays. By the Rev. H. R. Reynolds, D.D., of Cheshunt College. Crown 8vo. 3s. 6d. cloth boards.

Biblical Geography and Antiquities. By the Rev. E. P. Barrows, D.D. With Appendices by the Rev. Canon Tristram, B. Harris Cowper, and others. With Maps. Demy 8vo. 6s. 6d. cloth boards.

The Companions of the Lord: Chapters on the Lives of the Apostles. By Charles E. B. Reed, M.A. Crown 8vo. 4s. cloth.

Standard Works.

The Home and Synagogue of the Modern Jew. Sketches of Jewish Life and Ceremonies. Engravings. Imp. 16mo. 4s. cloth.

The Story of Esther the Queen. By the Rev. A. M. Symington, D.D. Small crown 8vo. 2s. 6d. cloth boards.

A New Companion to the Bible. An Introduction to the Study of the Scriptures for Bible Classes, Sunday Schools, and Families. With Maps. Crown 8vo. 2s. 6d. cloth.

A Biblical Cyclopædia. Edited by J. Eadie, LL.D. 8vo. 7s. 6d. cloth boards; 10s. 6d. half-bound; 12s. 6d. calf; 13s. 6d. morocco.

The Last First. Sketches of some of the less Noted Characters of Scripture History. By Alexander Macleod Symington, D.D. Crown 8vo. 2s. 6d. cloth boards.

Elijah, the Tishbite. By Dr. F. W. Krummacher. 12mo. 3s. cloth; 4s. half-bound.

The Great Problem; or, Christianity as it is. By a Student of Science. Crown 8vo. 5s. 6d. cloth boards.

A New Introduction to the Study of the Bible. By E. P. Barrows, D.D. 8vo. 6s. cloth boards.

The Critical Handbook. A Guide to the Study of the Authenticity, Canon, and Text of the Greek New Testament. By Edward C. Mitchell, D.D. Illustrated by a Map, Diagrams, and Tables. Crown 8vo. 3s. 6d. cloth boards.

Grounds of Christian Hope; a Sketch of the Evidences of Christianity. By Stanley Leathes, M.A. 4s. 6d. cloth boards.

The Judgment of Jerusalem—Predicted in Scripture, Fulfilled in History. By Dr. Patton, of New York. 2s. 6d. cloth.

An Exposition of the Book of Ruth. By the Rev. Samuel Cox. 2s. cloth boards.

How to Answer Objections to Revealed Religion. By Miss E. J. Whately. Fcap 8vo. 1s. 6d. cloth boards.

Angelic Beings: Their Nature and Ministry. By the Rev. Canon Bell. Crown 8vo. 2s. 6d. cloth boards.

The Analogy of Religion to the Constitution and Course of Nature; also, Fifteen Sermons. By Joseph Butler, D.C.L., Bishop of Durham. With a Life of the Author, a copious Analysis, Notes, and Indexes. By Joseph Angus, D.D. Crown 8vo. 2s. cloth boards.

Ditto, The Analogy, with the Three Sermons on Human Nature only. Crown 8vo. 1s. cloth boards.

Nehemiah: His Character and Work. A Practical Exposition. By T. Campbell Finlayson. 2s. cloth boards.

Standard Works.

The Pattern Prayer. By the Rev. F. Bourdillon, M.A.
Fcap 8vo. 2s. cloth boards.

The Resurrection of our Lord Jesus Christ: an Historical Fact.
With an Examination of Naturalistic Hypotheses. By the Rev. J. Kennedy, D.D. 2s. 6d. cloth.

The Rock of Ages; or, Scripture Testimony to the One Eternal Godhead of the Father, and of the Son, and of the Holy Ghost. By the Rev. E. H. Bickersteth, M.A. Crown 8vo. 4s. cloth boards.

The Spirit of Life; or, Scripture Testimony to the Divine Person and Work of the Holy Spirit. By the Rev. E. H. Bickersteth, M.A. Crown 8vo. 4s. cloth boards.

The Bible and Modern Thought. By the Rev. Canon Birks, M.A., Professor of Moral Philosophy, Cambridge. With Appendix. 12mo. 4s. cloth boards.

Outlines of the Life of Christ. A Guide to the Study of the Chronology, Harmony, and Purpose of the Gospels. By Eustace R. Conder, M.A. With Map. Crown 8vo. 3s. 6d. cloth boards.

Vox Clamantis.—The Life and Ministry of John the Baptist. By Alexander Macleod Symington, D.D. Cr. 8vo. 2s. 6d. cloth bds.

Thoughts on Prayer. Extracts from Modern Writers. Crown 8vo. 3s. cloth boards.

The Lord is my Shepherd. A Popular Exposition of the Twenty-third Psalm. By the Rev. James Stuart, of Stretford, Manchester. Small crown 8vo. 2s. 6d. cloth.

Symbols of Christ. By the Rev. Charles Stanford, D.D. Crown 8vo. 3s. cloth boards.

The Progress of Divine Revelation; or, The Unfolding Purpose of Scripture. By John Stoughton, D.D. Crown 8vo. 6s. 6d.

The Christian Garland. A Popular Exposition of 2 Peter i. 5-7. By the Rev. F. A. C. Lillingston, M.A., of Holloway. Crown 8vo. 2s. cloth boards.

The Epistle of Paul to Philemon. An Exposition for English Readers. By the Rev. A. H. Drysdale, M.A. Crown 8vo. 2s. 6d. cloth boards.

The Great Cloud of Witnesses, or Faith and its Victories. By the Rev. W. Landels, D.D. Crown 8vo. 4s. cloth boards.

Saving Faith: what is it? A Scriptural Inquiry and Appeal. Crown 8vo. 8d. cloth boards.

Bible Sketches and Their Teachings. For Young People. By Samuel G. Green, B.A., D.D. Fcap 8vo. I. The Creation to the Israelites' Entrance into Canaan. 2s. 6d. cloth boards. II. From the Israelites' Entrance into Canaan to the end of the Old Testament. 2s. 6d. cloth boards. III. Life of Christ. 2s. 6d. cloth boards.

www.ingramcontent.com/pod-product-compliance
Lightning Source LLC
Chambersburg PA
CBHW031819220426
43662CB00007B/711